The Last Called Mormon Colonization

The Last Called Mormon Colonization

POLYGAMY, KINSHIP, AND WEALTH IN WYOMING'S BIG HORN BASIN

JOHN GARY MAXWELL

THE UNIVERSITY OF UTAH PRESS
Salt Lake City

The Defiance House Man colophon is a registered trademark of The University of Utah Press. It is based on a four-foot-tall Ancient Puebloan pictograph (late PIII) near Glen Canyon, Utah.

Library of Congress Cataloging-in-Publication Data

Names: Maxwell, John Gary, 1933- author.
Title: The last called Mormon colonization : polygamy, kinship, and wealth in Wyoming's Big Horn Basin / John Gary Maxwell.
Description: Salt Lake City : University of Utah Press, [2022] | Includes bibliographical references and index.
Identifiers: LCCN 2021042444 (print) | LCCN 2021042445 (ebook) | ISBN 9781647690588 (cloth) | ISBN 9781647690595 (cloth) | ISBN 9781647690601 (ebook)
Subjects: LCSH: Mormon Church—Bighorn Basin (Mont. and Wyo.)—History. | Polygamy—Religious aspects—Church of Jesus Christ of Latter-day Saints. | Bighorn Basin (Mont. and Wyo.)—History. | Bighorn Basin (Mont. and Wyo.)—Colonies.
Classification: LCC BX8615.W8 M39 2022 (print) | LCC BX8615.W8 (ebook) | DDC 289.3787/4—dc23
LC record available at https://lccn.loc.gov/2021042444
LC ebook record available at https://lccn.loc.gov/2021042445

Errata and further information on this and other titles available online at UofUpress.com

Printed and bound in the United States of America.

Cover photograph of companies of organizing Latter-day Saints (photograph 602d8727b2277092a.jpg) courtesy LDS Church History Library.

to her who makes,
then remakes our world whenever needed

Contents

Contents

Figures, Maps, and Tables

Acknowledgments

As an only child I was brought on the more than occasional Sunday afternoon with my parents to visit my aunts and uncles. At times, while near torpor from a midday meal, I listened but never spoke. Word-of-mouth stories were told and retold, mostly by the women, about the Maxwell family's origin in Ireland, their life in Scotland, and their trek to the United States to gather with the Latter-day Saints in Utah. Usually featured first in these folksy accounts was John Maxwell, my great grandfather, who immigrated to the United States in 1854. Traveling without relatives or friends, he left behind the mills of Carlisle, England; Lanarkshire, Scotland; and whatever had been his life in Glasgow. He boarded the *John M. Wood* in Liverpool and arrived weeks later in New Orleans. A paddleboat steamer struggled up the Mississippi and dropped him at St. Louis. Another shallow draft vessel carried him on the Missouri's waters to Westport Landing at Kansas City. Driving a wagon pulled by two oxen, he brought himself and an unknown cargo to Salt Lake City, arriving in September before winter weather closed the route.

As each Sunday's topic turned to the extended Maxwell family's arrival in 1856, the tone became animated. There were the difficulties of their handcart march, their hunger, privations, and the death of Elizabeth Donnelly Maxwell, the maternal family head, and her burial near Cache Cave in Utah's Echo Canyon. While deserving admiration, these stories were weak in historical accuracy. Years later our searching revealed that starvation and illness had forced her delay at Fort Laramie. Without any family to give aid or comfort, Elizabeth was removed from that year's Second Handcart Company and taken into either the ill-fated Martin or Willie Companies. She became one of three hundred or more deaths in the faulted emigration experiment that stands as the worst tragedy and debacle in America's history of western colonization.

These stories did not catch the child's attention as fully as did the next chapter in the family's adventures, however. The Wyoming emigration was told by those still living—my uncle and aunts who had been "called" to the Big Horn Basin in 1901. Leaving their Summit County farms and livestock, my grandfather and great grandfather left a newly built sawmill on the Weber River. They followed their LDS leader's instructions and started over. Stories of attempts to dig a canal, to farm, to raise cattle, to become carpenters—all had their place. Recounts of my father's life in the Big Horn Basin included logging trips that encountered a grizzly bear; his mother's early untimely death without medical care; and his being considered, but not allowed, to go to a tryout as a Cincinnati Reds pitcher. My father's youngest brother, Everett, crashed the family's newly purchased Ford automobile in 1918; this brother's needless death came shortly thereafter in the WWI artillery massacre at the Argonne Forest. Until my Big Horn research of their colonization gave them personality and color, the surnames of Johnson, Marchant, Tippetts, Welch, Crosby, and Croft were obscure and had little meaning for me.

Therefore, it is these several long-dead relatives that I must gratefully acknowledge for their part in persevering through this period of western development. First, to my father Grant Verl Maxwell who was barely two years old when the family started from Utah in early spring 1901; to aunt Elizabeth "Nellie" Maxwell Johnson; to uncle John Alvin Maxwell and his wife Mildred Aldora Wilson; and to aunt Martha Mae Maxwell Tippetts who was sixteen years old when she drove a horse and wagon the full distance from Peoa, Summit County, Utah, to Cowley, Big Horn County, Wyoming. Gentle in spirit and supremely kind, Martha's description of that journey is included in this work. Any formal medical education of my great grandfather, John Maxwell, is uncertain for lack of documentation; however, he somehow learned enough from schooling or life experience to carry the title of doctor in many times of emergent need. Doctor Edward Woolley Croft was the bonafide medical doctor who later came to the Big Horn to fulfill the area's medical and surgical needs for many years.

Later in adult life I returned with expanded perspective to examine the history of my relatives within the larger canvas that is the Latter-day Saints' complex, contradictory, and partisan narrative. This work attempts to flesh out the story of this last "called" Mormon colonization by hundreds of faithful settlers who faced unforeseen obstacles in reach of their own and their leader's goals.

I owe credit to the late Dr. Floyd O'Neil, the honored historian at the University of Utah and the American West Center. He suggested that peeling off several layers from traditional historical wrappings might reveal that the Big Horn Basin's colonization under Abraham Owen Woodruff was possibly a small part of a larger dispersion of selected men among the Mormon leadership. He questioned whether they had a special purpose: to secretly sustain polygamy in perpetuity within the United States that might be added to those outside its geographical limits, such as in Canada and Mexico.

Thanks goes to Dr. Todd Compton, Utah and LDS historian and author of several acclaimed works, including a biography of Southern Utah's notable Jacob Hamblin. His treatise on the Nauvoo wives of Joseph Smith and others in the Nauvoo period acknowledge him as an expert on the subject. He kindly offered valuable suggestions for the chapter that attempts to distill an immense field of study to a manageable primer on early LDS plural marriages. To the late historian D. Michael Quinn I owe thanks for his review of several manuscript elements and for his unselfish sharing of his September 2019 update of his articles "John W. Woolley as a Highly Trusted Mormon From September 1886 to 1913," and "Lorin C. Woolley as a Faithful Mormon From September 1886 to 1913."

I owe thanks and recognition to Cowley, Wyoming's, mayor Roland Simmons, who helped me appreciate the city's progress in present days. Thanks also to Shirley Ann Lewis Busteed, the director of Cowley's Town Hall and History Museum, and Nick Sponsel, Town Manager, for access to its artifacts. To the many residents of northeastern Wyoming cities who responded anonymously to my unofficial survey of existing polygamy in their cities and towns, appreciation is also due.

With little accurate knowledge regarding the Rocky Mountains' early explorers and trappers, I was fortunate to learn from Jim Hardee's *Pierre's Hole!* His extensive knowledge of fur trade history accrues from experience in the Sublette County Historical Society, the *Museum of the Mountain Man*, and the Fur Trade Research Center. He generously reviewed and corrected several matters in the Big Horn Basin for that early era and called my attention to Mike Bryant's *Rocky Mountain Fur Trade Journal* article "Bad Pass Trail" containing Clint Gilchrist's beautiful Basin map.

Thanks to Butte, Montana's Richard I. Gibson, former national and international geologist, journalist for Butte's *Montana Standard*, and guide at Butte's World Museum of Mining. Dick conducts walking tours of the city and served as a guide for the Utah Westerners 2016 trip to Butte. I credit

Dick with teaching me how Butte railroads became part of hundreds of railroad companies before and after east and west were joined at Promontory in 1869. He helped clarify the route and names of railroads that served the Big Horn Basin and were used by LDS Church leaders and Mormon colonists in 1900 and 1901.

Dr. Jeremy M. Johnston holds the Hal and Naoma Tate Chair and is curator of Western American History, the Ernest J. Goppert curator at the Buffalo Bill Museum in Cody, Wyoming, and the managing editor of *Papers of William F. Cody*. He kindly reviewed several elements in this work and helped me understand the complicated history behind the water rights and land irrigation systems that arose in the Basin after the Carey Act's passage. His particular knowledge of Cody and his friends and their dealings with Abraham Owen Woodruff helped clarify a complicated story.

To the professional staff at The Church of Jesus Christ of Latter-day Saints Library in Salt Lake City, and especially to the patient and courteous archivist Jay G. Borup, my sincere thanks are owed. Church history specialist Megan McShane was extraordinarily helpful with downloading digitized files from the library.

Joseph W. Geisner, Clair Barrus, and Hugh McKell are among a band of selfless supporters of others, myself included. I wish to thank Holly Rogers, the most courteous and encouraging copy editor that I've had the good fortune to work with.

Recognition and thanks are gratefully given to my wife, Cheryl Gunn Maxwell, whose sharp eye kindly noted material that was unclear or in need of development. She unmuddles my sentences and fixes many that are overlong. She remains my most trusted judge, my most honest critic, and my best friend.

Preface

As the sun rose over Wyoming's Big Horn Mountains on a mid-June day in 1900, it warmed the tent and body of a little-rested construction foreman. It also rekindled his days-long anxiety over the unsolved task at hand. Dressing hurriedly, he went without awakening his workers to a ditch in the earth, twelve feet deep. There, on his knees, he poured out a prayer asking how to remove a gigantic rock of immense weight that blocked the only path possible for the water canal his teams were digging. After what an observer might consider a long time, he gradually experienced a sense of assurance that all would be well.

As the workers returned to removing earth and gravel with their horse-drawn bucket scrapers and long-handled shovels, a deep space seemingly developed beneath the rock's bottom edges. When one or two loose stone fragments were removed from the spot, it became apparent that the rock's base was not flat but somewhat rounded. The construction foreman seemed to hear a voice in his mind saying, "call the men out now." Immediately, he ordered all men and tools out from the canal ditch. Only moments later the rock spontaneously split into two fragments whose surfaces, smooth as plastered wall, fell harmlessly, with a loud boom, and became level with the ditch bottom.

This event, given little attention by modern western historians, was given long life in the memories of witnesses as the Prayer Rock Miracle.[1] The construction foreman, Byron Sessions, had been a successful farmer and rancher in Cache County, Utah Territory. With his wife and family, they had given up all they had to answer the personal call from LDS Church president Lorenzo Snow to settle the Big Horn Basin.[2] The rock experience underscores the simple faith that underlay the actions of hundreds to colonize a forbidding spot in what was still frontier in the Rocky Mountains' massive basin. Digging a thirty-seven-mile-long canal with primitive, dangerous tools, along with setbacks and failures, were threatening their task's completion and the promises of success from their leaders. A miraculous resolution of this seemingly impossible impediment confirmed to them that in bringing water to fertile soil they were doing God's work, and another community to expand God's church would follow.

The episode at Prayer Rock also underscores the colony's disparity at the century's turn. Elsewhere in the country, transformation from an agricultural economy to a science-driven, industrialized society was accelerating.[3] Steel production by companies formed by Andrew Carnegie and John Pierpont Morgan Sr. changed the course of industrialization in the nineteenth century's last years and after 1900. In 1903 the Wright Brothers successfully made the first heavier-than-air machine that flew on its own power at Kitty Hawk, North Carolina. As 1904 dawned, the Sidon Canal was still a work in progress, with horse-drawn scoop scrapers, faith, and prayers.

This book's title lays claim that the last colonization called by The Church of Jesus Christ of Latter-day Saints' leadership was in Wyoming's Big Horn Basin in 1900 and 1901. This is not in ignorance of William H. Smart's colonization efforts in Utah's Uintah Basin starting in 1905 or with disrespect for the award-winning biography titled *Mormonism's Last Colonizer: The Life and Times of William H. Smart* published in 2008 by authorship of his grandson, William Buckwalter Smart, a distinguished *Deseret News* journalist, committed Mormon, and acclaimed historian.

While this present work lays out several noteworthy similarities and interconnections between the two colonization efforts, its most important difference from that of Smart is its emphasis on the roles of four ardent apostles: Abraham Owen Woodruff, Matthias Foss Cowley, John Whitaker Taylor, and Marriner Wood Merrill. These Latter-day Saint apostles were not only the prime movers in the 1900 Big Horn Basin colonization, they were inarguably the most adamant and active defenders of post-Manifesto polygamy within the seventeen topmost men comprising the Mormon leadership. The reasons behind colonization of an isolated western frontier by these men and their families cannot be understood without considering the extraordinary depth of their devotion to continuing polygamy.

To avoid confusion between the claim of this work as the *Last Called Colonization* and Smart's *Last Colonizer* publication, clarification is mandatory. Both titles are correct; they are not in conflict. Both were last colonization drives, and both studies illuminate the serious, relative land shortage problems facing The Church of Jesus Christ of Latter-day Saints' leadership and Utah's citizenry near the end of the nineteenth century and into the twentieth.

William Henry Smart's life was as a faithful Mormon in Franklin, Idaho, and Cache Valley, Utah, "in the second level of Mormon leadership."[4] A complex human who struggled with physical and mental health, he made extraordinary contributions to his faith and state, as is well detailed in his biography. Smart's last church assignment as a stake president, which lasted much of his adult life, was to oversee matters in a very large geographical expanse, with some lands to be opened to colonization. Today's map shows the Uintah Basin including portions of Summit, Duchesne, and Daggett Counties, and it encompasses the massive Uintah-Ouray Indian Reservation. A 1905 land rush colonization initiated by the federal government and the unexpected involvement by LDS Church leadership made Smart the last LDS colonizing leader.

The 1900 and 1901 efforts of Abraham Owen Woodruff were a calling from LDS president Lorenzo Snow, which comprised the Latter-day Saints' last *called* colonization. A call was far more than an invitation. It was rarely contested and understood by the faithful to be almost an order, especially if it emanated from the highest level of leadership.

William Henry Smart was a post-Manifesto polygamist, not unlike many prominent men from Preston and Franklin, Idaho; Afton and Star Valley, Wyoming; and Utah's Cache Valley. However, he did not share the unshakable resolve to sustain and continue to perform plural marriages that was held by several Quorum of Twelve Apostles who were his respected contemporary friends, the four men earlier mentioned.

The lives of Abraham Owen Woodruff and William H. Smart were closely, unusually entwined. Woodruff was one of three apostles under whose hands Smart was set apart as president of Wasatch Stake on February 10, 1901.[5] Owen owned land and raised cattle in the small community of Charleston in Wasatch County, and on the day following Smart's ordination, Woodruff entered into his journal: "Drove to the farm, looked after affairs..... Took train for home," during which he "had a pleasant con[versation] with Prest. Wm. H. Smart and with Apostle [Francis M.] Lyman from Provo."[6]

Owen Woodruff mentored Smart on the virtues of marrying plural wives and counselled him regarding what he and the other three Mormon leaders considered an unrevoked, holy principle. Woodruff writes of a temple fast meeting where "Pres[idents] Jos[eph] F. Smith and John W. Taylor discussed the doctrine... that in Eternity one man will have but one wife [was] a 'Doctrine of Devils.'"[7]

Owen Woodruff was invited into a partnership that William Smart and his brother-in-law and business partner James W. Webster had established. They had planned to begin a livestock ranch in the Big Horn Basin in the winter of 1900–1901. They also hoped to run sheep on land part of the Wind River Shoshoni Indian Reservation or the Crow Reservation north of the Big Horn Mountain range. In spring 1901 Owen wrote to Utah Senator Thomas Kearns asking that he submit a request to the general land office commissioner for William H. Smart to graze sheep on the Teton Forest Reserve.[8] Kearns was out of his office, but his secretary forwarded the request. Owen was answered that Commissioner Binger Herrman declined permission to graze fifty thousand sheep as requested "since sheep are absolutely prohibited in the ... Reserve," but that "sheep, in limited numbers, are allowed in certain portions of the Big Horn Forest Reserve, but not elsewhere in the Wyoming reserves."[9]

William H. Smart also had connections to other Big Horn Basin apostles. Matthias F. Cowley was who Smart called on to perform his post-Manifesto, post-statehood plural marriage in 1902 to Mary Eliza Wallace. Cowley and Smart were additionally connected by Cowley's marriage to Luella Parkinson, the daughter of Smart's older sister, Maria. John W. Taylor was Smart's instructor during Smart's compressed two-hour preparation for his first mission call to Constantinople, Turkey, in 1889.[10] Smart's first marriage to Anna Haines on October 3, 1888, was performed by Marriner W. Merrill, a polygamist and Logan Temple president.[11]

In 1902 Congress moved to open the Uintah-Ouray Reservation in the northeastern corner of Utah to settlement.[12] This was subject to a preceding allotment of 180 acres to any individual Ute who applied and received official consent from a majority of resident Utes. Consent from the tribe to open the reservation to white colonization was not addressed in the legislation, however. Federal action moved ahead. One Ute said, "Look what has happened to us already in the last 40 years, and now you want us to give up the remainder of our reservation.... After the white people come in here, they will say, 'We took your land, now we will take your water, and your house, so you get off this land, go to some other country and find some other place!'"[13]

By 1903 William H. Smart was no longer residing in Cache County, having been called as president of the geographically huge Wasatch Stake, with his home in its ecclesiastical seat at Heber City, Summit County, Utah. The lands occupied by the Uintah Reservation were included in the LDS Church's Wasatch Stake. In a meeting on November 13, 1903, Smart met with Apostles John Henry Smith and Hyrum Mack Smith, along with First Presidency members Joseph F. Smith, John R. Winder, and Anthon H. Lund. At the meeting it was made clear that LDS leadership "considered the Uintah Basin to be Mormon Country."[14] In 1903 and 1904 Smart traveled the Strawberry, Duchesne, and Uinta river drainages, noting the suitability of the lands for agriculture. He brought in surveyors to identify the best sites for homesteading. He also organized Mormon leaders residing in the few existing small settlements to participate in the LDS stake's expansion and prepared them for the allotment draw that would attract many non-Mormon "Gentiles" as well as Mormons. Smart spearheaded the coming land-rush project with approval from LDS leadership.

Anticipating the water needs of an agriculture-based economy, Smart added the anticipated acreage to the existing and successful Wasatch Development Company. He named himself president. Joseph R. Murdock, his first counselor in the Wasatch Stake presidency, was made board chair; his stake clerk and fellow post-Manifesto polygamist, Joseph White Musser, vice chair; and second counselor James C. Jensen was company auditor.[15] Surveying identified existing and prospective townships as well as water sources. Soil experts from Utah State Agricultural College inspected the land for suitability for the anticipated land lottery. Mormons in Wasatch County and elsewhere were prepared to select, locate, file, and claim the most advantageous sites.

In June 1905 Smart and his counselors wrote to LDS stake presidents inviting bishops and church members "to seek the best lands on the reservation, pointing out the church's desire that young people stay to build up Zion rather than seeking livelihoods elsewhere, and promising to help them." They wrote, "We are acquainting ourselves with tracts of land which we feel are most desirable for settlement, and which, through land office connections being formed by us, can be chosen by those who may be in touch with us."[16] Smart's letter was published in the *Box Elder News* to alert Mormons in northern Utah to the opportunity. These actions immediately "launched a full-throated attack not only on Smart and his associates, but also on the First Presidency and [Utah's] Senator Reed Smoot."[17] Smart's letter was republished in full by the *Salt Lake Tribune*, whose editors responded that it "completely establishes the fact that there is a conspiracy among the Mormon hierarchy to steal the lands of the reservations when the opening comes."[18]

Registration for the land draw began on August 1; over seventeen days, more than thirty-seven thousand applications were submitted from stations in Provo, Price, and Vernal, Utah, and from Grand Junction, Colorado. The drawing began August 17 for approximately 5,880 individual applicants, whose religious affiliations were not identified. However, most settlements later formed were overwhelmingly Mormon. These sites were assigned to the LDS Wasatch Stake's Duchesne division, with Joseph Murdock at its head. Branches were also set at Whiterocks, Leland, and Myton.

While Smart intended the lands for white purchase, it is puzzling that he recorded that the land was dedicated "to the Lord for the settlement of the people and for the preaching of the gospel to the Indians."[19] Not anticipated was the immediate, crushing impact of white colonization on resident White River Utes. In 1906 several hundred Ute men, women, children, and animals fled north in "an anguished odyssey" to join the Sioux on their reservation to unify in opposition to the loss of their homelands.[20]

Smart's final years were without criticism by LDS Church leaders for his post-Manifesto polygamy. However, Smart and his wives, Anna and Mary, descended into "genteel poverty," with their money "exhausted in church service and in good works and bad loans for the community."[21] Ironically, Matthias Cowley, the close friend who married Smart to Mary, was excommunicated for his stand on polygamy and lived much of his remaining life in a degree of public dishonor. Smart's former mentor, John W. Taylor, met a similar fate.

In the long view, appraising the success of Smart's Uintah Basin's colonization is much like judging the success of Abraham Owen Woodruff in colonizing the Big Horn Basin. When Smart arrived, Duchesne County did not have a single LDS ward; by 1930 the combined membership of Uintah and Duchesne Counties totaled thirteen wards.[22] By this standard Smart met the charge given him, but his final years were not spent in reward, but in privation. Had Abraham Owen Woodruff not died before he reached age thirty-two, and had the LDS leadership not acted against John W. Taylor and Matthias Cowley, the Big Horn colonization almost certainly would have had a different outcome. When Woodruff arrived in the Big Horn Basin, the scant number of Mormons were scattered in several small communities. Woodruff died prematurely of a possibly preventable infectious disease only three years into his effort, and further advancement was lost without him. Success of both colonizations might have been attained by commercial agricultural advancement, but the Uintah and Big Horn ventures both struggled against the same obstacles: high altitude, severe weather, short growing seasons, undependable rainfall, the costs of obtaining and maintaining water supply by irrigation canals, and soil alkalization.

Lack of railroad service also prevented movement of agricultural products and livestock to markets.

Both last colonization efforts deserve a historical record. That of William H. Smart has been written. It remains for this work to examine those who answered the "last called colonization" in meeting the challenges of Wyoming's immense, arid Big Horn Basin.

Introduction

if you plant for a year, plant rice;
if you plant for ten years, plant trees;
if you plant for a hundred years, plant men.

—Chinese proverb

THE COLONIZING ACCOMPLISHMENTS of Brigham Young, the second prophet and president of The Church of Jesus Christ of Latter-day Saints, are well known. Through focused purpose, top-down organization, enforced unity, and immense sacrifice by thousands of Latter-day Saints, over three hundred settlements were founded on orders from this remarkable leviathan. Apart from the contiguous settlements to the north of Great Salt Lake City and in the valley's southern end, the first colonization group was officially called by Brigham Young to the Pacific Islands on June 3, 1849.[1]

Under Young's leadership, a man holding a priesthood office in the LDS church would often first hear of his call from the pulpit. This call to duty from the prophet was not received by the faithful as an option, even though its immediate fulfillment might be attended with great personal, family, and financial hardship. Calls may have appeared as random choices, but a closer look reveals that certain occupations and skills were often held in common by those who prospered in their callings.

In the decade before Brigham Young's death in 1877, at least 127 new colonies were founded. However, according to historian Richard Sherlock, the four-year period from 1876 to 1879 saw one hundred new settlements in Arizona, Idaho, Colorado, and Wyoming. According to Sherlock, "In the 1880s major new settlements were founded from Mexico to Canada with the important settlement at the Snake River Fork area around Rexburg beginning in the late 1870s. Others swell[ed] to a flood tide in the years 1882–84."[2] By 1880 Utah Territory was unlike any other territory in that its steady growth was due "almost entirely to its agricultural capabilities."[3]

Arable land had been eagerly taken up. Maturing young people who wanted to farm or those who lived in the rural periphery, miles distant from urban loci, were increasingly forced to look elsewhere—even beyond Utah Territory—for their future.

Following Young's death in 1877, colonization efforts continued under the tenures of succeeding church presidents John Taylor, Wilford Woodruff, and Lorenzo Snow. From 1870 to 1880, the average number of immigrants was 1,620 per year. From 1880 through 1883, 8,318 immigrants arrived, averaging 2,079 newcomers per year.[4] Mormon historian Leonard J. Arrington claims that if the "number of people involved" is used as the measure, the period 1896 to 1904 occurred "one of the most intense colonization efforts in Mormon history."[5] Coincident with the escalating disparity of relative overpopulation for the available productive land and the outward migration of families, a breakdown began of the structured Mormon-village system.[6] Additional change came from the shift from subsistence to self-sufficient farming to commercialized agriculture that began first in the territory's northern counties then gradually expanded across other rural Mormon communities through the 1890s. When that "decade ended, evidence was everywhere at hand that self-sufficiency had been abandoned," and farmers were reaching for success in commercial enterprises with organized land and irrigation companies.[7]

Simultaneous with these interrelated socioeconomic challenges was the drive for sovereignty for the peculiar people living in Utah Territory. The bane to achieving statehood arose from three obstructions within the Mormon's basic religious doctrines. The first was self-rule by an inseparable fusion of church and state believed superior to—and independent of—control by laws of the United States. Citizens were to answer to God's laws, not those of man. This had strength since the territory's people were predominantly members of The Church of Jesus Christ of Latter-day Saints. Through allegiance they were led and controlled by a single man, their president and prophet.

The second obstruction was their drive for *terra firma*, for taking ownership of Utah Territory's land and controlling its use. Here they could establish and defend their independent State of Deseret of the Kingdom of God on Earth. The third obstruction to statehood received the most attention and criticism. Latter-day Saints held that marriage of a man to more than one woman was a God-given commandment—even a sacrament—that they must follow to achieve the highest rewards in a life to come. In this hereafter, their human body would transition to a divine form and they would become masters of their own planet somewhere in the universe.[8] Many LDS members believed that this unique variation from traditional marriage was a religious right—superior and overriding any civil instrument—and was entitled to them by the United States Constitution's protection of freedom of religion.

Through the Antebellum and Civil War years, Utah Territory's demands for sovereignty were not unlike those held by most southern states as properly within the rights of an individual state's government. While the Latter-day Saints' unyielding doctrine of plural marriage was generally repugnant to Protestant Victorian America, it was considered analogous with the South's unshakable, Bible-based, doctrinal belief in the necessity and correctness of human slavery.[9]

Non-Mormon opponents of Utah's demands for sovereignty found the widely held and passionate disapproval of polygamy to be a convenient tool, a handle, to use to attack the greater issue: Mormon theocracy. Criticism especially of polygamy from non-Mormons lasted sixty years, from the tenures of church presidents Joseph Smith Jr., Brigham Young, and John Taylor through the disingenuous acts—publicly decrying polygamy but continuing to engage in it privately, even fathering children—of presidents Wilford Woodruff, Lorenzo Snow, and Joseph F. Smith. Polygamy's opposition held a significant role in the federal government's delay of statehood for Utah, not granted until 1896. Nonetheless, the performing of secret polygamous marriages continued as an insoluble issue for the Mormons and their critics for at least ten years into the twentieth century.

The two Mormon colonization groups described herein, sent during the administration of President Lorenzo Snow in 1900 and 1901, were unusual if not unique for several reasons in addition to both being the last called colonization.[10]

First, the Big Horn Basin effort was pre-capitalized within a formal company, "The Big Horn Basin Colonization Company." This was a "corporation duly organized and existing under and by virtue of the Laws of the State of Wyoming."[11] Other colonization companies, such as the Mexican Colonization and Agricultural Company[12] and the Juarez Tanning and Manufacturing Company, appear to have been created for profit well after the Mormon leaders had begun colonization, rather than as a preplanned enterprise.[13]

Second, the Big Horn groups were sent to an area that pushed the limits of Utah's adjacent theocratic influence at the time. Wyoming, with fewer than sixty thousand people and in many ways still a frontier, had been granted statehood in 1890. Fortunately, this Mormon enterprise was not opposed by Wyoming's people or the state's elected government. To the contrary, this migration had the approval and cooperation of Wyoming's governor, topmost civil officials, and its most widely known and acclaimed citizen, William F. "Buffalo Bill" Cody.[14]

Third, the colonists were made up of both those called and not called, but the latter volunteered for various reasons after hearing the venture discussed in public or from the *Deseret News* or other newspapers.[15]

Fourth, the enterprise was saved from almost certain financial failure by a substantial infusion of cash from the Chicago, Burlington and Quincy Railroad Company, in payment for services rendered by the Big Horn colony's men, teams, and equipment.

However, the most remarkable feature of this group, particularly considering its remote, hard-to-reach northern Wyoming location—only fourteen miles from Montana's state line—is the circumstantial evidence that it was designed by a special high-ranking young Mormon leader for it to become an out-of-the-way station for polygamy's survival. Abraham Owen Woodruff, the son of President Wilford Woodruff, was only twenty-four years old when he was ordained as an LDS church apostle by his father. He was the rising star among the brethren and at only age twenty-eight was the prime mover, under the approval of Lorenzo Snow, of the effort to found new colonies for Mormons.

While they had less direct feet-on-the-ground roles in Wyoming's colonization than Woodruff, three other Quorum of Twelve members shared his passion for plural marriage as an unchangeable doctrine. To varying degrees, they also continued to perform the marriage ceremony post-Manifesto. They were apostles John Whittaker Taylor, son of John Taylor, Matthias Foss Cowley, and Marriner Wood Merrill.[16]

Taylor and Cowley were expelled from the Quorum in 1905 when their unwavering support of plural marriage and active involvement in performing them became a national embarrassment for the church. This was a politically motivated, sacrificial act by LDS church leadership, precipitated by the scrutiny and criticism in the US Senate during hearings that followed the election of Apostle Reed Smoot. Not a polygamist, Smoot was told by other senators that he was not their target. Many political leaders across the nation knew that plural marriages continued to be performed in secret, despite repeated promises and false claims to the contrary by Wilford Woodruff, Lorenzo Snow, and Joseph F. Smith. Cohabitation with plural wives and children born to these unions also continued. Most fundamental was the primacy of federal law wherein these acts were illegal, overriding the theocracy of Utah's legislature, controlled as it was by LDS church leadership.[17]

In the spring of 1900, several hundred men, women, children, and animals started their journey toward Wyoming, leaving their homes and farms. A second group, substantial in size but smaller in number, came in spring 1901. The second group has received far less historical attention than the first. Colonists in smaller groups continued arriving in the basin from 1902 to 1905. Almost all were LDS church members, coming from nineteen Utah counties, including Millard, Morgan, Iron, and Summit. They came from Bear Lake and Madison County, Idaho, and smaller numbers from Arizona, Indiana, Massachusetts, and Wyoming. Many came seeking a better life, traveling by horseback, covered wagon, and on foot, just as many among them had done decades before, in handcart companies during the 1850s and 1860s.

Some colonists left behind a substantial level of comfort and accomplishment.[18] Byron Sessions and his wife, for example, sold shares they held in the Bear River Land and Livestock Company at a substantial loss and left a recently completed, well-appointed, two-story brick home in Woodruff, Rich County, in answer to the face-to-face call from Lorenzo Snow. As did many, Sessions and his family lived in a tent from April 22, 1900, to late October or early November that year, when they moved into the log cabin he had built for them.[19]

The destination was a piece of western America little known to them. It was readily apparent some had left behind hard-earned rudiments of progress: irrigated farms that sustained gardens and field crops, safe drinking water, secure shelter from weather, social networks, some schooling for their children, and a small but significant amount of medical care.[20] At their destination they found isolation, dust-laden wind, rattlesnakes, and arid land—much that would soon become leached with alkali. Undeterred, the faithful relied on prophecies from their leaders and immediately started over, scraping and scratching the ground for the necessities for survival.

This last colonization used the standard village template that had been successful in hundreds of earlier settlements. In Cowley, for example, homesites were placed centrally with farmlands and pasture at a distance, ensuring the people's unity and security. This time-tested plan also assured control by religious leaders who were also civil leaders. Top-down communication came from the pulpit and through the priesthood's high priests, seventies, and elders. Dissent or misbehavior were readily apparent and could be readily dealt with by priesthood leaders.

Several among the 1900 Big Horn colonists or their descendants have published their remembrances of hardship, endurance, faith, and accomplishment. The first was Charles A. Welch in his 1949 work, *History of the Big Horn Basin*. Mark N. Partridge's book *With Book and Plow* followed in 1967 and was revised in 1976. Attorney and artist Melvin M. Fillerup wrote his paean of faith—*Sidon, the Canal that Faith Built*—that appeared in 1988. The final work, *Wyoming's Big Horn Basin to 1901*, by Lawrence Milton Woods, was published in 1997 but does not cover the years of this study.

The present work frequently calls on these contributors while attempting to place the colonization within the broader context of financial, socioeconomic, and political crises of their time. No mention is made by authors Welch, Partridge, Fillerup, or Woods of plural marriage being a motivating factor for migrating to the Big Horn. Thus far the writings of Owen Woodruff, Mathias Cowley, and several other general authorities of their time have not been found to contain that specific admission. However, it is an underlying thesis of this work that this last officially called colonization by The Church of Jesus Christ of Latter-day Saints and Apostle Abraham Owen Woodruff was intended to preserve, in frontier isolation, a place to continue plural marriage.

CHAPTER I

A Primer on Latter-day Saint Polygamy

We hardly dared speak of it.
The very walls had ears. We spoke of it only in whispers.[1]

—Zina Diantha Huntington Jacobs Smith Young

THE DISCERNING READER may justifiably ask whether it is necessary to cover the distinctive marriage practices among LDS church members shortly after they came into existence in 1830. This primer is intended to set the polygamous marriages performed by a handful of high-ranking LDS leaders from 1890 to 1907 within the broader framework of Mormon marriages that began shortly after the church's organization and spanned approximately eighty years. Polygamy was a highly significant part of life for almost all leaders in the Nauvoo era, involving many Mormon women and the birth of many children. This background is essential to understanding that the several Mormon leaders whose unbending allegiance to continuing plural marriage were the same who led the extraordinary 1900 and 1901 migration to Wyoming's Great Basin.[2]

It is beyond the scope of this work to provide full treatment of the numerous sexual unions, plural marriages through sealings, possible wives, posthumous marriages, polyandry, and proxy unions of Joseph Smith and others of high rank among the early years of Mormon leadership.[3] My brief review is simply intended to supply a general background sufficient for understanding the depth of commitment to this principle that nearly destroyed The Church of Jesus Christ of Latter-day Saints by federal legislation between 1887 and 1890.[4]

The LDS church's first president and prophet, Joseph Smith Jr., "began to tamper . . . with one of the most basic mores in Occidental society" in the early years of the church's existence. In her 1945 biography of Joseph Smith, Mormon historian Fawn Brodie presented details regarding twenty-one "wives" of Smith. These were in addition to twenty-seven whose names were previously compiled by LDS Church Historian Andrew Jensen in 1887, bringing the total number to forty-eight.[5] Because such unions were neither performed under civil law nor recorded in official available church records, they were uncovered from miscellaneous, often secondary, or questionable sources. Therefore, other historians later arrived at varying total numbers: D. Michael Quinn lists forty-six marriages and George D. Smith, forty-three.[6] In his detailed award-winning publication of 1997, *In Sacred Loneliness*, author Todd Compton applied more stringent criteria to the accumulated evidence. He accepted only thirty-three wives for Joseph Smith.[7]

The LDS church's official founding was on April 6, 1830, in Fayette in the northern Finger Lakes area of New York, about fifty miles due west of Syracuse. Joseph Smith's Book of Mormon was published in March of that year in nearby Palmyra, New York. The evidence from Brodie and other historians suggests that Smith's first sexual pseudoconnubial actions date near that time. By spring of 1831 Joseph and his legal first wife Emma, with other church members, had moved from New York to Kirtland, Ohio. Here they remained for six years, during which time Joseph claimed more than sixty revelations from God regarding the LDS church, its organization, and its doctrines.

As early as 1832 Joseph Smith was linked to a "celestial" marriage with Nancy Marinda Johnson. In that year the prophet lived for a time in the home of John Johnson, Marinda's father, in Hiram, Ohio. It was alleged that her "brother Eli led a mob against Joseph ... because 'he had been too intimate with his sister.'"[8] Brodie's accounting of Marinda is disputed by Compton as lacking evidence, noting that Marinda had no brother named Eli. Compton accepts that Smith's tar and feathering from a mob as well as their plan for his castration on the night of March 24, 1832, could have been caused by knowledge of a sexual liaison, but Compton claims there were other equally plausible causes for the violence. Ten years later, in April 1842, Smith entered into a union with Marinda in Nauvoo, Illinois, while her legal husband, Orson Hyde, an early LDS leader and apostle, was absent on a mission in Jerusalem. Compton records, "As Miranda was apparently sincerely in love with Orson Hyde, polyandry must have been enormously difficult for her."[9]

In 1833 Fanny Alger, a comely seventeen-year-old young woman, was taken into the family household by Emma. Compton notes that Brodie considered Joseph's relationship with Fanny to be an affair, but he cites the testimony of Mosiah Hancock that a marriage ceremony took place in February or March of that year after Mosiah's father, Levi Hancock, acted as intermediary for Fanny.[10] The prophet's grammar teacher, Chauncey G. Webb, had recorded that the woman "was 'unable to conceal the consequences of her celestial relation with the prophet,'" and Emma drove her from the house.[11] Compton notes that "since there is no record of Fanny having a child, either Webb was mistaken (although this seems unlikely if Fanny lived in his home after leaving the Smith home), or the child was miscarried or died young, or was raised under another name."[12]

In his 2005 analysis of Smith's early marriages, historian Gary J. Bergera does not accept the criteria for Fanny Alger to be considered a wife.[13] Historian Richard L. Bushman disagrees, pointing out that Smith never denied a sexual relationship with Alger but insisted it was not adulterous. Bushman wanted it on record that Joseph had never confessed to such a sin with Fanny. Presumably, Smith felt innocent because he had "married" Alger.[14] Bushman adds that neither Joseph nor Hyrum Smith taught against the doctrine of plural marriage from the pulpit. "Joseph insisted 'the Church had not received any license from him to commit adultery, fornication, or any such thing but to the contrary if any man Commit adultery He Could not receive the Cel[e]stial kingdom of God.'"

Some evidence suggests that Lucinda Pendleton Morgan Harris was in a relationship with Smith as mistress or wife around 1838. Lucinda was born in 1801; she first married William Morgan then George Washington Harris. Notably, Joseph Smith lived in the Harris family home in Far West, Missouri, in 1838. In 1842 when a disturbed Sarah Marinda Bates Pratt (married to Orson Pratt) sought Lucinda's solace regarding Smith's recent marriage proposal to Sarah, Lucinda replied that Sarah had been foolish for not accepting, explaining that "I am his mistress since four years" (although this was prior to Nauvoo's founding).[15]

Compton claims that a non-Mormon journalist, B. W. Richmond, allegedly checked into the Nauvoo House in mid-June 1844 to call on Lucinda and ask about her dead husband, William Morgan. Richmond would later claim that when the bodies of Joseph and Hyrum Smith were brought to Nauvoo from their death site at Carthage jail, he observed that when Emma Smith and Mary Fielding Smith grieved over their dead husbands, that onlookers could not help but notice "a lady standing at the head of Joseph's body, her face covered, and her whole frame convulsed with weeping." Richmond implied that this was Lucinda Harris, grieving over the death of another husband. Andrew Jenson's list of Smith wives included Lucinda, but Jenson did not cite date, place, or source of this claim.[16] The tenuous evidence of Lucinda's marriage to Smith would mean that Louisa Beaman's marriage to Joseph on April 5, 1841, "in the City of Nauvoo" proved that Smith's polygamous marriages did not begin before the Nauvoo time.[17] According to Bushman, the former city of Commerce, Illinois, was renamed Nauvoo by Smith in May 1839.[18] G. D. Smith records that Beaman did not live in Nauvoo until after Smith's death in 1844. She later married Brigham Young and bore him five children.[19]

Fanny Young, the older sister of Brigham Young, is commonly listed as Joseph's thirty-third and last plural wife. Both Brodie and Compton judge this marriage solidly documented. She was twice widowed and, at age fifty-six, one the oldest of Joseph's wives. Fanny was nearly fourteen years old when Brigham was born on June 1, 1801, in Whitingham, Vermont, where the Young family had lived for some eight months. Because their mother, Abigail Nabby Howe Young, suffered from pulmonary tuberculosis and was "too weak to properly care for the new infant," Fanny became Brigham's surrogate mother.[20] The family's cow only allowed Fanny to approach her to get milk for her newly born brother. Fanny was "beloved by all . . . with her sympathies always exercised for the poor and distressed." In 1815, at age twenty-eight, Fanny Young married Robert Carr in Hopkinton, Massachusetts. As Carr proved "unfaithful and profligate," the marriage did not survive, and the couple had no children.

In 1830 a Book of Mormon was left by missionaries with the Young family. Fanny read the book along with their father John and her brothers Phinehas and Brigham, thus "the course of Mormon and western American history was thereby changed." Fanny was married in 1832 to Roswell Murray who was unwilling to join the LDS church even though Fanny was baptized; they moved with the Mormons to Ohio, Missouri, and Nauvoo. Murray was said to be "an enormously kind, unselfish man." He died in 1839, leaving Fanny single again. In a conversation in Nauvoo on November 2, 1843, Fanny expressed that she did not want a marital companion in a life to come, but Smith immediately dismissed this and—addressing Brigham Young—bluntly instructed him to "seal this lady to me." Without attempting to dissuade Smith or influence Fanny, Brigham immediately did so. Compton stresses that Fanny's marriage to Joseph Smith "shows how casual and unromantic polygamy could be." As did hundreds of other Latter-day Saints, Fanny traveled from Nauvoo to Winter Quarters and from there emigrated to Salt Lake City in 1850. Fanny's health rapidly declined, and by 1856 Brigham offered his sister lifetime living quarters in his newly completed Lion House.[21] She died there in June 1859, aged seventy-one years.

From the time of Joseph Smith's first plural marriage in 1841 to his death in 1844, twenty-eight men and 106 women who had been previously married, either civilly or in plurality, entered the prophet's order of celestial matrimony, according to historian Gary Bergera.[22]

Polygamy was high on the list of public opposition to the Mormons in 1838, which caused Smith and many followers to move to Caldwell County, Missouri. Violence erupted and David Wyman Patten, an early apostle, was mortally wounded.[23] When a report reached Missouri's governor Lilburn Boggs, he issued an order for all Mormons to be expelled or exterminated. Soon thereafter, a local mob massacred seventeen Mormons, including young children, at a site called Haun's Mill.[24]

By 1839 the Mormons, due to local tensions and their unusual marriage practices, were forced to migrate northward into Illinois where they established the city of Nauvoo on the Mississippi River's east bank. Polygamy in various forms veritably blossomed there for Joseph Smith and many other Mormon leaders.

Compton lays out the record for the several years before Smith's death:

> In 1841 Joseph cautiously added three wives. Then in 1842 he married eleven wives in the first eight months of the year. New marriages then stopped for five months . . . possibly due to [the] exposé of its practice by disaffected [member] John C. Bennett who had been a prominent Mormon leader in Nauvoo and participant in plural marriages.

By 1843 Joseph publicly claimed to have received God's revelation regarding the principle of plural marriage. In that year he married fourteen more wives during the first six months. According to Compton, Smith married no women in the final eight months of his life, perhaps out of self-doubt or because of Emma's threat to leave him.[25]

The intimate details of Joseph Smith's life as a polygamist and his purported seductions of young women remain an interest to dozens of historians to this day. Recent publications give substantial evidence that in the final months of Smith's life he engaged in sexual impropriety, even with no new marriages. In May 1844 the circuit court of Hancock County subpoenaed the Nauvoo stake president, William Marks, to select a grand jury. Among the jurors were other Mormons, including Edward Hunter and Daniel H. Wells. On May 23, 1844, the jury brought an indictment of "The People of the State of Illinois v. Joseph Smith, Sen. for adultery and fornication."[26] The indictment was based on several counts; all on "good and sufficient evidence." Bail was set at three hundred dollars.

The first count dealt with the crime of adultery. It stated that Smith lived in open adultery with Maria Lawrence on October 12, 1843, but that he also did this "divers [sic] other days & times before" that date and up until the finding on the indictment. Count two was less specific, charging Smith with living in an open state of adultery and fornication with "certain women to the jurors unknown." The final count dealt only with adultery and charged that Smith lived in an open state of adultery with women unknown on January 1, 1844.[27]

Historian John S. Dinger explains that specifically naming the women involved with Smith risked charges of slander. This and other legal issues resulted in Joseph Smith not being brought to trial on the indictments before his death, only thirty-four days later. According to author Jim Whitefield, Smith married sisters Maria Lawrence, age nineteen, and Sarah Lawrence, age seventeen, on May 11, 1843, some four years after taking over their guardianship and estate management of eight thousand dollars in gold from their deceased father's estate. Joseph and Emma had taken the two girls into their home around 1842.[28]

On June 27, 1844, while they were imprisoned and charged with treason at Carthage, Illinois, brothers Hyrum and Joseph Smith Jr. were assassinated in a lopsided battle exchange, where they attempted to protect themselves with pistols from a fully armed local mob.

Throughout the late 1830s, and until the Latter-day Saints left Nauvoo in 1846, a significant number of prominent men in church leadership were secretly "taken into the system" of plural marriage. While detailed treatment of these marriage events is beyond this study's scope, historians cite the names of Hyrum and William Smith, Brigham Young, Heber C. Kimball, William Clayton, Willard Richards, Benjamin F. Johnson, John D. Lee, Theodore Turley, Ezra T. Benson, Reynolds Cahoon, Howard Egan, Parley P. Pratt, Erastus Snow, Lorenzo Dow Young, and Edwin D. Wooley as marrying multiple wives with Joseph Smith's permission in this period.[29]

Following his 1822 marriage to Vilate Murray and before leaving Nauvoo, Heber C. Kimball "had been sealed in some fashion to more than thirty women." While historian Linda Thatcher Ulrich considers that "the majority of these 'marriages' were purely ceremonial," when "the Kimballs left Nauvoo, five of Heber's plural wives … were pregnant."[30] Subsequently, at least sixty-eight children were born to women who married Kimball while living in Nauvoo.[31] The score of men participating with a large but unknown number of women suggests that the details of plural marriage was far more porous than appreciated.

Most LDS men participating in polygamy, both in the pre-Utah period and after Utah's settlement, held two features in common: priesthood leadership positions and a privileged socioeconomic status. Polygamy was never universal among LDS men, for "only certain men were appointed to marry multiple women. This became a marker of power, representing a higher status, higher authority, and stronger masculinity within Mormon society."[32] Estimates of polygamy's prevalence among Mormon men have varied widely. One study in 1913 cited a range of 15 to 20 percent, a commonly accepted figure.[33] Carmon Hardy emphasized that "it was Mormonism's elite that was mostly involved," and "more than half had been called as branch presidents, bishops, stake presidents, or other high offices."[34] If men in these offices were not well-to-do before their rise in a priesthood office, they often became so.

During this period, bishops "could draw at will from the primarily non-cash tithing," and stake presidents received money from the tithe they collected from their congregations. By 1884 bishops were limited to 8 percent of tithes collected, while stake presidents received 2 percent of what the bishops collected.[35] Brodie was emphatic in appraising this aspect of leadership's benefits: "Wealth and power [were] considered basic among the blessings both of earth and of heaven, and even if they were to be denied them in this life, then they must assuredly enjoy them in the next." She considered Joseph Smith as "no hair shirt prophet. He believed in the good life, with moderate self-indulgence in food and drink.... And it is no accident his theology in the end ... became an ingenuous blend of supernaturalism and materialism, which promised in heaven a continuation of all earthly pleasures—work, wealth, sex, and power."[36]

For a period of time after the Homestead Act of 1862, plural marriage was linked to land acquisition and bettering the financial status of those who entered into the practice. The act allowed any male age twenty-one or older, who was a citizen or any head of family, to make an entry for 160 acres at $1.25 an acre. The term "head of family" was interpreted by Mormons to include plural wives, and instances of such abuse were published in the *Salt Lake Tribune*, the tireless critic of LDS practices of polygamy in its various scenarios: "In one day 1250 acres of public land were gobbled up by the wives of two men in clear violation of the spirit of the homestead law." The lands taken up were "in the vicinity of a located station on the proposed Utah Southern Railroad, to be built by the Church of Jesus Christ of Latter-day Saints," almost assuring their increase in value. While the genuine head of a Utah family could take only one quarter section of land, a polygamist man could file on as many homesteads as he had wives, accruing clear financial and economic advantages.[37]

From his study of Joseph Smith's wives, Compton also viewed plural marriage from the perspective of female participants: "polygamous wives, even those married to prominent, well-to-do men, were often not supported adequately financially." He cites one notable example of Annie Clark Tanner, the second of six wives of church educator Joseph Marion Tanner. Tanner's plural marriages were secretive; three were done post-Manifesto, including to Sarah Taylor Evans performed by Matthias Cowley in 1903. Annie wrote, "We returned from Provo after a single school year there. All of us were conscious now that we would have to make our own way, if possible, independent of help from Mr. Tanner." She was later told by her husband that she should "look to [her] stalwart sons for support." Being one among several wives often extracted other costs for the women, such as loneliness, despair, depression, helplessness, abandonment, anger, and low self-esteem. The hidden end result for many wives was solitude.[38]

Some have made counterarguments for polygamous unions performed after Joseph Smith's death and in Utah Territory. Yorgason asserts that for some wives, polygamy "helped relieve loneliness," but not through her husband. He cites that polygamy "provided opportunities for intimate female friendship, made sharing household and child-care responsibilities possible, and emancipated wives from many marital duties." Further, polygamy challenged the contemporary view of female dependency; feminism was nascent, for women no longer needed to live for men. Women even called into question romantic love. Female bonding, independence, and mother-child bonds were strengthened.[39] Other scholars object to the term "emancipated" for women in polygamy, noting that some—especially those in homes with many children—often were required by patriarchal oppression to take outside employment.[40]

Following the deaths of Joseph and Hyrum Smith, Mormons increasingly fled from several counties of Missouri and Illinois because of unwarranted persecution and violence against them—as they claimed—and because they were forcibly expelled for their unlawful practices and unacceptable sexual unions—as critics insisted. Fraudulent acts, political manipulations, and devotion to a one-man civic rule proved more causative than the standalone issue of multiple wives. The result of this aggregated antipathy was the crossing of the Mississippi River's frozen surface by upwards of ten thousand church members in the bitter winter of 1846. In a hegira of immeasurable personal sacrifice, they forged westward to an interim refuge they called Winter Quarters, about six miles directly north of midtown in present-day Omaha, Nebraska. From this place Brigham Young led a vanguard in the spring of 1847 to found what he named Great Salt Lake City in the West's Great Basin. The Latter-day Saints requested statehood with the name Deseret, but in September 1850 they were given only territorial status as Utah Territory, a name derived from an Indigenous tribe, the Utes. Here they continued plural marriage—without public acknowledgement by Brigham Young—until 1851 as an integral part of society, even an essential sacrament for attaining the highest level of reward in an afterlife.

The isolated refuge provided by the Great Basin's vastness was short-lived, as Utah was situated as a waystation on a path of massive western migration. Passing thousands grew to tens of thousands with migrants seeking gold in California or agricultural paradise in what would become Oregon and Washington. Polygamy in Utah soon became apparent across the continent, reaching even Europe where LDS missionaries had denied polygamy as only a rumor planted by critics. Brigham Young first admitted his personal polygamy in a discourse on February 5, 1851, in Great Salt Lake City:

> So if the Latter-day Saints wish to have more wives than one to live holy, and raise up Holy Seed unto the Lord, let him enjoy that privilege. . . . I have more wives than one: I have many and I am not ashamed to have it known. Some deny in the States that we have more wives than one. I never deny it. I am perfectly willing that the people in Washington should know that I have more than one wife and they are pure before the lord and are approved of in his sight. I have been commanded of God to pursue this course.[41]

More than a year later, on August 29, 1852, Young instructed Orson Pratt, an apostle and member of the Council of Fifty, a secretive political body organized by Joseph Smith in 1844, to take the public pulpit to unashamedly announce to the world polygamy's continued existence as doctrine and practice.[42]

England's mission president Samuel W. Richards had written in April of that year:

> Much opposition has existed in this country for a few months past and much still continues. The report . . . in relation to polygamy, etc.

in the [Great Salt Lake] Valley has been one great cause of it. Many [Mormons] are turned out of employment for embracing the work, and . . . attempts are made to poison elders, etc. . . . [Mormon] women in this country are shamefully abused with [strong] language."[43]

The first admission to Latter-day Saints in England of the LDS church's official sanction of plural marriage was on December 25 and 26, 1852, in a London Conference meeting in an area called Whitechapel. Elder James Marsden read the revelation (now in the Doctrine and Covenants, Section 132) to the congregation.[44] After the doctrine regarding polygamy was published in Liverpool's *Millennial Star* in January 1853, baptism rates in England fell by 88 percent, and church membership dropped 60 percent in Great Britain from 1853 to 1863.[45]

From 1858 to 1860 and 1863 to 1867, non-Mormon newspapers in Utah Territory published articles critical of Mormon society, the practice of plural marriage, and LDS theocracy that attempted to supplant national laws governing states and territories. The *Valley Tan*, the official newspaper of President James Buchanan's federal army sent to Utah in 1857 to replace Young as territorial governor, treated the subject repeatedly. The *Daily Union Vedette*, published by a second US army, became another independent press voice. The California and Nevada Volunteers' commander, Colonel P. Edward Connor, was sent to protect overland migration and keep watch on the Mormons whose fealty to the Union was much in doubt and its favoritism to the Confederacy apparent.[46] *Valley Tan* editors produced at least thirty articles critical of polygamy. Talented journalists and editors recruited by Connor for the *Vedette* placed more than four hundred citations containing the words "polygamy," "polygamous," and "plural marriage."[47] Its pages also spoke boldly against the ruling monarchy's many murders in the territory and the theocracy that defied federal oversight. It was common practice at the time for any newspaper's articles to be reprinted by other newspapers, east and west, and this was true with the *Valley Tan* and *Vedette*. The subject of multiple wives for one man was titillating. It sold newspapers.

The increasing weaponization of polygamy against the theocracy of Utah Territory from the 1870s onward seems to distract historians from two other elements that were raised by LDS prophets but given only transient treatment in modern works. In 1866 Brigham Young prophesied that monogamist Latter-day Saints could enter the Kingdom of Heaven, but only polygamist men and women in plural marriage could achieve deification and create children in the afterlife:

If you desire with all your hearts to obtain the blessings which Abraham obtained, you will be polygamists at least in your faith, or you will come short of enjoying the salvation and the glory [of eternal offspring] which Abraham has obtained.... The only men who become Gods, even the Sons of God, are those who enter into polygamy. Others attain unto a glory and may even be permitted to come into the presence of the Father and the Son; but they cannot reign as kings in glory, because they had blessings offered unto them, and they refused to accept them.[48]

Annie Clark Tanner wrote: "It was taught at that time that the second wife opened the door of salvation in the Celestial Kingdom not only for herself, but for the husband and his first wife."[49]

The transcontinental railroad's completion in 1869 furthered the presence and permanence of non-Mormons in Utah Territory. Scores of business leaders interested in commerce, mining, and manufacturing, as well as professionals such as the retired general P. Edward Connor, US Marshal George R. Maxwell, William Godbe, Charles C. Goodwin, Orlando Powers, Patrick H. Lannin, Henry W. Lawrence, William Nelson, and many others formed the non-Mormon Liberal Party. A major party tenet was to influence federal lawmaking to bring about changes in Mormon practices—including polygamy—that were holding in limbo statehood for Utah.[50] In Washington, no less than twenty-seven federal bills were introduced and failed until the Edmunds and Edmunds-Tucker bills were enacted in 1882 and 1887, dissolving the LDS church's incorporation with seizure of its cash, assets, and property.[51] Arrests and imprisonments of several notable Mormon leaders for cohabitation and the death of President John Taylor added to their burdens.

In January 1880 Apostle Wilford Woodruff was in a sheep herder's camp along the Little Colorado River when he awoke at night "full of the Spirit of the Lord, and he received a revelation" that stressed several principles, among them the divinity of plural marriage. The revelation was presented to the Quorum of Twelve and approved in April 1880. It contained a comprehensive list of individuals who were destined to receive the Lord's wrath, including "that Nation, or House or people who seek to hinder my People from obeying the Patriarchal Law of Abraham which leadeth to a Celestial Glory which has been revealed unto my Saints through the mouth of my servant, Joseph."[52]

In the spring of 1890 legislation written by Robert Newton Baskin, Salt Lake City's non-Mormon mayor and an outspoken activist, was introduced as the Cullom-Struble Bill and was favorably reported out of committee. The bill called for the disfranchisement of all LDS church members unless polygamy was relinquished. With the prospects for passage very high, the controversial young Mormon luminary Frank J. Cannon spoke persuasively before the Senate Territories Committee and interviewed senators privately, asking for a delay and reporting that church leaders were soon "to make a concession concerning . . . polygamy."[53] On October 4, the LDS newspaper *Deseret News* published a proclamation by President Wilford Woodruff as an "Official Declaration," later described as the "Manifesto," denouncing the practice of polygamy but not the theological principle of celestial or eternal marriage.[54]

Now that Mormons no longer intended to enter plural marriages and polygamists would live with only one wife, opposition to statehood diminished, and Utah became the forty-fifth state on January 4, 1896. Woodruff had not publicly addressed the issue of continuing open cohabitation, but "in a meeting with members of the Quorum of the Twelve shortly after the issuance of the Manifesto, [he] indicated that 'This manifesto only refers to future marriages, and does not affect past conditions. I did not, could not, and would not promise that you would desert your wives and children. This you cannot do in honor.'"[55]

Only thirteen months after statehood, ninety-year-old President Wilford Woodruff, who had reluctantly issued the 1890 Manifesto that disallowed further plural marriages, appears to have been secretly married or sealed in the final year of his life to a forty-nine-year-old married woman. In Salt Lake City on February 5, 1897, President Woodruff wrote the first of ninety references concerning this woman during the remaining months of his life: "I had a visitation at the Office to day of Mrs. Lydia Von Pinklestein [*sic*] Mountford A Russian from Jerusalem. She was Accompanied by another Lady."[56] The historian Susan Staker explains, "here begins one of the more remarkable relationships of Woodruff's final years—perhaps of his life." Staker notes, "nothing rivals the intensity of interest displayed in the pages of his journal on Lydia Mountford."[57] Multiple entries through February, March, and April document this with recurring references to her visits, and of Woodruff's "concerns about the affairs, personal and financial, of Madame Mountford." Woodruff's entries do not comment on Mountford's LDS church baptism by Anthon H. Lund sometime in February.[58]

Throughout the remainder of 1897, Woodruff's apparent secrecy in his diary regarding matters with Mountford was abetted by his personal secretary and fellow polygamist, L. John Nuttall.[59] Around April 28 Mountford left Salt Lake City to travel to San Francisco, and letters were exchanged through June and July. On her return she met with Woodruff on July 21 at his home when he was feeling feeble, and there she gave him a sample of her "massage treatment." Several August days—up to the 16th—were marked by exchanges of floral bouquets. On August 24, Nuttall brought the president a letter from Mountford that they read together, but the contents were not recorded. In early September Woodruff discussed a trip to the Pacific Coast with Nuttall, "for a change of air and exercise," but the two would only go "on the quiet and avoid newspaper men and interviews." Woodruff's wife Emma and daughter Alice wished to accompany him but were told they could not go, for the visit would be short. The women "did not feel well about it."[60]

Nuttall and Woodruff left Salt Lake City on September 9, traveling by rail to Oregon. Outside of Baker City they stopped, supped, and spent the night with a family named Meacham. They arrived in Portland on September 11. Here they took quarters and remained until September 16. Another rail trip on the Southern Pacific's Shasta route brought the two to San Francisco early on September 18. Two days later they boarded the steamship *Columbia*, arriving in Portland on September 22. They left Portland by rail on the 24th and returned to Ogden early in the morning of September 25.

Depending on Mountford's physical location or her ability to move efficiently on available transportation, the alleged marriage—with Nuttall officiating—could have taken place in Portland between September 11 and 16; on the train on September 17; in San Francisco between September 18 and 20; on the ship *Columbia* between September 20 and 22; in Portland between the 22 and the 24; or in Ogden on September 25 or 26.[61]

It is relevant to Mountford's whereabouts that a Sacramento newspaper published a personal note on September 11, that "Mrs. Lydia von F. Mountford is visiting the city, a guest of Mr. and Mrs. J. A. Woodson."[62] Several advertisements told of her appearance discussing "Village Life in Palestine" at the *Clunie Theatre* beginning September 27.[63] Since precise information placing Woodruff, Nuttall, and Mountford simultaneously in one of several possible locations is lacking, the marriage remains uncertain, and historians differ still. It is noteworthy that Matthias F. Cowley later told the Quorum of Twelve, "I believe President Woodruff married a wife the year before he died, of course, I don't know, I can't prove it."[64]

Four years after L. John Nuttall accompanied President Woodruff on the trip to the Pacific coast, Mountford wrote him a letter from New York City, to which Nuttall responded, "I have not forgotten the Ogden & other days with our Mutual friend."[65] According to Staker, Apostle Anthon H. Lund performed a vicarious sealing on November 20, 1920, for Woodruff and Mountford with Woodruff's son, James Jackson Woodruff, and Susa Young Gates, a friend of Mountford's, standing in as their representatives.[66] Staker notes that further details of this alleged event are not yet documented.[67] Mormon historian Thomas Alexander gives the date of November 23, 1920, for this union, and he notes that on the same day Mountford's sister, Anna, who died in March 1920, was sealed to Jacob F. Gates, Susa Young's husband.[68]

In the absence of verifiable facts, a historian can imagine a character's place and time to induce a plausible explanation. Would a ninety-year-old man whose health was fragile, who daily struggled with the tenuous state of church finances, who was beset by intense national criticism of illegal marriages, suddenly opt to embark on a sixteen-day vacation, not with his wife or family, but with a highly trusted friend merely "for a change of air and exercise"? Three trips by rail, totaling more than two thousand miles, and one six hundred–mile ocean voyage were more likely to tax a nonagenarian's health than improve it. The simplest explanation is that the trip was purposeful, that Woodruff and Mountford were joined by Nuttall in eternal marriage in one of several possible locations.[69]

Compton records ten marriages for Wilford Woodruff, and a marriage to Mountford would make eleven. Hardy also considers this marriage as Woodruff's post-Manifesto union.[70] Alexander does not accept that a sealing took place during Woodruff and Mountford's lifetime, but that the two were merely close friends.[71] However, beginning in 1835, "eternal marriage" meant that a man and woman could be married in a sealing and that their marriage would persist beyond the grave. Vicarious ordinances such as baptism for the dead are accepted by LDS doctrine as operative in the afterlife. In an example, David H. Cannon, the son of George Q. Cannon, was not officially betrothed to Lillian Hamlin. The two "had a romantic understanding" but were not sealed to each other until after his death. On June 17, 1896, Lillian was sealed to David for eternity, with Abraham H. Cannon presumably acting as proxy for his deceased brother. "By the Leverite principle, they could 'raise children' to David"; however, Abraham died just two weeks later on July 1. Lillian moved to Pennsylvania where she gave birth to a daughter nine months and five days later, on March 22, 1897.[72]

Lydia Mountford was a progressive national and international figure before and after her brief appearance in Utah.[73] She so "impressed Henry Ward Beecher with her eloquence" that she received an invitation to lecture on the chautauqua circuit.[74] She was the final speaker to the delegates at the Pan-American Congress of Religion and Education in Toronto, Canada, in July of 1895. She delivered "a thrilling address, telling of her own upbringing in the City of Jerusalem, and the congeries of races and creeds which she had seen gathered together in that city, and she went on most graphically to plead for greater religious unity."[75] Mountford from 1900 to 1920 spoke in Egypt and Jerusalem on women's suffrage.[76] She and her brother left a splendid high-valued collection of artifacts:

> Madame Lydia M von Finkelstein Mountford the known lecturer has consented to deposit the university her rich and extensive collection of objects gathered in Palestine illustrate her teachings on the Bible. Mountford museum comprehends also collection of Madame Mountford's brother the late Peter von Finkelstein Mamreov. Experts have pronounced this assemblage of Oriental objects unique. There is none like it in the world. It is valued at $50,000. During the lifetime of Madame the museum is to be a loan collection. Upon her death, Madame Mountford deems the collection to become the property of American University as a memorial of her and her brother Peter.[77]

While it may be chance, it was only eleven days after returning from his quixotic rail and sea expedition that Wilford Woodruff led a prayer ceremony that made his twenty-four-year-old recently married son, Abraham Owen, an LDS church apostle. At the same gathering Matthias Foss Cowley, equally fanatic as Owen about advancing polygamy, was ordained an apostle under the hand of a defender of polygamy, George Q. Cannon, first counselor to Woodruff in the presidency.[78]

The precarious state of health and vigor of Cannon and Wilford Woodruff was journaled by Brigham Young Jr., who on July 12, 1898, wrote that President Lorenzo Snow opened the Twelve's meeting with a "stormy refference [*sic*] to our financial Condition.... Pres. [George Q.] Cannon is feeble but he will not trust the Twelve in financial matters." Owen Woodruff asked the Quorum to take action on behalf of his father, that he not be indebted to Cannon's actions:

> "While we all belve [*sic*] in the integrity of Pres. Geo. Q Cannon still we belve [*sic*] that he has nearly ruined the credit of the Church with schemes that have failed, and the responsibility rest now upon Pres. W. Poor man, ... we now find ourselves with a very aged man

at the head and a badly paralyzed man to arrange all his public affairs.... Now it seems ... his own health and the welfare of the church demanded his complete isolation from all business cares and a strong hand to guide church business considering Pres. Woodruff's enfeebled condition."[79]

On August 28, 1900, almost two years after the death of Wilford Woodruff, L. John Nuttall received a letter from Mountford "in which she expressed a desire to come out here from New York, for a short visit and rest, but that she did not feel herself financially able to pay her expenses." Nuttall "concluded to appropriate her railroad fare and expenses." Additionally, Mountford was to accompany Susa Young Gates to a National Household Economic Association conference in Toronto, and she asked if the Church would pay her railroad fares to accompany Gates. Nuttall responded that this would also be paid.[80] On November 16, 1903, Nuttall received another telegram from Mountford asking for a $500 loan from the presidency to Charles Ellis Johnson who she wanted to accompany her to Jerusalem, presumably to photograph the expedition.[81] When Nuttall presented the request to President Joseph F. Smith, he was dismissively told to "bring it up in the morning."[82]

Less than a decade after statehood, the seating of a newly elected Utah senator, Reed Smoot, would trigger congressional investigations revealing that the LDS church president Joseph F. Smith had lied before Congress, and that LDS fusion of church and state continued. Investigations proved that new leadership-authorized plural marriages in significant numbers were still matters of fact, and many men continued living in the same households with their many wives.[83] President Smith admitted in 1904 that he himself had fathered eleven post-Manifesto children.[84] Further, as historian Ken Cannon II writes, the "First Presidency and at least seven members of ... the Twelve strongly supported ... new plural marriages on a limited, secretive basis."[85] During the fourteen years following Woodruff's Manifesto, "the members of the First Presidency—individually or as a unit—published twenty-four denials that any new plural marriages were being performed."[86]

Admirable yeoman's work by historians B. Carmon Hardy, Michael Quinn, and many others has documented at least 262 post-Manifesto plural marriages involving 220 individual men between 1890 and 1910. Hardy stressed, "the precise number authorized to enter polygamy after 1890 ... is less significant than the general magnitude of such activity."[87]

Abraham Owen Woodruff, John Whittaker Taylor, Matthias Foss Cowley, Marriner Wood Merrill, George Teasdale, and Anthony W. Ivins were
prominent high-ranking Mormon leaders throughout most of their adult
lives. They were the most active and most visible among the church hierarchy in performing what they firmly believed were leadership-authorized
plural marriages that supported the survival of polygamy and cohabitation
demanded by specific, God-given revelation. Foremost among these six men,
Abraham Owen Woodruff was the most deeply committed to the turn-of-
the-century Mormon colonization in Wyoming's Big Horn Basin.[88]

CHAPTER 2

Idealists Among the Pragmatists

The whole question of plural marriage and its abandonment by the church is still a Pandora's box the church authorities would just as soon keep closed for a long time.[1]

—Dale Morgan

FOUR LATTER-DAY SAINT APOSTLES were deeply dedicated to The Principle's survival after the Manifesto, yet they received neither an outpouring of public support nor behind-the-scenes appreciation from their leaders. In varying degrees, each was an idealist, a doctrinal purist, but these men were opposed by those who did not accept the alleged revelations that they cited. Higher-ranked leaders felt that compromise on plural marriage was required for the LDS church's very survival. The four men were not delusional. They were intelligent, vigorous, and mentally healthy, who saw plural marriage as basic, unchangeable doctrine, critically endangered by church leadership capitulation to political pressure.

One man, Abraham Owen Woodruff—probably the era's brightest young Mormon star of promise—died unexpectedly, prematurely. Death erased his potential, removing him as the church's prime mover in colonizing the Big Horn Basin and elsewhere.

Two men, John Whittaker Taylor and Matthias Foss Cowley, were born within three months of each other during the haste of 1858's surprise flight south from a US army entering the territory that the Mormon people feared. Throughout childhood they became close, high-achieving friends in Great Salt Lake City's Fourteenth Ward. Both became official outcasts from the tribal body of their fellow polygamist brethren in the Latter-day Saint hierarchy.

Two men, Woodruff and Taylor, were both born in polygamy to fathers who were or would become the LDS church president. They were companions during their first missions.

Two men, Woodruff and Cowley, were ordained as LDS apostles on the same day and hour. Both ordinations were performed by polygamists.

Only one of these apostles, Marriner Wood Merrill, came to the end of a long life in good standing with LDS church governance, blessed with impressive wealth and an admirable congregation-sized family.[2]

ABRAHAM OWEN WOODRUFF

Owen, as he preferred to be called, was the sixth of eight children born to Wilford Woodruff and his seventh wife, Emma Smoot Smith.[3] Owen's birth took place on November 27, 1872, in a log house south of Salt Lake City, built twelve years earlier by his father. Owen was four years old when Brigham Young died, and he later recalled his mother lifting him up to see the prophet's remains in the casket. He began district school at age six, bending to duties of farm life throughout his youth, while earning money by herding cows and gathering watercress at Liberty Park, which he sold for use in salads. Through his teens Owen attended Latter-day Saint College, where he had the good fortune to be a student of James E. Talmage, Karl G. Maeser, and the faculty president, Willard Done.[4]

With Owen's work ethic, his privileged status in Mormon society, and his knowledge acquired from a sound college-level education, labor in the fields was not to be his future. However, at no time in his life did he shirk physical labor when it was needed, whether on his livestock ranch in Charleston, Summit County, in Germany while a missionary seeking converts, or with his brethren in the Great Basin in need of encouragement. Owen's first employment was at Zions Savings Bank and Trust in Salt Lake City, whose officers and investors read as a Who's Who in Utah, and, with few exceptions, were polygamists.[5]

Owen was called to a mission in Germany in 1893 and served as branch president in Dresden. Because the German government did not permit LDS church proselyting, Woodruff and his fellow missionaries "were often compelled to employ most subtle methods in order to carry on their labors without detection and consequent interruption." Woodruff disguised himself in "rude garb and heavy clogs, and, with the other peasants, toiled in the shop or field during the day.... No sooner, however, did the evening shades fall, when he would meet in some humble cottage, a company of eager Saints, who would perchance bring some trusted friend with them, whom they hoped to lead into the gospel light."[6]

Returning to Utah in 1896, Owen Woodruff resumed employment at Zions Bank; his marriage followed shortly, on June 30, 1897, to Helen May Winters. She descended from Mary Ann Stearns, who had been married to Joseph Smith and Parley P. Pratt.[7] Their Salt Lake temple marriage was performed by Owen's father.[8] Owen shortly rose "to a position of great preferment in the ecclesiastical hierarchy of the Church of Jesus Christ of Latter Day Saints."[9] In fact, he was elevated to membership in the select Council of Twelve Apostles at the extraordinarily young age of twenty-four, on October 5, 1897, the same day as Matthias Cowley.[10] They were colleagues through their tenure, and in 1904 Cowley admitted that Owen Woodruff was his "best friend" among the apostles.[11] Owen was ordained by his father, who praised this son: "I had Great Joy in Listening to the first Discourse I Ever heard Owen Deliver. . . . Owen had a fund of knowledge and all truth necessary at his Tongues End."[12]

A new program was inaugurated by the LDS leaders in 1896. This was the "Colonization Committee," consisting of apostles Abraham Owen Woodruff and John Henry Smith. J. H. Smith, already a polygamist with two wives, would father nineteen children, and Owen Woodruff would shortly follow the same multiple-wife pathway. Utah historian Leonard Arrington confirms the Colonization Committee's special purpose as arising from the economic depression in Utah, its relative overpopulation, and its paucity of water-rich land.[13]

When President Lorenzo Snow assigned the responsibility for all contemporary Mormon colonization efforts to Owen Woodruff, Owen was instructed "to give his personal attention to establishing new settlements where good locations could be found." By "good locations," this likely meant good for agriculture.[14] Under Snow's assignment to Woodruff and J. H. Smith,—who were openly committed to continuing polygamy—church colonies were established or expanded in Millard County, Utah; White Pine County, Nevada; the upper Snake River Valley of Idaho; in southern Alberta, Canada; in Mexico's states of Chihuahua and Sonora; and the Big Horn Basin and Star Valley in Wyoming. Polygamy was present in all these areas, with the possible exception of White Pine County, with Ely the major city.[15]

Joseph Eckersley, a Mormon from Wayne County, Utah, worked for a time as an agent of Midland Mail Company, making deliveries in Wyoming's Big Horn Basin. He was an early instigator in the LDS church's interest in the area for colonization. While in the city of Basin around 1896 or 1897, he became acquainted with David Patten Woodruff, the half brother of Owen Woodruff.[16] David Woodruff had emigrated earlier to the area

Figure 1. Abraham Owen Woodruff as a young apostle, a rising bright star in LDS leadership. Fox and Symons Photography Studio, Salt Lake City, not dated. Courtesy of LDS Church History Library.

and was "held in high esteem by all persons in the county." David Woodruff asked Eckersley to visit the community of Burlington and take "note of the facilities afforded for settlement of the country by members of our Church seeking homes and that on my return to Utah would I call on his father" and make a report, asking for missionaries to be sent there.[17] Eckersley made the Burlington visit and wrote a letter to President Woodruff as requested, but he received no response. Some weeks later, Eckersley met Owen Woodruff by chance at the Wayne Stake Conference. Owen explained that the letter had been referred to him, and he was planning a visit to the Basin.[18] A short time later, at a conference at Woodruff, in Utah's Cache County, Eckersley again met Owen, this time accompanied by a Quorum of Seventy member, Joseph William McMurrin Jr.[19]

McMurrin and Owen together made a midsummer visit to the Big Horn Basin.[20] While there, they organized the Burlington Ward, selecting William Henry Packard as bishop, with David Woodruff and William Neves as counselors.[21] This small ward was made part of Woodruff Stake of Zion, which was located four hundred miles distant, in Evanston, Wyoming. Eckersley was invited by Owen Woodruff to join the colonization, but Eckersley was seriously injured in a stagecoach crash and post-recovery was sent to Great Britain on a mission. Owen Woodruff and McMurrin traveled over twelve hundred miles in six weeks of summer in 1899, traveling as far as the original Mormon emigrant road of 1847. They found large tracts of land on "both sides of the Shoshone River that were capable of sustaining thousands of people when water could be taken out and used for irrigation of crops." The two took samples of crops and returned to Salt Lake City, where they reported their findings to the general authorities.[22]

In January 1899 before leaving Salt Lake City to travel with McMurrin, Owen spoke in a Quorum meeting expressing his gratitude for Heber J. Grant's promise that Owen would have sons, a good name, and great financial influence. These blessings were said to be in store for John W. Taylor as well.[23] Two years later, both Owen Woodruff and John W. Taylor were present in a fast meeting in the Salt Lake temple, where Joseph F. Smith read from the Doctrine and Covenants revelation on plural marriage, adding "as a servant of God I warn you not rejt [reject] this princp [principle] or you will be damned & Jno. [John] Taylor has told me [by his own] lips that Jos [Joseph Smith] comd [commanded me] to entd [enter] into plur [plurality]."[24]

In February 1899 there was discussion within the LDS apostles' meetings that George Q. Cannon should run for the US Senate. By February 23, 1899, Owen Woodruff wrote in his diary that President Lorenzo Snow announced that "it was the will of the Lord that we do all we can to elect Pres[iden]t. [George Q.] Cannon to the U.S. Senate." On February 25, Owen wrote, "Bro[ther]. [Matthias F.] Cowley and I spent the whole day in trying to bring about the accomplishment of the mission assigned us."[25] Another source notes for September 25 that Owen Woodruff "discussed the status of his Wyoming efforts with President Snow."[26] On March 1 the entry read, "The movement to elect President Cannon to the U.S. Senate has become generally known in political circles, and has created quite a stir." Then on March 3 Owen wrote, "Spent most of the day at the Office straining every point possible to accomplish the will of the Lord."[27]

These fragmentary notes beg the question: was the secrecy over the mission assigned to Woodruff and Cowley that they were to continue polygamy in Wyoming or support George Q. Cannon's improbable reelection? Cannon had already served as Utah Territory's non-voting senator fighting passage of several anti-polygamy bills, including the Edmunds, Edmunds-Tucker, and Cullom bills.[28]

When Eckersley returned from his mission in the fall of 1903, he was made second counselor in Utah's Wayne Stake Presidency. Matthias Cowley, present at Eckersley's ordination, confided to him that it was "not the policy of Presid[ent]. Joseph F. Smith to censure any man for entertaining the order of plural marriage since the days of the Manifesto," provided he had the sanction of proper authority. In the Twelve Apostles' meetings the preceding September and October, at least two members, John W. Taylor and Marriner W. Merrill, were still urging that some plural marriages be solemnized to keep the institution alive.[29]

The special achievement in the short life of Owen Woodruff was his part in the Big Horn country's colonization. That work, placed in his hands by the first presidencies of Wilford Woodruff and Lorenzo Snow, was carried successfully until Owen's untimely death. Throughout his life, Owen possessed the gifts of humility and sociability. He was in close touch with common, toiling people, thereby gaining their confidence and love.[30] Professor Willard Done said of his former pupil, Owen Woodruff, that "he made an outstanding contribution as the chief colonizer and spiritual and temporal leader of the Latter-day Saint settlement in the Big Horn Basin of Wyoming. There his affable nature won him a place in the hearts of the people."

A friend described Owen's influence in these words:

> His was an affectionate disposition. He was loving and lovable. The ice of reserve always melted before the warmth of his nature. He was

like a brother to all his associates. In whatever relationship of business or social life he stood to them, they knew him first and foremost as a friend. In the Big Horn colony, that feeling of love for him was most intense.[31]

Benjamin Erastus Rich—one of fifty-two children of Charles Coulson Rich and his six wives—and a close friend to Owen, left his tribute:

> An Apostle of the Lord Jesus Christ for eight years and his mortal career ended when only 31 years of age . . . He was the very embodiment of gentleness kindness and Godly charity. His aim in life was to be a true representative of the divine Master a special witness for Him to Gods children on earth. We doubt if there be a member of the Church who was personally acquainted with this young Apostle who would not willingly have died in his stead had it met with God's approval. He was so much beloved by all he seemed so much more capable of doing good than the majority of us who have been spared for a season.[32]

MATTHIAS FOSS COWLEY

Matthias Foss Cowley was born at 44 South West Temple Street, in Salt Lake City's Fourteenth Ward, on August 25, 1858.[33] His father, Matthias Cain Cowley, was born on the Isle of Man. His mother, Sarah Elizabeth Foss, was a native of Maine, a schoolteacher, and a lover of education; she taught him at an early age to read and write.

When Matthias was five or six years of age, his father drowned in the Jordan River. His widowed mother survived by forming a private school and by selling carpets she made by weaving them from cast-off rags. Matthias tried to assist her in this. Rags that were not suitable for rugs she saved for papermaking. The *Deseret News* press was frequently in need of rags to manufacture newsprint. Matthias carried rags to the *News* and traded the proceeds earned for church books. Two Doctrine and Covenants copies were his first purchase; one he kept and the second was presented to his boyhood friend, John Whittaker Taylor. The Cowley house was located in the same block where apostles John Taylor, Brigham Young Jr., and President Wilford Woodruff all lived.

Figure 2. Matthias Foss Cowley, whose passionate belief in everlasting polygamy brought about his sacrificial removal from apostleship and excommunication. Courtesy of LDS Church History Library.

Early in his life Matthias read the Bible, the Book of Mormon, the Doctrine and Covenants, and the autobiography of Apostle Parley P. Pratt. In addition to John W. Taylor, his boyhood companions were Brigham Y. Woodruff, Brigham S. Young, and Howard Young. President Heber J. Grant's mother and his mother were close friends, and for many years Matthias held Heber Grant as an example of faith and devotion to God with honorable parentage. Matthias made an astounding claim to have had—in a preexistent life—the same superior class of people for associates. "My pre-natal conditions were in harmony with those of the pre-existence, for I had a father who held and honored the Holy Priesthood and a mother who was one with him." When Matthias was about twelve years old, his widowed mother married Jesse W. Fox Sr., a Utah Territorial surveyor. Matthias worked with his stepfather as they surveyed for the Utah Southern Railroad and performed construction on the south, west, and north Jordan canals. Around this time, he made acquaintance with Judge Elias Smith, cousin to Joseph Smith, who was then probate judge of Salt Lake County. Matthias's mother urged him to pursue surveying, but studying books on engineering and science did not interest him. The Bible remained his favorite; he carried a King James version in his pocket, which he read whenever brief leisure moments allowed it.

After being ordained as a Deacon and Teacher in the Aaronic priesthood, Matthias visited the homes assigned to him as a "block teacher." This duty made him the bishop's agent, responsible to report on any issues and to collect money for the Salt Lake Temple construction. Among his assignments was to visit apostles John Taylor and Wilford Woodruff, who both later became church president. From these one-on-one experiences, Matthias saw John Taylor as having "the most dignified bearing and personality of any man I ever beheld in mortality." He also developed a lifelong love and respect for Wilford Woodruff that would ultimately inspire him to write Woodruff's biography.[34]

When sixteen years old, Cowley was ordained an Elder in the Endowment House, an experience that he claimed "made a new being out of me. I felt the distinct change—an uplifting to a higher platform," with "more power than ever before to resist temptation and lay aside the evil tendencies of human nature." Shortly thereafter, he and John W. Taylor were made counselors to the Elders Quorum of Edward Davis. From this time until his first missionary call in 1878, he continued in his ward assignments and worked part time with the Fox engineering parties surveying the Utah Southern Railroad pathway.

Cowley's first of two calls to the Southern States Mission began in February 1878, with Henry W. Barnett of Payson, Utah, as his companion. Barnett had been a missionary in England for ten years before coming to Utah, and was, according to Cowley, "a very gifted preacher." The two worked for a year in Graves County, Kentucky, and in Franklin and Bedford Counties, Virginia. Cowley's next companion was Frank A. Benson from Logan, Utah, and they proselyted in the Virginia counties of Tazewell, Bland, and Smith. Several other companions were assigned to Cowley as they extended their work to other areas of Virginia. Cowley tallied up their work, having "baptized 114 people, blessed many children, and witnessed cases of healing the sick under the sacred ordinance established by the savior for the purpose." He concluded this mission with a horseback visit to rural Surry County, in the northwest corner of North Carolina, that adjoined Virginia on its northern edge. He proudly reported having spent "no more than $3.00 a month, aside from railroad and steamboat fare on the Ohio and Cumberland Rivers."[35]

Cowley returned to Utah in May 1880, but in early November he was assigned to conduct a company to Manassa, on the southern edge of Colorado. The group was comprised of 119 migrants from Virginia, Georgia, Alabama, Mississippi, and Tennessee. Among them were fifty-seven who had been converted to the LDS gospel. Later in November Cowley was called a second time to the Southern States Mission. Rather than returning to Virginia, as he wished, he was sent to Georgia, fulfilling a dream that had made that prediction. "My dear friend and boyhood companion, Elder John W. Taylor, was my comrade." In the deep south of rural southwestern Georgia in Terrell and Randolph Counties, their success was disappointing, with only three baptisms. In the spring of 1881, John W. Taylor was sent to the Kentucky Conference, and Cowley to St. Louis, where his companion was George C. Parkinson—with whom he would later serve from 1884 to 1895 as counselors in Idaho's Oneida Stake and for whom he would perform a post-Manifesto marriage in 1902. In St. Louis, meetings were held in the Odd Fellows Hall; they were well-treated, formed many friendships, and baptized fourteen souls. Cowley returned to Utah in June 1882; Parkinson was sent to England.

Later in June, Cowley made a trip east with John Morgan, where they took a second group of Latter-day Saints to join the Manassa settlers who Cowley had earlier escorted, then they revisited St. Louis. On their return they stopped at Richmond, Missouri, and visited David Whitmer and General Alex W. Doniphan.[36] Whitmer "was true and loyal in his testimony of the Book of Mormon, and related to us the miraculous sowing of fertilizer on his field by other than human hands"; Doniphan was "glad to see us and still friendly to the Latter Day Saints." By age twenty-four, Matthias Foss Cowley had completed two missions, as had been predicted in blessings he received when he was eighteen years old.

Returning to Utah, Cowley worked in the city recorder's office for John T. Caine and Heber M. Wells, and he was in the city hall office when City Marshall Andrew Burt was shot and killed by a prisoner who was being arrested.[37] Cowley was appointed—with Joseph F. Smith and Moses Thatcher—as Young Men's Mutual Improvement Association (YMMIA) superintendent. He canvassed widely to urge members to subscribe to its monthly periodical, *The Contributor*, founded by Junius F. Wells. Soon circulation increased from fourteen hundred to forty-two hundred with his efforts.

Matthias Cowley's first marriage took place in Logan, Utah, to Abigail Hyde on May 1, 1884, the first day the Logan Temple was open for such endowments. The marriage was performed by Daniel H. Wells. In October, Matthias and Abbie were called to strengthen Idaho's Oneida Stake, where many polygamists had congregated. Living in Preston, Idaho, he was ordained a High Priest by Apostle Francis M. Lyman, assigned to lead the stake's YMMIA. Three years later Cowley was appointed as a counselor in the Oneida Stake Presidency to fill the vacancy created by the arrest of his former mission companion, George C. Parkinson. Elected as superintendent of public schools, Parkinson also ran a cooperative store. When a suspected polygamist was found hiding in the store's basement, Parkinson was charged and convicted of concealing a criminal. After serving eleven months in prison, Parkinson was again made stake president, and Cowley his second counselor, where he served until ordained an apostle. Not surprisingly, Parkinson chose Cowley to perform his post-Manifesto marriage to Fannie Wooley in Colorado Springs, Colorado, in June 1902.[38]

Matthias F. Cowley explained that he performed plural marriages in "obedience to the Patriarchal order of Celestial Marriage as revealed to the Prophet Joseph Smith, and virtually re-enforced by the Revelation of God to President John Taylor of date October 13, 1882.[39] This unpublished revelation was nearly four years earlier than a similar one dated September 27, 1886, in Centerville, Utah, to John Taylor and later cited by John Whittaker Taylor in his trial.[40] Cowley's second marriage was to Luella Smart Parkinson, daughter of Patriarch Samuel R. Parkinson, in the Endowment House on September 22, 1889; the ceremony was performed by Daniel H.

Table 1A. Post-Manifesto marriages performed by select leaders, by date of marriage

Marriner Wood Merrill

Husband	Wife	Date of marriage	Place of marriage
Charles Edward Merrill	Chloe Hendricks	March 14, 1891	
John William Barnett	Hattie L. Merrill	July 16, 1894	Logan Temple
George W. Teasdale	Letitia Thomas	May 17, 1900	

Abraham Owen Woodruff

Husband	Wife	Date of marriage	Place of marriage
Edward William Payne	Lucy Alice Farr	November 26, 1899	Colonia Juarez, Mexico
Louis Paul Cardon	Mary Irene Pratt	November 11, 1903	
George Conrad Nagle	Jennie D. Jameson	November 18, 1903	
George Conrad Nagle	Philinda Keeler	November 18, 1903	

John Whittaker Taylor

Husband	Wife	Date of marriage	Place of marriage
Theodore Brandley	Emma M. Biefer	August 11, 1893	Canada
Charles Whipple	Mary Louise Walser	March 6, 1898[a]	Colonia Juarez, Mexico
George William Hardy	Emma S. Rowley	March 8, 1898	Colonia Juarez, Mexico
Lucian Morgan Mecham	Mary Ann Hardy	March 9, 1898	Colonia Juarez, Mexico
Brigham Strowell	Ella Marie Skousen	March 10, 1898	Colonia Juarez, Mexico
Anson Bowen Call	Dora Pratt	March 11, 1898	Colonia Juarez, Mexico
Heber S. Allen	Elizabeth Hardy	September 19, 1903	Cardston, Canada

Table 1A (*continued*). Post-Manifesto marriages performed by select leaders, by date of marriage

Matthias Foss Cowley

Husband	Wife	Date of marriage	Place of marriage
Benjamin Erastus Rich	Laura Bowring	April 13, 1898	Preston, Idaho
Joseph Morrell	Mary Ann Daines	October 23, 1898	Logan, Utah
Douglas McClain Todd	Hannah McMurray	May 22, 1899	Salt Lake City
Hugh Jenne Cannon	Vilate Peart	July 18, 1900	
John Mousley Cannon	Margaret Peart	July 18, 1900	
Thomas Chamberlain II	Mary Eliza Wooley	August 6, 1900	Salt Lake City
Arthur William Hart	Evadyna Henderson	August 21, 1900	Salt Lake City
Arthur William Hart	Ada D. Lowe	August 22, 1900	Salt Lake City
John Mousley Cannon	Harriet Neff	November 3, 1900	
Frank Young Taylor	Alice May Neff	November 3, 1900	
Frank Young Taylor	Annie S. Campbell	November 3, 1900	
Abraham Owen Woodruff	Eliza Avery Clark	January 1901	Preston, Idaho
Jesse Moroni Smith	Priscilia Smith	January 5, 1901	Salt Lake City
Henry Smith Tanner	Mary I. Richards	January 6, 1901	Salt Lake City
Marriner Wood Merrill	Hilda M. Erickson	April 7, 1901	
Joseph E. Robinson	Wilmia Brown	April 7, 1901	Salt Lake City
George Mousley Cannon	Katherine V. Morris	August 7, 1901	Salt Lake City
Brigham Young Jr.	Kirsty Maria Willansden	August 8, 1901	Salt Lake City
John Whittaker Taylor	Eliza Roxie Welling	August 29, 1901	Farmington, Utah
John Whittaker Taylor	Rhoda Welling	August 29, 1901	Farmington, Utah
Joseph Charles Bentley	Mary Maud Taylor	September 23, 1901	Colonia Juarez, Mexico
Daniel Skousen	Sarah Ann Spillsbury	September 24, 1901	El Paso, Texas
Joseph E. Robinson	Harriet Spencer	October 3, 1901	Salt Lake City
Mahonri M. Steele Jr.	Martha J. LeFevre	November 1, 1901	

Table 1A (*continued*). Post-Manifesto marriages performed by select leaders, by date of marriage

| | Matthias Foss Cowley | | |
Husband	Wife	Date of marriage	Place of marriage
John Fielding Burton	Florence Porter	November 15, 1901	Salt Lake City
Henry Smith Tanner	Clarice Thatcher	December 19, 1901	Salt Lake City
William Henry Smart	Mary Eliza Wallace	1902	
Joseph Edwin Hickman	Helen J. Hansen	January 1902	
Edwin Cutler	Caroline Erickson	January 27, 1902	Preston, Idaho
Joseph White Musser	Mary Caroline Hill	March 13, 1902	
George C. Parkinson[b]	Fannie Wooley	June 17, 1902	Colorado Springs
Joel Sixtus Eager	Emily Jane Lee	August 16, 1902	Colonia Juarez, Mexico
John Jacob Huber	Percis Lula Maxham	August 16, 1902	Colonia Juarez, Mexico
Charles W. Lillywhite	Abigail Lee	August 16, 1902	Colonia Juarez, Mexico
David King Udall	Mary Linton Morgan	1903	Preston, Idaho
Joseph Marion Tanner	Sarah Taylor Evans	1903	
John Allen Bagley	Mary M. Peterson	February 12, 1903	Preston, Idaho
Louis A. Kelsch	Mary Lucretia Lyerla	April 24, 1903	Preston, Idaho
Rueben G. Miller Jr.	Martha Nelson	June 25, 1903	Preston, Idaho
James Gledhill Duffin	Amelia Carling	July 27, 1903	
Byron Sessions	Janet Easton	August 13, 1903	Byron, Wyoming
Olonzo David Merrill	Mary Laura Hansen	February 23, 1904	Preston, Idaho
Rudger Clawson	Pearl Udall	August 3, 1904	
Alonzo Leander Taylor	Katie P. Spillsbury	January 1, 1906	Colonia Dublan, Mexico
John Whittaker Taylor	Ellen Georgina Sandberg	June 23, 1909	Salt Lake City
John William Woolf	Name unknown	Post-Manifesto	

[a]Apostle John Henry Smith, who was present, gave this date of marriage. White, *Church, State, Politics*, 392.
[b]Cowley served for eleven years, 1884–1895, as a counselor to Parkinson in the Idaho Oneida stake presidency

Table 1B. Post-Manifesto marriages performed by select leaders, alphabetical by husband

Marriner Wood Merrill

Husband	Wife	Date of marriage	Place of marriage
John William Barnett	Hattie L. Merrill	July 16, 1894	Logan Temple, Utah
George W. Teasdale	Letitia Thomas	May 17, 1900	

Abraham Owen Woodruff

Husband	Wife	Date of marriage	Place of marriage
Louis Paul Cardon	Mary Irene Pratt	November 11, 1903	
George Conrad Naegle	Jennie D. Jameson	November 18, 1903	
George Conrad Naegle	Philinda Keeler	November 18, 1903	
Edward William Payne	Lucy Alice Farr	November 26, 1899	Colonia Juarez, Mexico

John Whittaker Taylor

Husband	Wife	Date of Marriage	Place of Marriage
Heber S. Allen	Elizabeth Hardy	September 19, 1903	Cardston, Canada
Theodore Brandley	Emma M. Biefer	August 11, 1893	Canada
Anson Bowen Call	Dora Pratt	March 11, 1898	Colonia Juarez, Mexico
George William Hardy	Emma S. Rowley	March 8, 1898	Colonia Juarez, Mexico
Lucian Morgan Mecham	Mary Ann Hardy	March 9, 1898	Colonia Juarez, Mexico
Brigham Stowell	Ella Marie Skousen	March 10, 1898	Colonia Juarez, Mexico
Charles Whipple	Mary Louise Walser	March 6, 1898[a]	Colonia Juarez, Mexico

Table 1B (*continued*). Post-Manifesto marriages performed by select leaders, alphabetical by husband

	Matthias Foss Cowley		
Husband	**Wife**	**Date of marriage**	**Place of marriage**
John Allen Bagley	Mary M. Peterson	February 12, 1903	Preston, Idaho
Joseph Charles Bentley	Mary Maud Taylor	September 23, 1901	Colonia Juarez, Mexico
John Fielding Burton	Florence Porter	November 15, 1901	
Hugh Jenne Cannon	Vilate Peart	July 18, 1900	
George Mousley Cannon	Katherine V. Morris	August 7, 1901	Salt Lake City
John Mousley Cannon	Margaret Peart	July 18, 1900	
John Mousley Cannon	Harriet Neff	November 3, 1900	
Thomas Chamberlain II	Mary Eliza Wooley	August 6, 1900	Salt Lake City
Rudger Clawson	Pearl Udall	August 3, 1904	
James Gledhill Duffin	Amelia Carling	July 27, 1903	
Joel Sixtus Eager	Emily Jane Lee	August 16, 1902	Colonia Juarez, Mexico
Arthur William Hart	Evadyna Henderson	August 21, 1900	Salt Lake City
Arthur William Hart	Ada D. Lowe	August 22, 1900	Salt Lake City
Joseph Edwin Hickman	Helen J. Hansen	January 1902	
John Jacob Huber	Percis Lula Maxham	August 16, 1902	Colonia Juarez, Mexico
Louis A. Kelsch	Mary Lucretia Lylera	1898	
Charles W. Lillywhite	Abigail Lee	August 16, 1902	Colonia Juarez, Mexico
Marriner Wood Merrill	Hilda M. Erickson	April 1, 1901	
Olonzo David Merrill	Mary Laura Hansen	February 23, 1904	Preston, Idaho
Rueben G. Miller Jr.	Martha Nelson	June 25, 1903	Preston, Idaho
Joseph Morrell	Mary Ann Daines	October 23, 1898	Logan, Utah
Joseph White Musser	Mary Caroline Hill	March 13, 1902	
George C. Parkinson	Fannie Wooley	June 17, 1902	Colorado Springs

Table 1B (*continued*). Post-Manifesto marriages performed by select leaders, alphabetical by husband

Matthias Foss Cowley

Husband	Wife	Date of marriage	Place of marriage
Benjamin Erastus Rich	Laura Bowring	April 13, 1898	Salt Lake City
Joseph E. Robinson	Wilmia Brown	April 7, 1901	Salt Lake City
Joseph E. Robinson	Harriet Spencer	October 3, 1901	Byron, Wyoming
Byron Sessions	Janet Easton	August 13, 1903	El Paso, Texas
Daniel Skousen	Sarah Ann Spillsbury	September 24, 1901	Salt Lake City
William Henry Smart	Mary Eliza Wallace	1902	Salt Lake City
Jesse Moroni Smith	Priscilia Smith	January 5, 1901	
Mahonri M. Steele Jr.	Martha J. LeFevre	November 1, 1901	
Henry Smith Tanner	Mary I. Richards	January 6, 1901	Salt Lake City
Henry Smith Tanner	Clarice Thatcher	December 19, 1901	Salt Lake City
Joseph Marion Tanner	Sarah Taylor Evans	1903	
Alonzo Leander Taylor	Katie P. Spillsbury	January 1, 1906	Colonia Dublan, Mexico
Frank Young Taylor	Alice May Neff	November 3, 1900	
Frank Young Taylor	Annie S. Campbell	November 3, 1900	
John Whittaker Taylor	Eliza Roxie Welling	August 29, 1901	Farmington, Utah
John Whittaker Taylor	Rhoda Welling	August 29, 1901	Farmington, Utah
John Whittaker Taylor	Ellen Sandberg	June 23, 1909	
Douglas McClain Todd	Hannah McMurray	May 22, 1899	Salt Lake City
David King Udall	Mary Morgan	1903	
Abraham Owen Woodruff	Eliza Avery Clark	January 1901	
John William Woolf	Name unknown	Post-Manifesto	
Brigham Young Jr.	Kirsty Maria Willansden	August 8, 1901	

[a]Apostle John Henry Smith, who was present, gives this date. White, *Church, State, Politics*, 392.

Wells. To make his "obedience more complete," Cowley's third and first post-Manifesto marriage was to Harriet Bennion Harker in 1899, widow of Benjamin E. Harker and daughter of John Bennion. Cowley's final marriage was to Mary Lenora Taylor of Colonia Juarez, the daughter of Ernest L. Taylor, performed on September 16, 1905, in Canada by John A. Woolf. It is noteworthy that Cowley's two post-Manifesto marriages were after he became an apostle.

While residing in Preston, Cowley was ordained an apostle on October 7, 1897, by George Q. Cannon, Wilford Woodruff, and Joseph F. Smith.[41] Abraham Owen Woodruff was ordained the same day by his father. In attendance were Lorenzo Snow, Franklin D. Richards, Brigham Young Jr., Francis M. Lyman, John Henry Smith, George Teasdale, John W. Taylor, Marriner W. Merrill—polygamists all—and one monogamist, Anthon H. Lund. Heber J. Grant was not present, seriously ill with suspected appendicitis.

Three weeks into his apostleship, Cowley with Francis M. Lyman embarked on an official visit—Cowley's third—to the Southern States Mission. Four months were devoted to visiting each conference and holding priesthood meetings. One day was spent visiting friends in Tazewell County. They concluded their tour in Washington, DC, spending several pleasant days with William H. King, Utah's member of Congress.[42] King arranged a personal interview for the two with President William McKinley. They then went to Brooklyn, Chicago, St. Louis, and Cincinnati, next visiting sites of early Mormon history at Independence, Kirtland, Nauvoo, and Carthage. On returning home, Matthias and Abbie moved from Preston to Salt Lake City, renting a home in the Nineteenth Ward. The following spring, he and Anthon Lund each bought homes just north and west of the temple, with the home of Supreme Court Judge Aurelius Miner and his two wives between them.[43]

Matthias Cowley was a Council of Twelve Apostles member for eight years. He claimed visiting nearly all stakes of Zion, attending conferences and speaking. He visited every US mission and attended meetings in every state.

In 1894 Cowley fulfilled a four-month mission to northwest Montana where thirty-nine converts were baptized. He and other members explained their beliefs to Montana's governor John E. Rickards. Thereafter, Cowley visited and preached in most wards of Alberta and in various stakes in Canada's provinces. He did the same in Arizona and Mexico. He told of a blessing given to him by Apostle George Teasdale who said, "the Lord will give you the gift of the Spanish language." Cowley gave credit to this blessing for his ability, with very little knowledge by study, to preach many times in Spanish for up to an hour without pause or hesitation.

Cowley's descriptions of Reed Smoot's hearing in the Senate—including fascinating details of his release as an apostle—seem understated and dispassionate:

> In 1905 the agitation of hireling priests and many misguided people was strong against the seating of Apostle Reed Smoot in the United States Senate. The hue and cry was that many individuals had entered Plural Marriage since the Manifesto, among others, Bro. John W. Taylor and myself. It was therefore thought advisable for us two to resign our places in the Council of the Twelve. Before doing so, President B. H. Roberts had made a speech, I understand, by the request of the Presidency, in which he said that unless individuals would shoulder the responsibility of these marriages, the Church had not a "foot of ground to stand on, and that they were guilty of duplicity and double dealing." We had meetings with the Twelve for about six days which the Presidency did not attend except a part of the first one. No minutes of the meetings were kept. In one of these meetings Elder Penrose said, referring to Elder Taylor and myself—these are very nearly his words but I don't say [them] verbatim—"These brethren are not on trial—they are not charged with disobedience nor transgression, but we've all got in a box with the Government and something must be done to meet this fight, and if these brethren are willing to be humiliated they can be re-installed," whereupon Brother John Henry Smith threw up both hands and said, "yes, I'll vote for them with both hands." This was the spirit of the occasion, we had no arguments against our brethren. After the last meeting, which meetings were held in the Temple, Brother Penrose brought our resignations to us . . . all written, with no suggestion from us (although Brother Taylor desired to write his own). We signed them, and after doing so Brother Penrose said he had no idea that they would go into effect, and would not, unless matters came to the last ditch of necessity. This was in the fall of 1905, and at the April Conference of 1906 they were made public and became of effect.[44]

After his removal from the Twelve, Cowley claimed to "have done very little preaching," but he remained a popular speaker in local church meetings. He continued regularly attending Sunday School, Sacrament, and priesthood meetings, while continuing in faithful payment of tithes and offerings. Income came in from collecting taxes for Salt Lake County, serving as court bailiff, and presumably from returns on his business involvement. He claimed having spent "about $7,000 supporting his sons and others in the mission field." Cowley expressed gratefulness to President Joseph F. Smith who, out of "kindness and [his] element of justice," continued Cowley's church allowance of $150 a month. After Heber J. Grant's succession to president, this money was not forthcoming, and Cowley was conflicted: "For aught I know it may have been ... right for President Grant to stop it. At any rate, I shall sustain and uphold President Grant in his administration as I did his predecessors, and I hope and pray that my wives and children will do the same."[45]

In Cowley's autobiography, he closed it with his fervent testimony of Jesus Christ as Savior, of Joseph Smith as a prophet, and the LDS church's importance in the world's salvation. He urged his descendants to remain faithful in their belief and activity in the church and gave no measure of anger at his fate at the hands of his fellow apostles or the first presidency. Cowley's narrative history is not dated, but since he did not address his 1911 excommunication, it is reasonable to assume it was written between April 1906 and May 1911.

Beloved by many church members, Matthias Foss Cowley died June 16, 1940, in Salt Lake City from kidney failure at age eighty-one. To the end he retained his memory and ability to write and speak. His memorial was held on the Salt Lake Temple grounds, not in the famous Tabernacle, but in a lesser building, the Assembly Hall. It was conducted not by President Heber J. Grant, but by the Seventeenth Ward bishop, Harold W. Langston. Tabernacle Choir members sang appropriate hymns; Hugh B. Brown was the principal speaker.

JOHN WHITTAKER TAYLOR

John W. Taylor—the abbreviated name most commonly used by historians—was born in Provo, Utah, on May 15, 1858, to John Taylor and one of his eight wives, Stephanie Whittaker Taylor. At the time of John W. Taylor's birth, the city of Provo was only a temporary home for the family. Utah County was awash with massive numbers of Latter-day Saints who had fled south from the Salt Lake valley and further north in Utah Territory. This flight was ordered out of fear by Brigham Young, but Colonel

A. S. Johnson's Tenth Infantry troops, wagons, teamsters, and hangers-on passed uneventfully through Great Salt Lake City without harming people or property. The thousands of displaced citizens gradually returned northward to their homes, including the John Taylor family, who returned to their Fourteenth Ward home in Salt Lake City. The father would become in 1880 LDS church president, after three years of leading the church from his position in the Quorum of the Twelve.

As earlier noted, the family of Matthias Cowley and Sarah Elizabeth Foss Cowley shared the same temporary migration south from Salt Lake City. Their months-long stay was in Springville, not far from Provo. They also returned to their former home in the Fourteenth Ward. It was shortly after their return that a son, Matthias Foss Cowley, was born to them on August 25, 1858.

John W. Taylor and Matthias Foss Cowley grew up as close boyhood and teenage friends in the city's same ward. They attended church meetings together and "studied the Scriptures and memorized scores of passages bearing upon the most important principles of the gospel."[46] John W. progressed quickly through the Aaronic priesthood offices. Shortly after his ordination as an Elder in the Melchizedek priesthood, he was selected as an Elders Quorum counselor—together with his friend Matthias—to the quorum's president, Edward W. Davis. While he was a Fourteenth Ward Sunday School teacher in a class of one hundred children, John W. was praised as "the best primary teacher ... in the Church."[47] Another of their boyhood friend was Abraham H. Cannon, who grew up in Salt Lake City in a large four-apartment home built by his father, George Q. Cannon, so that his wives could live close together yet be apart. Cowley wrote of Abraham that "he was given the best opportunity that the times afforded for an education and ... he availed himself of that privilege, finishing his studies in the Deseret University." Abraham also learned the carpenters' trade, worked on the temple block, studied architecture under Obed Taylor, and "became an architect."[48] Later, the performance of plural marriages would also link the lives of Abraham H. Cannon and Cowley.

In the fall of 1880, Taylor and Cowley continued their friendship in Dawson, Georgia, as ordained companions in the Southern States Mission. They would introduce the gospel for the first time in Georgia's southwestern Terrell and Randolph Counties. In 1881 they went north to the counties of Clayton, Campbell, and Henry. Taylor was shortly assigned a new companion, William J. Packer, and they worked in Haralson and Polk Counties where thirty to forty converts were baptized. From Georgia, Taylor was moved to Kentucky's Rochester and Butler Counties where he and his companion, Jacob G. Bigler, baptized about eighteen people.

Taylor wrote on March 19, 1882, to his earlier companion, Matthias Cowley, now a missionary in St. Louis, Missouri. In his letter Taylor predicted Cowley's future: "I believe I speak by the spirit of prophecy when I say if you are faithful you will yet become one of the Twelve Apostles of the Church of Jesus Christ in all the world and by the power of God and the eternal Priesthood will become great in wisdom and knowledge, Amen."[49] This was an early instance of Taylor's remarkable gift of foreseeing the future that biographers claim he possessed.

Taylor was released from his Southern States mission and shortly thereafter, on October 19, 1882, was married to May Leona Rich. They moved to Cassia County, Idaho. After 1882 to 1909, Taylor was married to five additional women, including to two half sisters on the same day. Taylor's marriage to Nellie Eva Todd was on September 25, 1889; to Janet Marie Woolley on October 10, 1890; to Eliza Roxie Welling and Rhoda Welling on August 29, 1901; and to Ellen Georgina Sandberg on June 23, 1909.[50] These marriages took place during times of immense risk for the LDS church, embattled by public criticism over their marriage practices and the federal government exposing the leadership's duplicity for publicly proclaiming in 1890, 1900, and 1904 that plural marriage had been relinquished when in fact it had not.

John W. Taylor was ordained an apostle on April 9, 1884, by his father—who by this time was LDS church president. This high status made the plural marriages of the younger a serious concern, as he was more likely to be exposed. Later in 1884, Taylor was sent as a missionary to Mexico. Before beginning his labors, he met with President Porfirio Diaz. On returning, Taylor was elected to the Utah Territorial legislature. A mission call followed to the Uintah Stake, led by William H. Smart, that extended from Summit County to the west edge of Colorado. A large number of stake members had become indifferent to their church's beliefs and duties and needed reawakening.[51]

An event in 1886 serves as an example of Taylor's passionate, impulsive defense of polygamy, in disregard for the consequences for the church. When the Edmunds-Tucker Act was being discussed in Congress, which would seize the church's assets, Taylor was arrested by US marshals in Pocatello, Idaho, accused of making treasonous remarks at a nearby conference:

> I want you people to go to the polls and vote every man of you and maintain your rights and defend them! What are you, a lot of cattle

only fit to be governed? Ten thousand of you in these counties? Send
in your votes, go to the polls and carry your case to the Supreme
Court of the United States. You are not to be controlled by a few
corrupt adventurers and sycophants! Fight every inch of the ground
and claim your rights; you that are not in polygamy have broken no
law. I believe in polygamy; I am the son of a polygamous mother and
I mean to practice it too.[52]

Taylor had various business enterprises in the LDS colonies in Canada
that were "persistent and fruitful . . . [and he] greatly encouraged the Saints
in that country." Canadian newspaper reports varied widely in their assessment of Mormons emigrating to Alberta. The *Edmonton Bulletin* wrote that
the Mormons were an "utter abomination which no effort should be spared
to rid the nation of," and that southern Alberta Province "was being taken up
by the filth of which the United States is ridding itself.[53] Winnipeg's *Manitoba Daily Free Press* took the line that Mormons were "very hard working
people . . . all the Mormons then in the settlements are monogamous, with
not one who rejoices in the possession of a second spouse."[54] The McCleod
Gazette held that Mormon colonists were "generally acknowledged to be a
class which make the most desirable settlers, and we have no hesitation in
giving them . . . a hearty welcome. These settlers have come here prepared to
obey the laws of Canada to the letter, and there will be plenty of time to warn
the government against them when they show the least inclination to break
them."[55] The *Lethbridge News* gave a backhanded racist insult to two other
groups in their assessment, that Mormons were "steady industrious men"
whose immigration "should be encouraged, for they were far superior to the
Chinese or the Jews.[56]

Taylor's concern for Latter-day Saints migrating to Canada grew, and
by November 1888 he was interviewed with several members by Canadian
Premier, John A. MacDonald.[57] On this visit to Ottawa, Taylor was in the
company of Mormon leaders Francis M. Lyman and Charles O. Card. They
discussed Canada's acceptance of Mormon colonists, including those fleeing
from harassment or arrest for practicing polygamy. MacDonald had indicated that Canada would allow emigrants seeking refuge from persecution.
One wife could come with as many children as she wanted, but two wives
and one man could not legally live in Canada. This conversation became of
grave importance when it was resurrected in the 1911 punitive action against
Taylor.[58] Taylor told colonists at Lee's Creek that they could still consider
Canada as a "place of refuge where we can raise one family and wait till the

clouds ... disperse." However, in February 1890 the US Supreme Court upheld the Edmunds-Tucker Act's constitutionality, and the Canadian Parliament followed suit, passing acts that "in essence made the same legislative interpretation" as in the US Edmunds law.[59]

The life and family of John W. Taylor were the subjects of an unusual work published in 1951. The book *Family Kingdom* by Samuel Woolley Taylor, son of John W.'s third wife, Janet Marie Wooley Taylor, or Nettie— is history-based fiction, suggested to its author by Mormon leader Hugh B. Brown. However, forty-three years after its publication, the author said, "I still feel that in *Family Kingdom* I did present the truth of our family's way of life as accurately as I could."[60] After its publication, Utah historian Dale Morgan described an article "Gallant Lady" by Samuel W. Taylor that had appeared several years earlier in *Holiday* magazine. "Gallant Lady" was "a reminiscence full of zest, of high good humor, and refreshing social insights," and now the author had "written an entire book about John W. Taylor and his variegated families, a book which has every good quality of the original article, and particular virtues besides." Morgan praised *Family Kingdom* as "an impressionistic portrait of both" Samuel's parents, "gay, and altogether engaging yet with an underlying sadness." Morgan wrote:

> John W. Taylor was a young man of distinguished presence, gay and gregarious, headstrong to the point of willfulness, brimming over with energy, a born promotor and plunger, yet a man whose essential spirituality was his most striking quality. He brought snap and sparkle into the lives of everyone who knew him, warmth and a sense of the richness of life, so that each of his friends regarded himself as his best friend and each of his six wives felt assured in her heart that she was his favorite wife, while he was adored by, as he adored, not only the three dozen children his own wives bore him but all the children of any neighborhood he lived in.[61]

Samuel W. Taylor described his father's spirituality as an inner "prompting" that he might instantly foresee future events. For example, John W. was said to foresee an adverse event happening to James A. Garfield on his inauguration day as the United States president. Less than seven months later, Garfield fell victim to a demented assassin. Taylor wrote to Matthias Cowley that Cowley would someday become one among the Twelve Apostles; this happened years later, in the same meeting Taylor himself was ordained. In Canada, Taylor convinced some Mormons digging a canal to leave their

Figure 3. John Whittaker Taylor, an apostle dedicated to plural marriage, was a single-minded visionary described as a human rocket. Fox and Symons Photography Studio, Salt Lake City, not dated. Courtesy of LDS Church History Library.

wheat unplanted until the canal was finished so that their contract would not be broken. Taylor claimed that he foresaw a mild winter and a good crop. While very reluctant to accept a wild weather prediction, the farmers complied. They finished the dig and planted late in the fall, and in fact normal winter freeze did not occur; consequently, they were still harvesting abundant crops in January. "Multiplied by dozens of such incidents . . . the spiritual man inevitably comes to depend on inner guidance at the expense of experience, convention, advice, logic." Taylor somewhat impetuously entered his six marriages because he did what he always did: trust his spiritual vision, his internal "prompting."[62] But John W. Taylor "was a man born too early or too late. In a time when the survival of his church depended on its capacity to compromise and change, he was hostile to compromise and uncapable of change."[63]

Samuel W. Taylor described his father's impulsive business decisions that made their family life one of alternating boom and bust. Often an endeavor was impractical but still embarked upon, driven by John W. Taylor's certainty that he could foresee the future. He was "at once a high Church official and also a big-time promoter—colonizing and constructing dam and irrigation projects similar to what the US government builds today. Taylor dealt in timber and coal properties ("Large tracts only," according to his letterhead) and "had a gold mine in Mexico." He often left his wives in such financial want that they were forced to run "their household like widows." Samuel claimed that despite these recurring cycles of success and failure, his father believed "that one result of his living the gospel will be that his business will thrive, and . . . a healthy business certainly does no harm to his progress in the church."[64]

Of his father, Samuel said he "was neither discreet or low profile."[65] Each of his six wives "hitched a wild ride for time and eternity with a human rocket."[66] His verve carried into his relations with other general authorities. Diary entries of Apostle John Henry Smith provide examples of Taylor's contentiousness regarding plural marriage and other issues. In a meeting on September 30, 1890, thirteen church leaders "spoke upon the President's Manifesto . . . and [all] endorsed it. [However] John W. Taylor was somewhat mixed but acknowledged the hand of the Lord in it."[67] On October 9, 1898, George Q. Cannon presented the names of all church authorities for a sustaining vote. All received unanimous approval save John W. Taylor: "Some few voted against him for remarks made on Friday about Kamas Ward and the Salt Lake Tabernacle Choir. . . . Bro. John W. Taylor at the close of the meeting met with the choir and arranged his trouble with them."[68] Apparently, Taylor had openly accused—from the pulpit—several members of the choir of visiting a Salt Lake City bordello after choir practice.[69] In a March 1889 meeting, President Woodruff sought the apostles' views regarding some words spoken by John W. Taylor against Senator John T. Caine, then in Washington attempting to take his senatorial seat.[70]

John Henry Smith's diaries also contain several examples of Taylor's persistent interest in polygamy. In Thatcher, Arizona, in early 1898, "Elder John W. Taylor made a ringing address on our duties to our families and on the sacredness of the doctrine of the Eternity of the Marriage Covenant, including the Plurality of Wives. He told the brethren to do their full duty to their wives but that man could not take more wives in the plural order." Contradicting his own words, Taylor performed five forbidden plural marriages in Colonia Juarez, Mexico, in a one-week period in March 1898.[71] Also, on Sunday, March 5, "Bro. John W. Taylor spoke one hour on polygamy."[72]

From the time of his second marriage in 1888, Taylor and his six wives lived on "the Underground," pursued by US marshals and bounty hunters. He scattered his wives and children to homes in Canada; Davis County and Provo, Utah; and Mexico. In 1904 Taylor successfully avoided subpoenas issued from the Senate to testify in the Reed Smoot hearings. Actions against him by LDS leadership took place in 1906 and 1911, near the same time as similar actions against Matthias Cowley. Samuel W. Taylor's grandson claimed that the church continued to pay Taylor a salary after his excommunication, but the amounts reported were inconsistent with other accounts.[73] Weak and wracked by stomach cancer, John Whittaker Taylor died at the home of his second wife, Nellie Eva Todd Taylor, in Salt Lake City on October 10, 1916.

MARRINER WOOD MERRILL

With ancestral roots in Canada, Marriner Wood Merrill was born in Westmoreland County, New Brunswick, in 1832. Merrill claimed to have visions and supernatural experiences, even as young as age nine. He allegedly saw the prophets Joseph Smith and Brigham Young, life in Nauvoo, and horses and mules (which he had never actually seen) pulling wagons. Merrill claimed to comprehend, in this semiconscious state, what he would later recognize as the LDS church's doctrines and principles.

Merrill first heard the Mormon gospel from missionaries John Skerry and Jesse Wentworth Crosby Sr. in 1852. In April, at the age of nineteen,

Merrill was baptized by Skerry, and on September 5 was ordained a Priest by Crosby. Another connection between Merrill and the last called colonization is noteworthy. By 1900 Merrill had been made an apostle, interested in continuing plural marriage, when Jesse's son, Jesse Wentworth Crosby Jr., a three-wife polygamist, came with that year's migrants as a colonizer to the Big Horn Basin.[74]

Crosby Jr., whose father had brought Merrill into the church, was living in Kanab, Kane County, in 1890 when he and other local church leaders brought charges against President Wilford Woodruff. Their complaint was that Woodruff "leaned on" men in Kanab who were "not friendly to the Ward Priesthood," rather than dealing with them as other leaders had done previously. John W. Taylor and two other apostles heard the case on September 18 and 19, 1890. John Henry Smith's journal cites four counts that were discussed and settled by the High Council.[75] When the junior Crosby came to the Big Horn Basin in 1900, it was with an Iron County contingent, not with fellow Kane County members.

About a year after his baptism and following his nonbelieving father's death, Merrill started west from Canada to join the Latter-day Saints in Utah Territory. He arrived in Keokuk, Iowa, in time to leave on May 18, 1853, with the William Atkinson Company, and he arrived in Salt Lake City around September 10. Also traveling in the company, returning from his mission, was Jesse W. Crosby Sr. Merrill later claimed Crosby was the company's captain, but this is not verified in LDS church records.[76] Once in the valley, Merrill hastened to find employment, then he married Sarah Ann Atkinson, William Atkinson's daughter, on November 11.

In the winter of 1855, Merrill sought firewood in Millcreek Canyon. Despite Sarah's pleadings that the snow and severe cold made it dangerous, he persisted. As he was loading his logs, some slid off his wagon and pinned him. Merrill later recounted severe pain, then losing consciousness, but he described a supranormal event wherein he awoke to find himself freed, with his logs properly loaded. Despite severe pain and the inability to move his lower extremities, Merrill was able to drive his team and cargo safely home.[77] Always reluctant to speak publicly, Merrill often spoke of his vivid dreams and unusual experiences while speaking in meetings or with church leadership. On October 1, 1899, in Logan he "related a dream about Satan."[78]

Merrill was advised by church authorities to move to Cache County northern Utah in 1859. There he became involved in large-scale agriculture; he was made the bishop of Richmond, Utah; and he became a contractor for the Utah Northern Railroad. He became prosperous. Merrill's next appointment was to serve in the Richmond Stake Presidency. He also served in the Utah Territorial legislature in 1876 and 1878. Federal census records show Merrill in 1870 living in Richmond, Cache County, with four of his wives and fifteen children, then in 1880 with twenty-four children. He was made Logan Temple president in 1884, and on October 7, 1889, Merrill was ordained as an LDS apostle by President Wilford Woodruff.

Merrill "directed his family, almost as if by divine right, as they operated numerous farms, mills, and dairy plants, controlled social affairs locally, and infiltrated the state's growing educational system." The Merrill family came to be recognized as an accomplished, prominent, American-born immigrant family in Cache Valley, along with the polygamist families of Peter Maughn, Ezra T. Benson, William B. Preston, and several others.

In meetings with fellow apostles, Merrill frequently supported polygamy. On April 1, 1896, he "told of his ordination to the Priesthood. He predicted we would practice plural marriage again and our Nation [would] endorse [it]."[79] In the temple on January 9, 1900, Merrill "stood strong for polygamy."[80] Merrill's deeply held commitment to polygamy was on a personal level rather than to perform marriages for others. Of his eight marriages, only one took place after 1890. This was on April 7, 1901, when he married Hilda M. Erickson, performed by fellow plural marriage enthusiast, Matthias F. Cowley. Merrill fathered only one child born after 1890.[81] He was sought by prosecutors to give testimony in Washington in 1904 and 1905 in the Smoot hearings regarding Mormon plural marriages, but he resisted because of failing health from progressing kidney failure. He was not forced to appear. Merrill died at his Richmond, Utah, home in Cache County in February 1906. He left many descendants from his forty-six children. Marriner W. Merrill was very active and admired by his community for his enterprising work, and he died with assets worth more than a million dollars.

The other three apostles highlighted in this chapter also devoted much of their time not only to church matters, but also to their diverse business pursuits in colonization companies, construction projects, and irrigation companies in the United States as well as Mexico and Canada. One might assume that these men of similar ecclesiastical rank, education, and energy would compile assets in general proportion to their length of life. Table 2 addresses this possibility. However, due to several factors, it is not possible to reach simple conclusions. Some factors are regarding Cowley, the longest lived, and the uncertain degree of negative financial impact that Cowley and Taylor experienced by the church's official actions against them. Measures of devotion to plural marriage by the four apostles are compared with that of President Lorenzo Snow in Table 3.

For thirty-eight church general authorities who died before 1911, the association between financial status at death with leadership position in the church hierarchy, their age at death, and their participation in plural marriage is addressed in Table 4. The mean age at death was seventy-five years. The strongest correlation was participation in plural marriage. Among these thirty-eight Utah-period church leaders, thirty-seven were polygamists. The only exception was Joseph A. Young. Thirteen were apostles or former apostles, ten were First Presidency members or president, and seven were seventies or former seventies. All four church presidents, Brigham Young, John Taylor, Wilford Woodruff, and Lorenzo Snow, died before 1902; all are on the list. Nine men, 24 percent, died as millionaires or multimillionaires. Twenty-three men, 60 percent, died with an estate worth $913,000 to $200,000.

There have been general authorities at various levels who received insufficient remuneration during their years of service and labored long years to repay their debts; others died while still in debt. Some even declared legal bankruptcy. The first to do so were Joseph Smith, his counselor Sidney Rigdon, his older brother and presiding patriarch Hyrum Smith, and presiding bishop-designate Vinson Knight. They sought relief from their indebtedness in 1842 by filing for bankruptcy in Nauvoo.[82]

Table 2. Business efforts of the four apostles dedicated to plural marriage

Name	Age at death	Citations of business involvement[a]	Assets at death in 2010 dollars[b]
Abraham Owen Woodruff	32	25	$60,427
John Whittaker Taylor[c]	58	27	$28,345
Marriner Wood Merrill	73	15	$1,022,250
Matthias Foss Cowley	81	17	Not listed

[a]Quinn, *Mormon Hierarchy: Wealth and Corporate Power*, Appendix 5, "General Authorities in Business Before 1933," 177–446.
[b]Quinn, *Mormon Hierarchy: Wealth and Corporate Power*, Appendix 4, "General Authorities Assets at Death in US Dollars," 173–76.
[c]John W. Taylor was listed as only one of two general authorities having less-than-average income for 1885 and 1886, and the only man in that category in 1888. Quinn, *Mormon Hierarchy: Wealth and Corporate Power*, Appendix 1, "General Authorities with Less-than-average Wealth," 158–62. The other three apostles do not appear in the list.

Table 3. Measures of devotion to plural marriage by select Mormon leaders

Mormon leaders championing Wyoming immigration and plural marriages	Highest office held	Plural marriages entered post-1890 of total marriages	Number of children	Number of children born in polygamy post-1890	Number of marriages performed post-1890
Lorenzo Snow	President	0 of 9	46	1	0
Marriner Wood Merrill	Apostle	1 of 8	46	1	3
Abraham Owen Woodruff	Apostle	1 of 2	5	3	4
John Whittaker Taylor	Apostle	4 of 6	36[a]	34	7
Matthias Foss Cowley	Apostle	2 of 4	15[b]	13	46[c]
Totals		8 of 29	148	52	58

Mormon leaders active in plural marriages, not part of Wyoming colonization	Highest office held	Plural marriages entered post-1890 of total marriages	Number of children	Number of children born in polygamy post-1890	Number of marriages performed post-1890
Anthony Woodward Ivins	First counselor First Presidency	0 of 1	9	0	43
Alexander Finley MacDonald Sr.	Patriarch and Seven President of Seventies	0 of 5	26	0	16[d]
Judson Tolman	Patriarch	1 of 5	Unknown	Unknown	15
George Teasdale[e]	Apostle	Unknown of possible 17	16 or more	1	3

[a] Samuel Woolley Taylor, John's son by third marriage, gives the number of his siblings "exactly three dozen." Taylor, *Family Kingdom*, vii.

[b] This number is from Cowley's autobiography.

[c] Smart lists only 43, *Last Colonizer*, 140.

[d] Most were performed in Mexico, in Colonia Diaz, Colonia Juarez, and Colonia Garcia.

[e] Incomplete data from Family Search, © by Intellectual Reserve, 2019, a service provided by the Church of Jesus Christ of Latter-day Saints, April 2019. https://www.familysearch.org/tree/person/collaborate/KWJC-FQB

Table 4. Plural marriage, financial standing, and ecclesiastical status among LDS general authorities who died before 1911

Name	Year of death	Age at death	Ecclesiastical status[a]	Polygamist	Net value 2010 dollars[b]
Brigham Young Sr.	1877	76	President	Y	$34,959,000
Horace S. Eldredge	1888	72	Seventy	Y	$13,875,016
George Q. Cannon	1901	74	FP counselor	Y	$5,311,106
John R. Winder	1910	89	FP counselor	Y	$3,455,598
John Taylor	1887	79	President	Y	$3,291,949
Moses Thatcher	1909	67	Apostle	Y	$2,318,278
Edward Hunter	1883	90	Presiding Bishop	Y	$1,541,128
Heber C. Kimball	1868	67	FP counselor	Y	$1,501,802
Marriner W. Merrill	1906	74	Apostle	Y	$1,022,250
William B. Preston	1908	78	Former Presiding Bishop	Y	$913,254
Wilford Woodruff	1898	91	President	Y	$813,000
George A. Smith	1875	58	FP counselor	Y	$683,309
Parley P. Pratt	1857	50	Apostle	Y	$670,800
Abraham H. Cannon	1896	37	Apostle	Y	$628,158
Lorenzo Snow	1901	87	President	Y	$499,403
Edward Stevenson	1897	77	Seventy	Y	$488,423
Charles C. Rich	1883	74	Apostle	Y	$439,425
Leonard W. Hardy	1884	79	PB counselor	Y	$377,238
Erastus Snow	1888	70	Apostle	Y	$352,962
Robert T. Burton	1907	86	PB counselor	Y	$329,621
Albert P. Rockwood	1879	74	Seventy	Y	$321,924
Joseph A. Young	1875	41	Former FP counselor	N	$256,289
Willard Richards	1854	50	FP counselor	Y	$226,299
John Van Cott	1883	69	Seventy	Y	$157,638

Table 4 (*continued*). Plural marriage, financial standing, and ecclesiastical status among LDS general authorities who died before 1911

Name	Year of death	Age at death	Ecclesiastical status[a]	Polygamist	Net value 2010 dollars[b]
Ezra T. Benson	1869	95	Apostle	Y	$93,877
Nathan H. Felt	1888	69	Former Presiding Bishop	Y	$88,875
Daniel H. Wells	1891	77	Counselor to Twelve	Y	$77,959
Orson Hyde	1878	73	Apostle	Y	$62,946
Abraham Owen Woodruff	1904	34	Apostle	Y	$60,427
Orson Pratt	1881	70	Apostle	Y	$56,456
George Teasdale	1907	76	Apostle	Y	$54,062
John E. Page	1867	68	Former apostle	Y	$40,955
William E. McLellin[c]	1883	77	Former apostle	Y	$31,214
Brigham Young Jr.	1903	67	Apostle	Y	$30,720
Zera Pulsipher	1872	83	Former Seventy	Y	$24,995
John F. Boynton	1890	79	Former apostle	Y	$24,700
Benjamin L Clapp	1865	51	Former Seventy	Y	$9,729
George Reynolds	1909	67	Seventy	Y	$4,940

[a]Quinn's ranking for ecclesiastical status is president or presidency counselor, Quorum of Twelve Apostles member, counselor to the Twelve, Presiding Patriarch, first counselor of the Seventy, Presiding Bishop, and Presiding Bishop counselor. Quinn, *Mormon Hierarchy: Wealth and Corporate Power*, 158.

[b]Quinn, *Mormon Hierarchy: Wealth and Corporate Power*, "General Authority Assets at Death in US Dollars," Appendix 4, 173–76.

[c]Although Quinn includes William Earl McLellin, McLellin is not included in the final calculations here. After a stormy and checkered history with the early Latter-day Saints, McLellin broke all ties with any religion from 1869 to his death in 1883. He married once but spent most of his life single.

Figure 4. "The Wealthy Polygamist" emphasizes the fellowship of conformity, polygamy, corporate business ventures, wealth, and high priesthood status in Utah's nineteenth and twentieth century LDS society. (Caricature by H. L. Stephens, from Fanny Stenhouse's 1872 *Expose of Polygamy*, 108.)

In his remarkably detailed 1997 study of LDS church finances, historian D. Michael Quinn discusses kinship as a significant variable among general authorities. Between 1832 and 1932, 123 men were appointed as general authorities. Sixty-three, 51 percent, were related within a two ancestral generation kinship to one or more living general authorities. The percentage of total kinship among general authorities was 70 percent for 1856–1866, 64 percent for 1900–1910, and 100 percent for 1922–1932.[83]

Thus, five variables—power, money, multiple sexual partners, many children, and kinship—characterized the all-male theocratic leadership within the LDS church from 1844 well into the twentieth century, decades beyond the time of Utah statehood.

For a variety of reasons, some not in their control, apostles John W. Taylor, Abraham Owen Woodruff, and Matthias F. Cowley failed to achieve power or wealth. However, they stood unyielding in what they firmly believed was their personal and divine requirement.

CHAPTER 3

The Big Horn Basin as Frontier

> Being on the frontier ... required doing rather than imagining: clearing
> land, building shelter, obtaining food supplies. Frontiers test ideologies
> like nothing else.[1]
>
> —Robert D. Kaplan

TOWERING ROCKY MOUNTAIN RANGES encircle the immense 12,000-
square-mile Big Horn Basin of north-central Wyoming. They deliver their
clear, cold waters into a plethora of rivers. Along these riverbanks and in
the mountains' vastness, such men as Jedediah Strong Smith, Manuel Lisa,
and brothers William and Milton Green Sublette trapped for furs and
sought buffalo hides in the mountain man era. In February 1803, President
Thomas Jefferson moved Congress to appropriate funds for a Pacific expedition, anticipating the outcome of what became the Louisiana Purchase
from Napoleon. France officially transferred the territory on December 20,
and the United States took formal possession on December 30. This nearly
doubled the land mass of the United States.

The British North West Company learned of Jefferson's massive land
purchase and that an American expedition was to start westward early in
1804. Explorers, commanded by Captain Meriwether Lewis and Second
Lieutenant William Clark, were to ascend the Missouri River to trap, trade,
and claim the land. The British company was alarmed. François-Antoine
Larocque was sent to investigate what the British fur outfit considered an
intrusion into their trapping and trading monopoly.[2] Starting from their
post in today's southwestern Manitoba, Canada, Larocque and four companions arrived at the Mandan villages on the Missouri River and soon met
the Lewis and Clark expedition there on November 25, 1804. On a second
journey in 1805, Larocque and his companions joined a large contingent of
Crow Indians on "an extended trading sojourn that would traverse a huge
expanse" across the Yellowstone River's headwaters. The trip lasted four and

a half months and covered some thirteen thousand miles. After Larocque's report of his 1805 experience, the British North West Company abandoned further attempts at trading and trapping on American lands.[3]

On his August 30, 1805, camp at the Big Horn River's northern mouth, Larocque wrote the first known description "of the fifty-mile long, steep, vertical-walled, Big Horn Canyon that would later be named the 'Bad-Pass.'" Larocque recognized that the Big Horn River's water did not originate in the mountains adjacent to the Bad Pass, but from mountains "30 or 40 miles" upriver, further to the south. He wrote that "Indians say it is a Man Wolf who lives in the canyon and rides out of it to devour any person or beast that go to [*sic*] near. They say it is impossible to Kill him for he is ball proof."[4]

These explorers and hundreds of others like Hugh Glass, John Frémont, and Peter Skene Ogden—American, French, Canadian, and Métis—sought pelts and dealt with the fearful Blackfeet and the horse-hungry Crow.[5] They also encountered the Shoshone, the Assiniboine and Gros Ventre, the Flathead and Nez Perce peoples. Colter's Hell, a region of sulfurous, subterranean belching of gases and molten debris to the earth's surface, was named for its first-known Euro American explorer, John Colter. Colter saw the awesome spectacle in 1807 while returning from an honorable discharge from his two-year trek with Lewis and Clark.[6] Contrary to modern folklore about its location, Colter's Hell was then close to but outside the region now designated as Yellowstone National Park. The original locale is only a modest-sized extinct geyser basin west of present-day Cody, Wyoming.

Nearby, the Demaris hot springs is active. Jim Bridger and Joe Meek were mountain men intimately familiar with the area and insisted it was "near the forks of the Shoshone or Stinking Water River." Colter's solitary mountain exploits, begun later that year, earned him the appellation as the original first mountain man. From a geographic perspective, Colter's Hell was not far from the north–south Absaroka Range that forms the Big Horn Basin's west wall and sends waters east in the Yellowstone River and west into the Snake and the Columbia.[7]

Perhaps the most well-known widely believed episode of Colter's early encounters was in 1808 when he ran for his life. He and another Corps of Discovery veteran, John Potts, were captured by a group of Blackfeet Indians near the Jefferson River.[8] Colter surrendered but Potts did not, and the latter was summarily killed. Stripped naked and without foot protection, Colter was told to run, pursued by several young Blackfeet seemingly determined to kill him. Nearing exhaustion, Colter stopped suddenly, turned, and surprised his leading pursuer, causing him to drop his spear. Colter picked up the spear

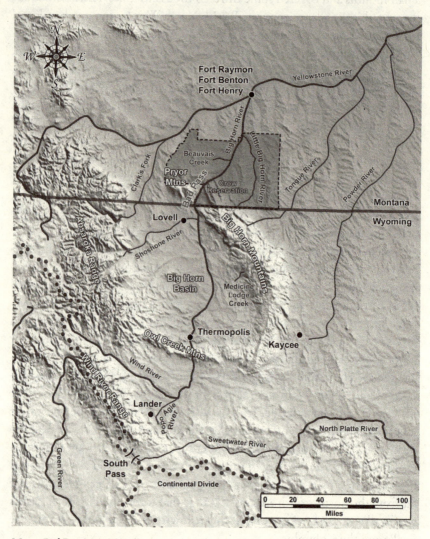

Map 1. Bad Pass Map. This thirty-mile corridor, used since prehistoric times, connects two important watersheds, the Wind and Yellowstone, and provides a detour around the 1,000-foot-deep Big Horn Canyon. Mountain men used it from 1805 through the end of the rendezvous era. The Pryor Mountains were named for Nathaniel Pryor of the Lewis and Clark Expedition. Reprinted with permission from Mike Bryant, "Bad Pass Trail: Gateway between the Wind and Yellowstone Rivers," *The Rocky Mountain Fur Trade Journal* 11 (2017): 89.

and killed the Blackfoot Indian, then he leaped into the river and hid inside a beaver mound or a logjam until the search was abandoned. Near starvation and naked save for what he could fashion, Colter made his way, walking 250 miles to Manuel Lisa's trading post at the Big Horn River's mouth.[9]

Another legendary mountain man, James Felix "Jim" Bridger, deserves remembrance for his extraordinary part in exploring the Big Horn Basin and the West. Union Major General Grenville Dodge, who served as Ulysses S. Grant's intelligence chief in the western theater, said this of Bridger:

> He was a born topographer; the whole West was mapped out in his mind, and such was his instinctive sense of locality and direction that it used to be said of him that he could smell his way where he could not see it. He was a complete master of plains and woodcraft, equal to any emergency, full of resources to overcome any obstacles ... and could live without food except what the country afforded in that wild region.[10]

Bridger was part of a Big Horn Basin trapping expedition in 1825, and in the spring of 1830, with Jedediah Smith and Joe Meek, Bridger brought a party of trappers through the basin, then he attended the annual rendezvous in mid-July at the Wind River's junction with the Popo Agie. In August, the firm of Jed Smith, William Sublette, and David Jackson sold out to the Rocky Mountain Fur Company, of which Bridger was a partner, along with Thomas Fitzpatrick, Jean Baptiste Gervais, and Henry Fraeb. Bridger, Fitzpatrick, and Milton Sublette led a party of approximately two hundred men through the basin to the Yellowstone River, which became Bridger's third visit of 1830.[11]

In 1864 Bridger guided at least ten trains of gold-seekers bound for Virginia City through the basin on the Big Horn Mountain's west side, which was then named the Bridger Trail. The Bozeman Trail, more exposed to Indian attack on the Big Horn Mountain's eastward slope, saw only four trains to Virginia City in 1864. Bridger guiding the west trail is the only time its use by immigrants in 1864 is documented.[12] Travelers on both trails indicated the Bozeman Trail provided better grass compared to the arid Big Horn Basin side. These facts were supported by an 1868 report to Congress by the US Topographical Corps' Captain William F. Raynolds, which read:

> This part of the country ... is repelling in all its characteristics, and can only be traversed with the greatest difficulty. ... The valley of the

Big Horn ... is totally surrounded on all sides by mountain ridges, and presents but few agricultural advantages. ... The region is totally unfit for either rail or wagon roads.[13]

This description immediately suggests a parallel with what author and historian Wallace Stegner wrote in his recall about Whitemud, the place of his boyhood, in Canada's Saskatchewan Province. "Has it anything ... that would recommend it as a human habit? ... low rainfall, short growing season, monotonous landscape, and wide extremes of temperature limit the number of people who can settle and the prosperity and contentment of the ones who manage to stick." The place also "raises the question, unthinkable to pioneers but common enough among their expatriate sons, whether any [place like] Whitemud can hope to develop to a state of civilization as high as that which some of its founders abandoned."[14]

On the basin's north side are the Beartooth and Pryor Mountains.[15] Marking the basin's east side, the 120-mile-long Big Horn Mountain range is the headwater source for the Tongue and Powder Rivers that join the Yellowstone and become the Missouri River. It was in these mountains, along the Little Big Horn River's course, where Lieutenant Colonel George Armstrong Custer and 260 Seventh Cavalrymen were killed by Lakota warriors on June 26, 1876. The Owl Creek Mountains were called the Littlehorn by the mountain men, which make the basin's south and southwest walls. The Wind River passes through the Wind River Canyon and becomes the Big Horn River at a site known as the "Wedding of the Waters." However, there is no junction of separate waters here; the same river changes names from Wind River to Big Horn River when it leaves the canyon and flows northward. Waters from the Wind River Range contribute to the Green, the Sweetwater, and the Colorado, flowing to the Pacific Ocean. With eight snow-capped peaks, each over 12,000 feet, the 170-mile-long Absarokas form the eastern boundary of Yellowstone Park, feeding the Shoshone, Greybull, and Big Horn Rivers, flowing eastward into the Missouri. Their peaks complete the circle on the basin's west side.

The country along the Big Horn Mountain's eastern slope, the Powder River Basin, was a favorite hunting ground for Indigenous groups where game, wood, and good water and grass were abundant. Consequently, they fought against encroaching US Army forces and killed all eighty-one of Captain William J. Fetterman's troops at Massacre Hill, near Fort Phil Kearny, and General Custer's force on the Little Big Horn River. The area later became "a number of well-known summer resorts ... being transformed

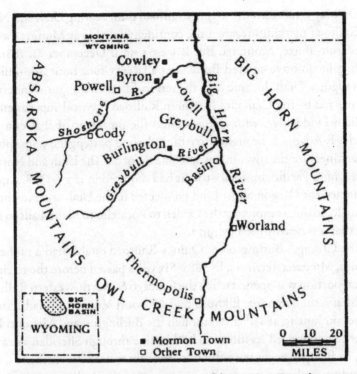

Map 2. A simple outline of the main rivers of the Big Horn Basin showing the ring of mountain ranges that define the basin. The Wind River Range spans the Southern Absarokas and the Owl Creek Range. Reprinted with permission from Bowen, "Migration," 210.

into a great dairy region," with a "diversity of scenery" with "rich agricultural possibilities." It was also "underlaid with unlimited coal deposits, [with] medium elevation, exhilarating atmosphere, much sunshine, and an agreeable climate the greater part of the year."[16]

These formidable mountain ranges on the compass four points made access for Euro American settlers very difficult prior to completion of various railroads. Wyoming was named a territory in 1868, and during that era the Union Pacific Railroad propelled economic growth through Cheyenne, Laramie, and Rock Springs in the territory's southern portion. On May 10, 1869, a golden spike was driven at Utah's Promontory, linking the westbound Union Pacific with the eastbound Central Pacific. East–west commerce was then assured as the nation's economy was recovering from its devastating Civil War years.

On May 9, 1880, a narrow-gauge railroad train bearing Utah and Northern Railroad markings reached the continental divide at Monida Pass, 125 miles from Butte, Montana. But it wasn't until December 21, 1881, that the first locomotive entered Butte after a twenty-four-hour 466-mile run from Ogden, Utah. It came over the ten-to-fifteen-mile spur clandestinely constructed by the Utah and Northern Railroad's general superintendent, William Doddridge, who circumvented the president of that company, Charles F. Adams. It brought forty Butte-bound passengers, 5,600 pounds of machinery for the silver mines, and one car of oil. The Utah and Northern was a Union Pacific subsidiary that it had acquired in 1877–1878. Another subsidiary, the Oregon Short Line, connected to the Utah and Northern at Pocatello, Idaho, completing the Ogden to Pocatello to Idaho Falls to Butte path that was heavily used by 1900.

The Chicago, Burlington & Quincy Railroad established a railhead at Billings, Montana Territory, by 1882. Six years passed before the territory's central portion was opened when the Chicago & North Western Railroad's subsidiary, the Fremont, Elkhorn and Missouri Valley Railroad, came to Casper on June 15, 1888.[17] Even though the Burlington and Missouri River Railroad announced its intent to build a line through Sheridan as early as 1888, its first passenger train did not arrive there until November 22, 1892. To "induce settlers to come to Wyoming in 1892 the Burlington offered passengers passage from Kansas City, Missouri to Gillette for $2."[18] However, even by the century's turn, the Big Horn Basin's cities and settlements west of the Big Horn Mountain's western side still had no railroad terminals.

According to railroad historian Robert G. Athearn, the Denver and Rio Grande Railroad completed a line of narrow-gauge track connecting the metropolis of Denver with Salt Lake City in late March 1883. It then opened a wider-gauge service from Denver to Ogden in 1891.[19] After the Union Pacific's reorganization in 1900, it completed its own lines to Butte. This route entered into Wyoming's southeastern corner at Cheyenne and Laramie. The course then went directly west to Granger, then to Evanston, to Ogden, then directly north to Pocatello, to Idaho Falls, and to Butte, all while staying on the Absaroka Range's west side and west of Yellowstone Park.[20]

When Abraham Owen Woodruff left his ranch in Summit County, Utah, or from Salt Lake City or Ogden to travel by railroad to what became Cowley, Wyoming, in the basin, the nearest railheads were at Bridger and Red Lodge, Montana.[21] Connections could be made by traveling from Park City to Kimball Junction to Coalville on the Utah Eastern Railroad; from Coalville to Echo on the Summit County Railroad; from Echo to Corrine on the Union Pacific Railroad; from Corrine to Brigham City to Franklin, Idaho, on the Utah Northern; from Franklin to Dillon, Montana, on the Oregon Short Line and Northern Pacific Railroad, then to Bridger or Red Lodge.[22] Travel for Latter-day Saints to distant destination cities east and south was available by 1904. The Burlington & Missouri Railroad's Passenger Agent in Omaha, Mr. J. Francis, mailed tickets on February 15 to apostles John W. Taylor and Owen Woodruff in Byron, Wyoming, for their trip by way of Garland, Wyoming, and Denver, Colorado's capital city.[23] As noted, rail travel through the basin's heart was not reached until 1909.

A letter from the Oregon Short Line Railroad's officials in Salt Lake City to the general passenger and ticket administrator for the Union Pacific in Omaha reveals details regarding the routes of travel for Latter-day Saints to the basin in February 1901. It also gives evidence that they attempted to negotiate a less costly fare for members traveling to and from Big Horn County. At the "earnest solicitation" by Latter-day Saints needing to travel to northern Wyoming in 1900, the Oregon Short Line took up with the Northern Pacific and arranged a special rate from Butte to Bridger, then the nearest rail point. Subsequently, "the Burlington have built their cutoff from Denver, and are now building a branch line known as 'Toluca-Cody branch' which when completed . . . will not be over 5 miles distant from the colony."[24] The letter continues:

> The Northern Pacific have been very arbitrary and unaccommodating to these people, and the Church officials here desire if possible, to change the routing of his business to Cheyenne and Sydney [Nebraska] and the B & M [Burlington & Missouri]. A further incentive for changing the routing of this business, is that the Mormon people in that section have a $75,000 [*sic*] grading contract with the Burlington road. They ask us if, in the future, the business cannot be routed from here via the Oregon Short Line, U.P. and the B & M. The rate we have made from Salt Lake to Bridger has been $17.05, divided as follows: $10.05 O.S.L. to Butte, and $7.00 [for the] Nor[thern]. Pac[ific] beyond, which is half rate; I understand that the Burlington people have solicited this business with the Rio Grande lines via Denver at $17.05 rate. If you desire to handle this business via Sidney or the B & M junction, at the rate named, I would suggest you take [the] matter up with Mr. Francis and arrange for division of revenue and advise us later. While of course, you readily appreciate that the Short Line are not anxious to lose this revenue,

at same time we do not wish to have the business routed via Denver if you care to handle it over your line in connection with the B & M. through Sydney. An early reply will greatly oblige.[25]

The Oregon Short Line ticket agent, D. E. Burley, wrote Woodruff again on March 8, indicating that discussions with the Union Pacific and Burlington concluded that they were not yet ready to provide service beyond Billings, and that the Northern Pacific must be used from Billings to Bridger.[26] In May an additional letter to Woodruff in Bowler, Montana, explained that the reduced fare of $7.00 beyond Butte applied only to groups of five traveling together.[27]

William F. Cody, best known as "Buffalo Bill," had been interested in the basin as early "as several times in 1891," when he visited Edward Gillette's surveying camps. By 1895 he was further interested in developing an eastern access to Yellowstone Park through the 8,553-foot altitude of Sylvan Pass that could be served by a new town to be named Cody.[28] Answering Cody's interest was in part the Chicago, Burlington and Quincy's motivation, but it also served as notice to competing rail lines that they were already present in force and influence. In 1899 surveying began, and in the spring of 1900 the Burlington awarded contracts to Mormon leader William H. Packard of Burlington to construct its 130-mile-long "line from Talooka, [sic] Montana to Cody."[29] From Toluca the railway line went to Pryor, to Bowler, Montana, and in Wyoming through Frannie, Deaver, Garland, and Powell to Cody. The grade through the Pryor Gap was the toughest, and in winter months young men from Cowley would jump on the coal cars to steal coal to heat their homes. The first train reached Cody on November 11, 1901, with notable passenger Colonel Cody himself. A second train soon arrived, this one from Billings, bearing Wyoming's senator Clarence D. Clark.[30]

The *Cody Enterprise* welcomed the endeavor:

There is an immense territory lying in the northwestern portion of Wyoming that is perhaps as little known as any region now open to civilization under the American flag. It is a country of great resources as yet almost absolutely undeveloped. This region has by common consent been given the name of the Big Horn Basin. A new line of railway has just been built into the heart of this country, extending from Toluca, Montana... to Cody... and daily train service in both directions is offered over it.[31]

The Toluca–Cody line was called the "Squaw Train," in part because its sizeable number of patrons were Crow Indians and because the Burlington sent many of them as laborers to build the line.[32] The Toluca line was expensive to repair, the demand was not great, and trains were rarely on time due to washed out track or damaged bridges. It ceased operation in 1911.[33] Strictly speaking, the Big Horn Basin's thin northern rim had some rail service by 1901, but it brought little more than contact and was not suitable for reliable import of freight or outgoing farm products.

In 1901 the Chicago, Burlington & Quincy was sold to the Northern Pacific and Great Northern, and from 1902 to 1905 this new line was developing plans "to connect the Pacific Northwest and the Gulf of Mexico with a line from the Big Horn Basin to the North Platte River." The Big Horn Railroad Company was set up as "a paper corporation for the work," and construction began at Frannie, Wyoming, in October 1905.[34] The work moved southeast "along the Big Horn River through Greybull, Basin, and Worland to reach Kirby, Wyoming, on September 3, 1907," and Thermopolis in 1909.[35] "The CB&Q operated an Immigration Bureau to lure settlers to take up land in the Big Horn Basin's new irrigation projects between 1906 and 1913. Railroad officials reported that their publicity brought an estimated 8,000 families to the Basin. Through a variety of nearly 400 mergers, the Burlington Northern Santa Fe rail is now among the largest networks in North America with more than 32,000 rail miles across the United States' western two-thirds."[36] While this line "continues to serve agriculture in the Big Horn Basin, most of its Wyoming business is hauling coal. Day and night, trains stretching a mile-long run from the Powder River Basin via the Orin Cutoff, bound for many power producing plants in the Midwest, South and East."[37]

Aridity was an additional reason the basin remained relatively untouched by general westward expansion during the nineteenth century's latter half. Despite the traverses by the Wind, Greybull, Shoshone, Big Horn, and other sizeable rivers through its central portion, the Big Horn Basin receives less than six inches of rain annually and is usually a candidate for the state's most arid region. The basin also experiences huge temperature variations, and "while generally it is not the coldest place in Wyoming, it is often the warmest in the summer."[38] Until nourished by water supplied by human-made irrigation canals, the soil yields little sustenance for human populations. Wyoming historian Phil Roberts credits early Hispanic farmers with the first irrigation projects in Wyoming, for they created primitive catch dams along the Laramie River to raise vegetables for sale in Fort Laramie.[39]

Small numbers of non-Mormon immigrants formed settlements on the basin's east side in 1886–1888 near today's cities of Ten Sleep and Shell Creek, but they were primarily would-be cattlemen, taking advantage of free grassland remaining from the former cattle-king heydays.[40] Wyoming Territory was granted statehood on July 10, 1890. At that time the vast majority of its 62,000 inhabitants lived in the state's southern half, while the northern Big Horn Basin's population was sparse, only about fifteen hundred.[41]

Notably, the 1890 federal census defined frontier as having an area average of less than two people per square mile, and the basin met that definition. By 1900 there were only 92,500 people spread over about 98,000 square miles of Wyoming, or slightly less than one person per square mile. Only the territories of Alaska and Nevada had fewer people per square mile. According to historian Frederick Jackson Turner's definition, Wyoming's north-central quadrant remained a frontier, an area unbroken by significant "settlements, out of which distinctive traits and institutions would grow."[42] Utah historian Dean May described frontier as "lands that from their perspective had a small, culturally less advanced population and an abundance of unclaimed and under-developed resources."[43] Without further interpreting the terms "frontier" versus "region" in western development, Turner claimed that frontier is an "elastic" term.[44] In many ways, the 1900–1901 colonizers were met by the harsh conditions of a frontier.

By 1895 the city of Otto in Big Horn County had fifteen businesses and a population of "about 70 people"—making it the largest town in the Big Horn Basin. The businesses included a saloon, barbershop, and blacksmith shop. The Greybull River's devastating flooding in 1914 led to efforts to move the town's structures on rollers made from cottonwood trees. It was not successful, and as author historian Loveland recorded, "like Brigadoon, Otto was there, then it was gone. What was once a thriving town is now a farmer's field."[45]

Overall, the basin remained a frontier population demographically. Of those older than age eighteen, 72 percent were men, mostly unmarried, while most women residents were legally married. The basin presented many frontier obstacles to the Mormon farmers who arrived. "The natural growth of the valley [soil] consists of . . . salt sage which grows very short and scrubby, just a few inches in height," with "prickly pears and little early spring grass," reported George C. Lustin, the agricultural superintendent for the Utah Sugar Company. "All the land has more or less gypsum [sic] which has the appearance of white alkali, but from the farmer's reports that have been there a number of years, it appears that all grain and nearly all kinds of vegetation will grow where this gypsom is most prominent, if the land is flooded when irrigated so that the gypsom [*sic*] will be dissolved and washed away."[46]

It was a frontier challenge for the Mormon colonists that all water for drinking and culinary use had to be hauled in barrels from the Stinking Water River.[47] Horses and other livestock were taken daily some distance to a small water source called Sage Creek, though not safe for human consumption.[48] No water would be available for growing crops for their livelihoods until the colonists completed—without outside help or modern machinery—digging a canal in the hard, dry ground. When finished it was more than thirty miles in length, measuring twenty-five feet wide at the water line, fifteen feet wide at the bottom, and five feet deep, with its grade dropping two feet per mile.[49]

The majority of men listed "farmer" or "farm laborer" as their occupation on the census, but historian John W. Davis notes that they were in fact ranchers or hired hands working on cattle ranches. Davis writes, "If the definition of 'farmer' extends only to one who raises crops for market, virtually no person before 1900 in Big Horn Basin could be considered a farmer." As noted, this frontier had no rail or other transportation to distant markets in population centers. Within the decade of 1900 to 1910, southwestern Wyoming's sheep growers were frequently Mormons who left crop farming.

The basin remained frontier-like in its judicial system. The courts of two northern Wyoming counties, Fremont and Johnson, were so widely spread it rendered a judicial system nearly nonfunctional. From the area around Cody, a trip to Fremont County's court in Lander involved crossing the Owl Creek Mountains, and Johnson County's court was in Buffalo, requiring justice seekers to journey across or around the formidable Big Horn Mountains to reach their eastern slope.

During the cattle range era, scores of murders occurred in the Big Horn Basin. Because of the area's poorly functioning judicial system, most violent crimes went unpunished, save for the operation of extralegal vengeance, notes Davis.[50] The pathetically inadequate system of law enforcement endured from 1879, when Judge William A. Carter, the sutler at Fort Bridger, brought a cattle herd of four thousand to the "sparse but nutritious grass" in its high valleys. These valleys developed into a cattle king's province, and law enforcement remained under their personal control through the nineteenth century's final two decades. A 1980 study of lynching in the United States after 1909 found that although the majority were committed in southern states, mostly on African American victims, the western states and territories were not unblemished. Montana was cited with eighty-four, Colorado with forty-three, and Wyoming with thirty-five, with most victims presumably white men.[51]

Even in 1902, when the Mormon colonization was only two years old, justice by vengeance was still very much in evidence, as in the case of Jim Gorman. He was convicted of murdering his brother, Tim, by burying a hatchet in his head. Jim was allegedly having an affair with Tim's wife, Maggie, who was complicit in her husband's killing. While Jim was being held in the Big Horn County jail awaiting trial, a mob broke into the jail and killed Jim, another prisoner, and a deputy sheriff.

It was not until 1909, when a Big Horn jury—with Mormon bishop William H. Packard and several other Mormons as jurors—delivered justice and legal punishment for the 1909 Shell Creek slaughter of sheepherders Joe Emge, Joe Allemand, and Jules Lazier by a band of cowboys. Convicted and sentenced to prison terms were George Saban, Herb Brink, Milton Alexander, Thomas Dixon, and Edward Eaton. With this, the operation of extralegal punishment by the euphemistical "Judge Lynch" in the Big Horn Basin finally ended. As the prosecuting attorney William Metz stated:

> The "gun-man" has had his day in Wyoming. From this time on set-tlers may come in assured that the law will give them its fullest pro-tection, that the open range will be as safe as the peaceful prairies of Iowa or Illinois. It is a triumph of law and order, the culmination of a struggle waged for two-score years . . . against the domination of its broad acres' usurpers of the open range who have opposed the passing of the old order of things and have desperately fought it.[52]

When the Mormon colonists arrived in 1900 and 1901, they did not find a godsent serendipity. Far improved over the ordeals of Colter, Bridger, and others, they still encountered a frontier. They found a demanding, challenging land, distant from population centers. It lacked schools, hospitals, doctors, sewage systems, and public utilities. However, they did not lack pluck, nor assurances from their leaders that they would be blessed if they remained obedient, hard-working, tithe-paying, and faithful. They were promised prosperity—in ways not described or defined—and that they would receive all the blessings of Jesus Christ's restored gospel.

CHAPTER 4

Dispossession and Elimination

> To have and to houlde, possesse and enjoy ... the foresaid lands, territo-
> ries, islands, ... precincts, seas, waters, fishings, and all that should from
> henceforth arise ... and every part and parcel thereof, unto said Councell
> and their successors and assigns for ever.[1]
>
> —Massachusetts Bay Colony Royal Charter

IN DEFINING THE BIG HORN BASIN as frontier in 1900, it is important to address the fact that significant numbers of Native inhabitants lived within its boundary. Neither Shoshone nor Arapaho moved against Abraham Owen Woodruff's colonization. Conversely, Woodruff's people made no moves against the Native Americans.

Wyoming's history reveals that "by the 1890s the Eastern Shoshone," under Chief Washakie, "had been living on its reservation in the Wind River Valley for more than two decades, under its treaty with the U.S. government." In 1878 about 950 Northern Arapaho people had been escorted into the valley by the US Army, where they awaited the government's promised reservation for their own. Buffalo herds had nearly disappeared from the Wind River Valley, save for a few hundred head in the western section, and by 1889 both tribes "were in a state of semi-starvation." The Eastern Shoshone's population fell from 1,259 in 1885 to 841 in 1900. Measles killed 153 people in 1897 alone. During this fifteen-year span, the Northern Arapaho population fell from 978 to 801.[2] Both tribes needed money for food and were under increasing pressure by the threat of land invasions by cattle outfits owned by whites.

The Eastern Shoshone and Northern Arapaho agreed to sell more than one million acres in the valley's north and east portions to the federal government. The tribes intended to use the funds for schools and cattle herds, with the rest to be placed in interest-bearing accounts. Opposition came from local ranchers, including Wilford Woodruff's son, John Dwight Woodruff. Congress refused to ratify the agreement. Finally, in April 1896, negotiations led to the sale of 64,000 acres, including today's site of Thermopolis, a magnificent hot springs.[3] The price was $60,000, with promised future financial installments. At the time of sale there were only 457 males of both tribes over the age of eighteen, and of them only 273—60 percent—signed the contract. Of these, 180 were Shoshone and 93 Arapaho.[4]

Only one encounter between the Mormon colonists and the Shoshone Reservation Indians had the potential for violence with other Big Horn colonists, but it ended peacefully. The incident arose from Owen Woodruff's assignment in May 1900 to colonist Hyrum King North to drive some two hundred head of cattle belonging to the forming 1900 Mormon colonists who had gathered at the Ham's Fork crossing. After entering the reservation where there were a number of farms, the cattle "plunged headlong into the ditches for water," and "the Indian police came out in force." Rather than immediately removing the cattle from the ditches, North invited the Indians to share his evening supper, after which "nearly half of the Indian village turned out and helped get the cattle together."

Shortly thereafter, North was searching for a missing cow and calf when he found them in an Indian shed. He placed the calf on his saddle and drove the cow, attempting to catch up with his moving herd, when he noticed an Indian riding fast after him. Still some distance away, the Indian dismounted and fired in North's direction. Fortunately, the shot was aimed not at him but at a large prairie dog that the Indian, now with a big smile, picked up and presented to North. In another incident, North was approached by two Native cowmen with rifles, pistols, and ammunition, saying they owned the lease on the reservation. They explained that all their cattle were branded, and they would take care that none of North's animals would become mixed into the herd. They dined together and North recalled, "It seemed that a good meal is not [only] the road to a man's stomach, but to his heart also."

North completed his task of driving cattle in a little more than two months; it was without friction with the Native people and with only one yearling lost. Whether his experiences with the Native groups had an impact on Hyrum K. North's commitment to colonization is uncertain. He had arrived in the Big Horn without his family, who remained near Mill Creek in Salt Lake County when he left in May 1900 with the main immigrant group. In June, at the time of that year's federal census, North was listed living in Lovell, Big Horn County, without his wife and children. However, the historian Welch records that North owned a city lot in Cowley with 160 acres northwest of town. By census time in April 1910, he had returned to Salt Lake City, where he, his wife, and their six children were living and operating a grocery store. North worked more than twenty years as an employee of

Deseret News Company and as district manager of paper carriers in Davis, Morgan, and Summit Counties.[5]

The most serious and tragic interaction between whites and Native Americans in Wyoming after Owen Woodruff's colonization was a direct but delayed outgrowth of Mormon colonization in Utah's Uinta Basin. The White River band of Utes was displaced and suffered severely through 1904 to 1908 in a long march from Utah through Wyoming and into South Dakota. This trying journey to find secure homeland had its beginnings forty years earlier, from federal acts in 1865 when they had been forced to move onto the desolate Uintah Reservation in Utah Territory. In October 1861, President Abraham Lincoln set aside the Uinta Basin in Utah Territory—"a vast contiguity of waste"—as land proper for a Native reservation.[6] In early 1865 Congress approved a bill to extinguish the "Indian Title to Lands in the Territory of Utah Suitable for Agricultural and Mineral Purposes." Thus, all Utah tribes were ordered onto the Uintah Reservation by June 1865 resulting from a treaty signing at Spanish Fork, Utah.

Even though he held no official Utah territorial or Indian Affairs position at the time, the LDS church president Brigham Young himself personally orchestrated the treaty with Indian Superintendent Orsemus H. Irish, who quietly did Young's bidding.[7] Ute chief Sanpitch initially declined to sign; he later went to Salt Lake City and very reluctantly did so. Less than a year later, in April 1866, Sanpitch was killed by local Mormon militia. "San-Pitch had warned, 'You may kill Black Hawk and all his band, but if you kill me, you will never have peace.'"[8] The Spanish Fort Treaty was never ratified. "Starvation, brutal winters, and epidemics compelled the various Ute leaders to resist the relentless seizure of their beloved lands" that had once been "a princely domain."[9] Soon thereafter, the Black Hawk War in Utah Territory ensued; it proved brutal and long.

The Uinta Basin's reservation remained a land of arguable value to the remaining defeated Ute occupants, and it was essentially unchanged until 1902 when Congress opened it to white colonization while making claims for Indian rights that were never recognized. This arose from influential Mormons in the federal government, including Utah senator Joseph L. Rawlins and other LDS church authorities. Project manager William H. Smart invested two years of on-site work preparing for the forced sale of this last site of refuge for the Ute tribe remnant.[10]

The US Supreme Court approved the action in 1903, clearing the way for Smart's preparations through 1903 and 1904. In 1905 President Theodore Roosevelt withdrew 1.1 million acres from the Uintah Reservation to create a national forest reserve. Also in 1905, LDS church leaders urged their Utah members to seek the choicest lands on the reservation that Smart and his team identified for them.

The government received nearly six thousand applications for land in August 1905; to no one's surprise, the better sites were drawn by Mormon applicants. The Utes then living on the Uintah Reservation were of two distinct bands, the Uncompahgres who were bewildered and shocked that the reservation lands were no longer theirs, and the White River band, the Yampahs, whose leaders were very angry and sullen. Immediately, the Yampahs made plans to move north en masse and unify with the Lakota on their South Dakota reservation for both tribes to unify and address their loss of homelands.[11]

In spring of 1906, a Ute named Red Cap spoke to his people during a bear dance: "The white people have robbed us of our cattle, our pony grass and our hunting grounds," and he urged his people to rally with the Sioux.[12] In the summer of 1906, Wyoming Governor Bryant B. Brooks wrote that a "band of renegade Indians from the White River Reservation in Utah made their appearance in Wyoming. Their number was estimated to be from two to five hundred, including squaws and children. They were heavily armed, well supplied with ammunition and had in their possession several hundred head of ponies." Brooks continued, seemingly to incite fear but writing incorrectly that "during the summer and early fall they traversed the entire width of the state."[13] Apparently not recognizing the irony, he added that the Ute band slaughtered "large quantities of antelope and other game in direct and flagrant violation of our game laws." Further, he wrote, "The presence of an armed band of Indians in the state caused great uneasiness, and frequent communications were received . . . [from whites] that something be done to get rid of them."[14]

When the main group of Utes arrived at the Lakota reservation, their plan for unity was rebuffed, for the Lakota considered their own campaigns against the US Army finished. They too were facing difficult times and had no hunting lands they cared to share with the Utes. Refusing to sell their horses or livestock, the Utes worked for wages on the Santa Fe Railroad. The main group of Utes were placed about two miles south of Fort Mead, South Dakota, and another band traveled to an area near Thunder Butte, about 140 miles northeast of the main group.[15] In January 1907, a Ute delegation went to Washington, DC to plead their case against returning to Utah to President Theodore Roosevelt. They were not successful. In late October 1907, whites in the Thunder Butte area were warned that they were in danger, as the Utes were angry and might destroy government buildings. No violence ensued, but the Utes encamped at Thunder Butte spent that next winter in desperate need of provisions.[16]

After about fifteen months, when no acceptable alternatives were presented, the Utes were forced to return to the Uintah Reservation in Utah. Great effort was allegedly expended by government and military agents to avoid violence; however, scores of Utes reportedly died on the 1,100-mile return journey. As historian Floyd O'Neil describes, "The melancholy spirit of the Utes was not assuaged by the journey, and they came to the position they had fled feeling very defeated.... Their hope of return to those happy days coming was tragically hollow."[17]

Recent work by British author Simon Winchester describes the sponsorship of religion-based colonization, beginning as early as 1493 in papal bull *Romanus Pontiflex*, which is now designated as the "Doctrine of Discovery."[18] By its contents, all lands one hundred leagues west of the Azores and Cape Verde Islands were assigned to Spain. Winchester explains that "any land not inhabited by Christians was available to be 'discovered,' claimed, and exploited by Christian rulers." It further declared that "the Catholic faith and the Christian religion be exalted and be everywhere increased and spread ... and that barbarous nations be overthrown and brought to the faith."[19] The Doctrine of Discovery "became the basis of all European claims in the Americas as well as the foundation for the United States' western expansion. Lust for land became the quintessential allure of America ... that transcended the more principled reason for migration, which had been the religious and political freedoms ... by breaking free of the stiffening constraints of the older world," writes Winchester.[20]

In 1628 the Euro Americans of Massachusetts Bay Colony reaffirmed the right of possession. In 1763 a brief respite from the lust for land came from England's King George III, with his proclamation that no English could henceforth seize, buy, or settle lands that lay west of the ridge of the Appalachian Mountains.[21] In the 1823 US Supreme Court case *Johnson v. McIntosh*, Chief Justice John Marshall wrote the opinion for the unanimous court. He held that "the principle of discovery gave European nations an absolute right to New World lands." American Indians were left with "only a right of occupancy, which could be abolished."[22] Nascent racism was thinly veiled in the 1879 Nebraska District Court trial for Standing Bear, a Ponca, that Indian natives were declared to be humans.[23]

In modern works of conventional Latter-day Saint scholars writing of intermountain colonization carried out by settlers, words like "dispossession,"

"elimination," and "genocide," are not commonly found. However, historians writing of colonization in British Columbia, Africa, Australia, and New
Zealand repeatedly use these words as part of a common, recurring theme
for the destruction of Indigenous peoples that took place across most of
America's westering colonization. Here colonization did not originate from
aristocratic rulers living thousands of miles distant, as in the late nineteenth-
century empires of French and British rule in Africa and India. However,
the difference was that "the primary motive in American colonization began
with the expropriation of *native land* rather than that of *native labor* as had
been by earlier empire."[24] Here, elimination—that is, outright killing—of
Native people was "not for race or religion, ethnicity, grade of civilization,
but for access to territory."[25]

Canadian author Cole Harris notes that trade was usually the first basis
for the relationship between British Columbia Natives and the small number of non-native colonizers. Trade might be started with trinkets, furs,
knives, horses, slaves, or children. No increase in the number of colonizers
was needed, for land acquisition was not then an issue.[26] As the settling
process moved on to agriculture, settlers first required land, and shortly
thereafter, their rising land hunger required more and more land. This was a
particularly attractive pull to emigrants who originated from Europe's landless masses.[27] Arable land could be acquired by dispossessing summarily,
by executing Indigenous people, or by using threats or lesser levels of violence that ultimately forced them onto fixed reservations with boundaries
imposed by terrain.[28]

Assimilation of Indigenous people by intermarriage, adoption, and
forced sexual submission was commonly attempted by American colonizers. Mormons sought assimilation under Brigham Young's leadership beginning in 1851, using the Book of Mormon promise that offspring of Mormon
men married to Native women (often in polygamous unions) would become
"white and delightsome." Few ranking LDS leaders acquiesced to follow
this principle, and this form of assimilation soon ceased. In historian Adam
Dahl's book on colonization, he considers that assimilation by white settlers
was preferred, for it offered "the gift of civilization" rather than annihilation.
Dahl also asserts that "Manifest destiny is one of the most enduring legacies
of American colonial thought," and that colonizers believed "the United
States had the right and duty, as a matter of divine providence, to expand
over the whole of the North American continent, spreading democracy
and freedom as settlers marched to the Pacific," no matter the price.[29]

In December 1862, the Dakota were given a hard lesson on the "established rules for empire, expansion and ... white supremacy," when thirty-eight of their men were hung in a mass execution in Mankato, not far from present-day Minneapolis.[30] Another instance of elimination followed in the severe cold of January's 1863 winter at Utah Territory's Bear River. Colonel P. Edward Connor, commanding 225 cavalry from Fort Douglas in Salt Lake City, made the final push in night's darkness against a group of Shoshone and a smaller number of Bannocks at Boa Ogi, a hot springs on the Bear River. Connor announced in advance that he did not intend to take prisoners. The estimated number of at least 250 Shoshone dead may not have included some women and children who perished in the melee that followed the main battle. Additional instances are Colonel Chivington's massacre of 163 or more Cheyenne and Arapaho at Sand Creek in Colorado; George Armstrong Custer's tally of up to 150 at Washita River, Oklahoma; and James W. Forsyth's Wounded Knee that accounted for at least 300 massacred Lakota in today's South Dakota.[31]

The LDS application of manifest destiny was theocracy rather than democracy, and control rather than freedom, as LDS settlers were impeded—even detained by violence or its threat—from marching west beyond the Salt Lake valley to the Pacific in California or Oregon.[32] The 1906–1909 dispossession of Utah White River Utes was a relatively recent reenactment of Brigham Young's colonization recipe. While it lacked a bloodbath—like Fort Utah's 1850 carnage at Utah Lake by the militia general Daniel H. Wells; or the militia major Warren S. Snow killing more than twelve Indians, including women and children, at Burrville; or the sixteen, including women, at the Circleville Massacre in 1866—it is yet another example of the many instances of Mormon leadership's pursuits of empire. These can be succinctly summed up in the few words of Mormon leader Willard Richards in 1850: "My voice is for War. . . . Exterminate them." Brigham Young added, "I say go & kill them. . . . We shall have no peace until the [Native] men are killed off."[33] It is possible that historians such as Michael Hardt, Patrick Wolfe, Collin Harris, Adam Dahl, and Peter Cozzens would agree with historian Will Bagley's conviction that the essence of Latter-day Saint colonization from 1847 to 1877, and seemingly to 1906, is distilled in the title of Bagley's final volume of the Kingdom of the West Series: *The Whites Want Every Thing.*[34]

CHAPTER 5

Penury, Depression, and Overpopulation

We are passing through a great financial difficulty, ... the Lord alone can
help us out ... Our debts are heavy ... money matters are crowding hard
upon us.[1]

—LDS church President Wilford Woodruff

THE CHURCH OF JESUS CHRIST of Latter-day Saints was in deep financial trouble in the nineteenth century's final twenty years. Funds had gone
to support families of men sentenced to prison for polygamy or unlawful
cohabitation under the 1882 Edmunds Act. Money was spent paying court
costs and lawyers' fees of many Mormon men arrested by United States
marshals or bounty hunters. A defense fund was maintained to pay for
the ongoing public relations and political efforts in Congress and among
non-Mormon luminaries in Washington, DC. Money was needed to fight
further federal anti-polygamy legislation, promoted without quarter by
Utah Territory's expanding non-Mormon faction or opponents across the
nation. The Edmunds-Tucker Act that passed in 1887 not only disrupted
the Latter-day Saint quest for the Kingdom of God by its breakup of church
and state unity, but the bill's provisions were also financially devastating in
mandating the confiscation of LDS church monies and property. By midsummer 1888, Fred H. Dyer, the federally appointed non-Mormon receiver
of LDS church assets, had taken possession of more than $807,000 worth of
church property. To meet their cash obligations to the federal government,
the church borrowed more than $239,000 from Salt Lake City banks.[2] LDS
church president Wilford Woodruff saw these federal interventions by non-
Mormons, in or out of Utah, as deserving divine punishment. He believed
that God's anger should bring about the "overthrow & final destruction of
the United States government."[3]

The short-term financial impact of adverse federal legislation placed
the LDS church debt at $500,000, or approximately $88 million in 2010

dollars.[4] These adverse financial conditions were compounded after 1887 by significant decreases in tithing payments by church members, who feared that their money would immediately be seized by Dyer and federal officials. This was particularly damaging to the church at this time since tithing was their chief source of revenue.[5] Historian Leonard J. Arrington estimates that annual tithing receipts dropped from more than $500,000 per year in the 1880s to about $300,000 in 1890. Michael Quinn's data shows that only 17 percent of church members paid some tithing in 1890, the year the Manifesto was announced. For the preceding decade, the percentage had hovered near 15 percent.[6]

Lorenzo Snow in April 1899 called for stake presidents and bishops to come to Salt Lake City for a conference specifically addressed to the topic of tithing. In May a revelation at St. George concerning tithing followed, and tithing payments began to improve by the next year. At this time, the tithing amounts given by the faithful were diminished, because 10 percent went to bishops and stake tithing clerks as a stipend.[7] Also, members of stake presidencies received as much as $300 to $500 a year for transportation expenses.[8] Further outlays continued for maintenance of LDS colleges in Logan, Provo, and Salt Lake City. From 1875 to 1910, "the LDS Church

Table 5. Percentage of LDS stake members who paid tithing (per capita for total membership[a]

Year	Percent tithe payers
1890	17.2
1891	15.1
1892	15.8
1893	14.9
1894	15.7
1895	15.3
1896	15.1
1897	15.6
1898	18.4
1899	25.6
1900	27.0
1901	28.9
1902	28.2
1903	28.5

[a]Quinn, *The Mormon Hierarchy: Extensions of Power*, 202.

also sponsored thirty-three 'academies' for secondary education in seven western states, Canada, and Mexico." These were formed because public educational facilities in Utah before 1900 were lacking, and non-Mormons launched competing academies that attracted many LDS youth. Additionally, quality schools were needed in new Mormon colonization areas in the western United States and adjacent nations. Appropriately, among the thirty-three schools was the Big Horn Academy in Cowley, which opened in September 1910.[9]

The LDS Trustee-in-Trust, the Corporation of the President, made personal loans to various general authorities that totaled $115,000 by early 1899.[10] Living allowances, travel expenses, and special expenses for widows of monogamist and polygamist general authorities added to the expanding deficits.[11]

In 1893, the soon-to-be-completed non-Mormon architectural flagship—the Salt Lake City and County Building—spurred Wilford Woodruff to speed up the Mormons' forty-year-delayed building project, the Salt Lake Temple. Woodruff expended an estimated $1 million—or $209 million in 2010 dollars—in what amounted to a race between Mormon and non-Mormon factions.[12] After all, the temple was the "greatest landmark in all Mormondom," and it was "to the Mormons what St. Peter's is to Rome and the Catholic."[13] The temple's capstone was laid on April 6, 1892, and by month's end the call was made by the First Presidency "to furnish as fast as it may be needed, all the money that may be required to complete the Temple" by the following spring's general conference.[14] Their appeal was heard by a population already severely stressed by a national and local depression but was nonetheless answered, for the temple was completed and dedicated in April 1893.[15]

President Woodruff's "days became consumed with a tenuous juggling act, keeping a stressed Mormon institution afloat financially." On September 17, 1896, he wrote, "Our Affairs are in a Desperate Condition in a Temporal Point of view." And on December 30 he added that the presidency was "so overwhelmed in Financial Matters it seems as though we should Never live to get through with it unless the Lord opens the way in a Marvellous [sic] Manner. It looks as though we should never pay our Debts."[16] An additional cash outlay was spent in 1897 for a stone and brass monument at Main and South Temple streets, near the temple block's southeast corner, honoring Brigham Young and the early pioneers.[17] By 1898 the LDS church debt amounted to $1.25 million, or more than $243 million in 2010 dollars.[18]

By the time Lorenzo Snow had taken the seat as LDS church president in 1898, he estimated the church business debt had increased to approximately

$2 million—or $366 million in 2010 dollars.[19] This would be approximately $1,300 for each man, woman, and child of its 284,000 members.[20] Sufficiently disturbed, and knowing that Woodruff's mind in his final years had not been attuned to financial details, President Snow assigned Rudger Judd Clawson to the task of setting the church financial books in order.

Clawson, the first polygamist to serve a prison sentence, had been recently released from his 1884 sentence.[21] Clawson formed a committee and announced on February 18, 1899, that the total church assets were $1,878,179.78, with total liabilities of $1,797,891.38, making a total of active LDS church assets at $80,228.40. If the fungible tithes on hand were required to be sold, the market value would be discounted 50 percent, making the church's net worth $233,082.90. Clawson concluded that it was "quite apparent that the church was dangerously near bankruptcy."[22] Two months after this alarming report, Snow announced a revelation stipulating that tithing meant one-tenth of gross annual income. Following this pronouncement, various leaders visited stakes and wards with the news. The percentage of payers of some tithes increased to 26 percent from an 1890 level.[23] It was not until January 10, 1907, that President Joseph F. Smith announced that the church was free of debt brought on by Edmunds and Edmunds-Tucker.[24]

During the Twelve Apostles' quarterly conference in October 1903, Rudger Clawson reported on his recent trips to Arizona and Mexico. He said that the enthusiasm for plural marriage was not dying out in these areas. In fact, one young woman, Pearl Udall, purportedly said that women "would much prefer to take a married man in the church, who had proven faithfulness and integrity, than to marry a single man, who was untried." The First Presidency entered the room too late to hear this remark, and when their business was finished, they left. Apostle Marriner W. Merrill then bore testimony to the other apostles regarding the truthfulness of plural marriage and exhorted the younger men—Rudger Clawson, Owen Woodruff, and Hyrum M. Smith—to marry plural wives and increase their families so that they would be "crowned with glory and exaltation in the presence of God."[25] Of note, Clawson's marriage linked him with the Big Horn Basin apostles. In a post-Manifesto ceremony in August 1904, with fellow apostle Matthias Cowley officiating, he was married to Pearl Udall who, as noted, had expressed interest in marriage to Owen Woodruff.[26]

Arrington judges the mid-1890s nationwide economic depression as "the gravest economic debacle in nineteenth century America." He notes that even the non-agricultural workforce was hit by 20 percent unemployment, 800 banks failed, and 156 railroad companies were in receivership. Utah was not spared. In fact, its distress, worse than other areas, resulted from its near-total dependence on agriculture. Farm income dropped, then silver, copper, and salt production fell drastically, resulting in additional income losses from falling rail transportation revenue.[27]

The civil leadership of Governor Caleb West, Salt Lake City Mayor Robert Newton Baskin, and Ogden Mayor C. M. Brough struggled with a massive influx in migration. Approximately fifteen hundred unemployed, destitute men from San Francisco, Oakland, and Sacramento arrived in April 1894, led by organizer "General" Charles T. Kelly. This army—driven by poverty to extremes—were brought by the Southern Pacific in twenty-seven unheated cattle cars that were without roofs, seats, bedding, food, or water. Kelly's plan was to travel eastward and join the unemployed thousands marching to Washington under Jacob S. Covey. They demanded federal action for employment or relief from the poverty and hunger afflicting them and their families. A solution was found when Kelly's army was moved eastward by a secret arrangement made by the Ogden mayor and the Union Pacific Railroad. Escorted by Utah National Guard troops, Kelly and his army marched into Weber Canyon, where it happened *by chance* that a Union Pacific train *incidentally* carrying empty boxcars was traveling east, stopped *briefly*, and the crew was *unable* to prevent the men from boarding.[28]

The First Presidency urged the unemployed men of Salt Lake City to volunteer in the Spanish–American War. With little money in circulation, the tithing office issued its own script redeemable only at the bishop's storehouse. Salt Lake City dwellers were urged by leadership to move to "country settlements," where they could grow their own food. Migration into Utah was discouraged; unused land in the city was converted to vegetable gardens.[29]

The call by church leadership for converts to gather to its mecca had been so successful that by the late 1870s and early 1880s, relative overpopulation became one of Utah Territory's underlying economic problems. Charles Card, a stake president in Cache Valley in 1884, wrote, "we have factories idle and others not run to their capacity.... It is no wonder that we have an unemployed element and many parents say what shall we do with our boys? Others appeal to the capitalists to start enterprises that the unemployed may obtain remunerative labor and [by] this gather means to sustain themselves."[30] Before his death in 1877, Brigham Young advised a man leading a group of converts from Alabama and Georgia to not come to Utah but go to western Texas or New Mexico.[31]

Conditions were worsened as Utah's population nearly doubled from 144,000 in 1880 to 277,000 in 1900. Arrington wrote that "in every valley there were signs that the continued flow of immigration, and the natural increase in population had filled up the suitable land."[32] Recently married couples were not able to find farms; older people found themselves under-employed. A *Deseret News* reporter wrote in 1885, "I find the settlements crowded up to their almost capacity, land and water all appropriated and our young people as they marry off have no place to settle near home."[33] The Census Bureau in 1890 reported a total of 11,884 farm owners or farm renters; however, only 461, or .04 percent, were under age twenty-five. Another 1,230, or 10 percent, were between ages twenty-five and thirty. The single largest group of owners or renters were over age sixty.

The Pahvant Valley in central Utah, the Uinta Basin of northeastern Utah, and the Grand Valley in southeastern Utah, called by Arrington as "waste space," were the last areas to be populated by white settlers within Utah Territory. From Cache Valley on the territory's north side to the southern counties and into Arizona, people were leaving settled valleys and moving elsewhere.[34]

While Utah's expanding population exceeded the territory's ability to provide agricultural land suitable for irrigation, the church's financial desperation prevented land purchase outside—or inside—Utah. One example is cited from a July 1897 First Presidency meeting, wherein a letter from M. L. Causey informed them of a tract of land for sale in Oregon's Grande Ronde Valley at $27.50 to $40 an acre.[35] But "it was decided the Church was not in a position to entertain this proposition."[36] D. Michael Quinn points out the church's financial stress was not only from external forces and events, but "from massive losses in the church's interlocked mining, sugar, real estate, banking and investment firms. For example, . . . the First Presidency in 1894 used $217,000 in tithing funds to establish the Sterling Mining and Milling Company. Within four years the church lost its entire investment in this speculative mining venture." Lorenzo Snow told the apostles in 1899, "the Lord was displeased with us for borrowing or going into debt to the extent of nearly two million dollars for business enterprises." First counselor to Snow in 1927, Anthony W. Ivins announced the church loss of $526,900 in transactions with the Utah State National Bank; it increased to $1.37 million by 1932. In 1930 Ivins cataloged church losses of "at least six million dollars" in bond and stock investments during the previous decade.[37]

By 1899 the mismatch of people and land led church officials to conclude that it was no longer advisable for converts to gather to Zion, even at their own expense.[38] Inducement for migration came from the Colorado Beet Sugar Company's representatives visiting Lehi, Utah, in January 1900, offering land to Latter-day Saints who would go to Colorado.[39] Land could be purchased for a modest price with payment as a percentage of the sugar beet crop, or rented if at least 75 percent of acreage would be in sugar beets. Charles N. Cox stated "that he would like a large colony to go and settle there and that the company will furnish ... every family every facility and give them land in one locality where they can all live together and name their own settlement."[40]

On a visit to Utah's arid Millard County in 1889, Abraham H. Cannon, George Q. Cannon's son, toured with the local bishop Joseph Black to scout possible water and land developments. Abraham wrote, "we also drove over hundreds of acres of unclaimed meadow lands skirting the [Sevier] river, which could sustain large herds of stock" with "an abundance of good land which will ... sustain a large population."[41] Black carefully outlined the potential for a new canal estimated at $10,000. This could open an entire new tract of land for settlement. Abraham agreed to be a financial supervisor and arrange for financing with outside banks. He organized a water and land development company for administrative and maintenance oversight. In Salt Lake City, Abraham met with LDS church officials, including his father and Joseph F. Smith. Abraham convinced them of the feasibility of developing the land and constructing a new canal in west Millard County.

The Deseret and Salt Lake Agricultural and Manufacturing Canal Company was incorporated with a capital stock of $50,000, with each of ten individual incorporators investing $500 cash in the company and project.[42] They intended to claim all unappropriated Sevier River water so members could secure claims to government lands under the Desert Land Act. Millard County Surveyor Joseph S. Giles prepared to file on the land at the federal land office on the company's behalf. Surveyor Jesse W. Fox Sr. of Salt Lake City was hired to lay out the project.[43] Within weeks, the company assessed the first of many additional levies upon the stockholders to commence canal construction. Superintendent William V. Black was instructed to proceed with "all possible speed so as to prevent apostates from securing water which we needed for our land."[44] Some early stockholders were the three Cannon sons, Abraham, John Q., and Frank Jenne. Others were Charles H. Wilcken, Alfred Solomon, Brigham Y. Hampton, Joseph S. and William V. Black, and Andrew Jensen.[45]

In a presidency meeting in August 1905, it was discussed that British Columbia's provincial government had offered a tract of one thousand square miles to be opened for settlement. Church leaders were asked if they would participate in colonization. "It was the sense of the Council that nothing could be done in this direction at present." At the same meeting, Montana banker W. G. Conrad offered fifty thousand acres of land, well supplied with water and already fenced, while he controlled an additional 150,000 acres of government land for $750,000. Again, the answer came that the church was not in a financial position to pursue this opportunity.[46] To the contrary, the sale of church property to its own faithful, wealthy members was now the source of income. The First Presidency instructed bishop William B. Preston in 1897 to "perfect the organization of the Parsons Ranch property," owned by the church, and have it "platted and appraised and offered to sale to *our people*."[47]

Utah Territory's problems of relative overpopulation for the available arable land and the financial depression of church and territory during the century's last decade were, in fact, severe. However, the communities from which Latter-day Saints had come as they migrated to the Big Horn Basin had progressed considerably, at least in some respects, beyond frontier conditions.

CHAPTER 6

Five Woodruff Men

All men were made by the Great Spirit Chief. They are all brothers.[1]

—Chief Joseph

THE FIRST THREE

The first three Woodruff men were blood brothers; two filled significant but disparate roles in the earliest migration of whites into Wyoming Territory. The mature years of two were spent in Utah, where they were active and contributed much within the non-Mormon society. All three were buried there.

The colorful and daring life of John Dwight Woodruff, born in 1847 in Boone County, Illinois, earned a historian's compliment as an early "Wyoming pioneer." His younger brother, Edward Day Woodruff, was also born in Boone County three years later. Edward Day came to Wyoming in 1880, where he lived a conventional life as a surgeon in Rock Springs for a decade. Moving to Salt Lake City, he became a highly successful entrepreneur. Their father, John Woodruff, was born in 1814 in Connecticut, which could possibly make him a distant cousin to Wilford Woodruff through one of two wives of Wilford's father, Eldad Aphek Woodruff, who was born in Farmington, Hartford County, Connecticut, in 1778.[2] However, none of the three—John Dwight, Edward Day, nor Russell Dorr Woodruff (another brother)—were at any time Mormon.

John Dwight Woodruff Sr. was born in Windsor, Broome County, New York, about 130 miles southeast of Palmyra. At the time of his birth in 1847, the Mormons had long before departed to Kirtland, Ohio; Nauvoo, Illinois; and west to Winter Quarters, Nebraska. Thus, it is likely John knew little of their history in New York. About 1849 his father, John, and mother, Lucinda Mariah Dimick Woodruff, moved their family to Bonus in Boone County,

Illinois, not far from present-day Rockford. Historian Lois M. Homsher relates that John Dwight Woodruff, at age fifteen, traveled west from Boone County New York into the Rocky Mountains in 1862.[3] Homsher is incorrect, for it was not until 1866.

In 1862 Boone County, like the entire nation, was experiencing the Civil War upheaval that threatened the country's survival and divided its people over slavery. Philo D. Woodruff, the firstborn son of John Woodruff and Lucinda Mariah Dimick, died in 1858, leaving the second-born son Russell Dorr to head the line for "the tenets of Abraham Lincoln and his Republicanism [principles that] burned ... deeply into their hearts and minds" in the highly patriotic family.[4] Therefore, to Russell Dorr fell the mantle while John Dwight and Edward Day remained at home to help their father shoulder the work.

Russell was twenty years old, unmarried, and a farmer when he enlisted in the 15th Illinois Infantry with others from Boone County in March 1863. He was a sergeant in Company B while the 15th was active at Fort Donelson, at Shiloh, and the siege of Vicksburg. There Russell was captured and sent to a Confederate prison in Millen, Georgia, in November 1863. Shortly thereafter, he was moved to the living nightmare of Georgia's Andersonville prison, where he somehow survived until war's end in 1865. In the ensuing years, he and his wife Laura Ann Ball Woodruff lived a conventional life in Chicago, where he drove streetcars and worked as a US postal service carrier. By 1900 Russell was in Salt Lake City, where his occupations were "a fresco painter" and a clerk in a jewelry store. Both he and Laura Ann died in Salt Lake City; Russell in March 1929, and Laura in 1927. Because both were buried in the non-Mormon Mount Olivet Cemetery, it is unlikely that they had embraced Mormonism.[5]

Out of his passion for maintaining national union and an equally strong sentiment against slavery, John Dwight Woodruff attempted three times to enlist with the Union. The recruiting officer turned down the sixteen year old each time, the third saying, "if he didn't go home, stay home, and stop being such a nuisance, it would be necessary to throw him out on his head and to notify his father in the bargain." Dwight did not follow the recruiter's admonition and dismissed whatever consequence might come from his father. In 1863, misrepresenting his age by a decade as twenty-six and claiming he was a married carpenter, Dwight found himself a private in Company A, 77th Illinois Infantry.[6] This unit saw action against the Confederate works at Chickasaw Bluffs, the siege of Vicksburg, and along the Red River in Louisiana, but John Dwight did not remain with them.

At some point his ruse was discovered, and he was sent back to Illinois. But the military record of his older brother Russell upheld the family's deep sense of honor.

J. Dwight Woodruff joined as a teamster with a group bound for Colorado in 1865. John Davis, historian of Wyoming, claims Dwight was the first white man to take residence in the Big Horn, traveling from Colorado in 1866.[7] Dwight wrote of his life at this time:

> About three or four years before the U. P. R. R. came west, another boy and I in our wanderings came to Crow Creek and camped about three miles below where the city Cheyenne now stands. We each had a saddle and pack pony and each a Hawkins muzzle loading rifle, some powder and lead. We had some flour, soda and salt and a sour dough pot. We lived mostly on wild meat and by a miracle escaped the Indians. Most people speak of Wyoming as being a wilderness at that time. It did not seem so to me then nor does it seem so now as I look back. To me it was always a land of many attractions. Its sagebrush plains, its grassy hills and valleys and most majestic mountains were always beautiful to me and I never got tired of looking at them. And when I ask my Great Spirit to take care of me, when I am through with this world, I do not ask for the pearly gates or golden streets, nor for harps, haloes, wings or white robes. Such … doesn't appeal to me in the least. But I ask Him for a good camping place in a beautiful valley like one of those in Wyoming, where I might stay through all eternity.[8]

Dwight told another story of this period, when he and three companions took refuge from Indians in a buffalo wallow, and after three days of intermittent fighting were "saved only by the appearance of a second Indian war party." This second group did not realize the whites were present, as they frightened the first party away. Dwight's younger brother Edward Day claimed that "'Indians were afraid of Dwight, he was so fearless and daring, so resourceful and his coolness carried him through so many tight places.'"[9]

Dwight early on survived in the basin by trapping and hunting; by the summer of 1870, he had become a wagon master in Rawlins, Wyoming Territory. In the 1870s the basin was still the hunting grounds of Crow and Shoshone tribes and was also subjected to raids by war parties of Arapaho, Cheyenne, and Sioux. Nonetheless, in 1871, after gaining the friendship and respect of Shoshone Chief Washakie, Dwight brought six thousand sheep,

"Oregon woolies," into the Owl Creek area and built a cabin said to be the first Euro American settlement in the Big Horn Basin. For a number of years he grazed sheep along the Wind River's north side and probably used the Owl Creek Mountains for summer pasture.

About 1880 Dwight brought cattle into the Owl Creek country and began a cow operation with his cabin as its headquarters. Early in the 1880s Dwight sold this cabin to Captain R. A. Torrey from the Fort Washakie garrison. Captain Torrey and his brother, Colonel J. L. Torrey, built up a large cattle and horse ranch. This Owl Creek operation developed into the Embar Ranch. At one time some forty thousand cattle and more than six thousand horses carried the phonetic version: "M–––" brand. Embar Ranch buildings gradually replaced Dwight Woodruff's original cabin, which is no longer in existence.[10]

J. Dwight Woodruff was an army scout with Captain Alfred Bates when his troops fought with the Arapaho Indians on the Norwood River on July 4, 1874. Woodruff guided US generals Phil Sheridan and George Crook in selecting a site for Fort Custer on the Big Horn River in 1877.[11] Dwight "knew all parts of Wyoming, Fort Laramie, Fort Bridger, Fort Brown and Fort Stambaugh. He was alleged to be among the first to investigate the reported gold fields at South Pass. He saw the Pony Express rider's times, the stage couches [sic], and the road ranches. He prospected and during the Indian troubles he became a scout, guide, and Indian fighter."[12]

Chronicler of Wyoming's early history, Tacetta Walker credits J. Dwight Woodruff with many stories of bravery as a hunter and trapper. When a group of four friends, including one Jim Lysite, decided to search for an alleged gold mine in the basin, Woodruff considered himself warned by a dream in which they were all killed by Indians, and he withdrew from the planned excursion. Several weeks later Lysite's body, together with three others, were discovered by Sheridan's guide, O. M. Clark. Woodruff insisted on venturing out to bury the four men's remains. General Sheridan allegedly sent troops to accompany Woodruff.[13] Walker's praise for Dwight Woodruff is unreserved, claiming he "should be considered in the same class with the Sublette brothers and Jim Bridger. Like them, he explored the country long before he settled down on his ranch. His life was a life full of stirring experiences. He knew Wyoming in all her moods and loved her as he did no other place."[14]

Dwight married Josephine Doty in 1883 in Chicago, and they had four children, all born in Wyoming. He remained in Laramie and Fremont Counties working as a stockman, lumberman, and wool grower. He served three

times as a Wyoming senator, the last in the fall of 1922. Dwight bought and
worked in coal mines in Converse County, and in the early 1900s he with
B. B. Brooks and C. B. Richardson invested in large tracts of timberland and
a lumber mill in Mexico. These new-century, entrepreneurial ventures were
interrupted by the Mexican peasant revolution championed by Emiliano
Zapata.[15]

John Dwight Woodruff died at his home in Shoshoni, Wyoming,
on June 6, 1925. However, he was buried beside his wife, Josephine Doty
Woodruff, who chose to be interred at Aultorest Cemetery, Ogden, Utah,
beside their two children whose deaths preceded hers. An accomplished
man, but never a Mormon or a sodbuster, he had little in common with the
last two more recent LDS Woodruffs in Wyoming's history, save a possible
distant, uncertain blood relationship and their shared commendable works
to improve Wyoming and the development of its Big Horn Basin.

Born in Illinois, Edward Day Woodruff spent time as a youth in Wyoming Territory with his older brother, John Dwight Woodruff. Edward later
returned to study medicine in Chicago. By 1880 he had finished his medical
studies, and that year's federal census recorded him as living in the Popo
Agie Valley, a physician, boarding with the Sweetwater County Commissioner, John Curry. While there he accepted an offer to become a surgeon
for Union Pacific Coal Company and Union Pacific Railway Company.
Edward married Minnette M. Roberts in 1882. In 1889 or 1890, the family
moved to Salt Lake City, where Edward became a successful businessman
in mining and merchandising. He proved active in civic affairs and entrepreneurial ventures. He formed the Brown, Terry, and Woodruff Company
and the Troy Laundry business. Edward was an active mason, a Commercial
Club member, the president of Utah's Chapter of Sons of the American
Revolution, and in 1913 he became president of Salt Lake City's Chamber
of Commerce.

The city's prestigious architectural firm Hedlund and Wood built his
family a luxurious 11,000-square-foot Renaissance-style home, among the
grandest on Capitol Hill, completed in 1906. By 1910 Edward had returned
to medicine as a surgeon in general practice. However, when he applied he
listed his major occupation as "banking." Edward died at age seventy-four
on April 9, 1925, and was buried at Mount Olivet Cemetery near his wife,
whose death preceded his by two months. The mansion overlooking Salt
Lake City was willed to his daughter, Lesley Day Woodruff, and her husband, Benjamin Franklin Riter Jr., who became a widely recognized and
highly accomplished Utah citizen. Edward served in both world wars, was

head of the Office of Judge Advocate General for the European Theater, and he later became the first Utah attorney to serve on the American Bar Association's board.[16]

THE FINAL TWO

The final two Woodruff men, like the first three earlier described, were blood brothers, and they too played significant roles in the development of the state of Wyoming. The fourth was David Patten Woodruff, born in Salt Lake City in 1854 to Wilford Woodruff and his seventh wife, Sarah Brown.

David Patten's name honored the memory of David Wyman Patten, his father's friend and a Danite leader, who was the second ordained among the earliest twelve Mormon apostles. He with three others remained loyal to Joseph Smith in a tumultuous period in Kirtland, Ohio. It was also he, "Captain Fearnought," who died from a wound received when the Mormon militia, under his command, attacked the Missouri state militia at the Battle of Crooked River in 1838.[17] In a posthumous tribute, Apostle Wilford Woodruff wrote, "Thus fell the noble David W. Patten as a martyr for the cause of God and he will receive a martyr's crown. He was valiant in the testimony of Jesus Christ while he lived upon the earth. He was a man of great faith and the power of God was with him. He was brave to a fault, even too brave to be preserved.... Many of the sick were healed and devils cast out under his administration."[18]

David Patten Woodruff was born into Mormonism, but he did not follow his father's path into church leadership in Great Salt Lake City. He first farmed in Utah Territory's northern area at Randolph, not far from the southern end of Bear Lake, then at Smithfield, also in Cache County, where two children were born to him and wife Arabella Jane Hatch Woodruff. The family moved around 1880 to the Uinta valley in northeastern Utah Territory. There seven children were born to them. After their move to the Big Horn Basin, the last two of their eleven offspring were added.[19]

David P. Woodruff first traveled to the Big Horn Basin on an exploratory trip with a Cache and Uintah County Mormon, William Henry Packard, in the spring of 1893.[20] Packard's wife, Christine Ernestine Perry Packard, tells the story:

> In the summer [of 1892] there was an excitement raised about ... the Big Horn country in Wyoming. We didn't know whether it would

be right to ... go where it would be all an outside [non-Mormon] population. David Woodruff, a son of President Woodruff wrote to his father and said he had to go somewhere as his circumstances made it necessary. His father said, "If you have to go, do so, and may the Lord bless you and also those that go with you." So David and Will [Packard] and two others [Henry Griffin and James Shaffer] made a trip up there to look at the country.[21] They were gone a month.... They told what a wonderful country it was, how high the grass grew. That was real encouraging as there was scarcely any grass in Ashley, just shadscale and in some places white sage grew.... Will was still trying to sell the place, but money was scarce. He finally sold it for mostly cattle. We had some real nice furniture ... but it had to go to buy feed for the cattle.... We did not get started on our journey till into May [1893]. There was a lot to be done to be ready, and the feed wasn't good enough for the cattle any sooner. There was [sic] several different crowds on their way to Wyoming that season.

On June 25, 1893, the Packard family arrived at a point in the Grey-bull River that came to be known as Mormon Bend.[22] It was the spring of 1893 when Packard, Griffin, David P. Woodruff, and around three hundred migrants from about fifty Mormon families—from Star Valley, Wyoming, as well as Bear Lake, Cache, Ashley, and Uintah Valleys in Utah Terri-tory—settled at what would become Burlington. They selected a flat area on the Greybull River's north side, about twenty-five miles from its conflu-ence with the Big Horn River.[23] Shortly after his 1893 arrival, W. H. Pack-ard became the Wyoming settlement's first bishop. Under his leadership, a rough-hewn church house was built from logs hauled from the Pryor Mountains. Although the group was comprised predominantly of Mor-mons, they did not come as called colonists and were not under the aegis of church sponsorship.[24] Historian Charles Lindsay clarified:

The Mormon migration in 1893 was in no sense a religious enter-prise. It is said that the church authorities learned nothing of the affair until it was so well under way that it could not be stopped, and that it was then disapproved.... it was each man for himself until he got there; then there was some cooperation. No arrangements had been made for either land titles or water rights prior to reaching the Basin.... David P. Woodruff, largely by virtue of ancestry, was looked upon as entitled to be the religious leader ... however he presently

left the main body of Mormons on the Greybull river, and moved up
on Wood river, where he established a horse ranch. Many members
of the community gravely disapproved of his action for it appears
that Woodruff's name had served to lend color of church authority
to an enterprise that had none.[25]

Bishop William Henry Packard is credited with a significant role in
bringing law and order to the area after a period of violence inflicted by the
livestock era's cowboys. He was selected as the jury foreman in the trial of
cowboy Herb Brink, indicted for the grisly murder of sheepman Joe Allemand at Spring Creek in 1909. A mistrial ended the first attempt, for a
number of jurors were hardcore livestock men. After the pool of jurors was
enlarged, a guilty verdict to murder in the first degree followed. At least four
Mormon men were included in the new jury.[26] Packard and these jurors,
who might have been influenced by knowledge of the violent treatment of
Mormons in Ohio and Illinois, were credited with successfully convincing
pro-livestock and anti-sheep jurors that justice and rule of law outweighed
their allegiance to the disappearing era of violence by cattlemen.[27]

It was not until July 30, 1899, that David Patten Woodruff was ordained
to the office of High Priest by his younger half brother, Abraham O. Woodruff; David became a High Council member in Wyoming's Big Horn
Stake.[28]

The fifth and most widely known and warmly admired Woodruff in
Wyoming was Abraham Owen Woodruff. Born in 1872, eighteen years
younger than David Patten, Owen was the son of Wilford Woodruff and
his sixth wife, Emma Smith. Owen was unlike his half brother and chose to
live in the heartland of Zion in his early adulthood, where he emulated his
father's service to the church. He also formed a strong bond with Lorenzo
Snow, who succeeded his father as LDS church president. Owen was chosen
as the instigator of expansion in Mormon colonization and the driving force
propelling the 1900–1901 Wyoming colonization.

CHAPTER 7

Whether Called or Volunteered, Plans and Progress Follow

I consider it a sacred matter.[1]

—Lorenzo Snow

THREE YEARS BEFORE OWEN WOODRUFF brought the 1900 group of Latter-day Saints to the area of Cowley, Wyoming, LDS settlers in Burlington, under William H. Packard, were already flourishing. According to a letter of recommendation from Ambrose Hibbert published in the *Deseret News*, all was plentiful:

> The Saints are feeling very much encouraged over the very mild winter that has passed. We expect to be plowing and putting in garden and grain soon. We have a good climate and good country, *plenty* of good land and plenty of water for irrigation purposes. ... There is *plenty* of work for laboring men, with fair wages, $35 to $40 per month in cash. All we lack is *plenty* of good Latter-day Saints.[2]

According to First Presidency meeting minutes in midsummer 1899, "The people settled in the Big Horn Country were also eagerly looking forward to the visit of an apostle."[3] In response, Owen Woodruff "thought these people should be visited and the country looked over." President Lorenzo Snow agreed and thought that Apostle Woodruff "had better arrange to visit those places and look over the land."[4] On August 25, 1899, Owen Woodruff traveled to Evanston, Wyoming, met with a Mr. J. L. Ham, and through him applied to the Wyoming state engineer for permission to irrigate certain lands in the state. Woodruff discussed these efforts with President Snow on September 25, and on November 8, Woodruff was officially sustained as Colonization Agent for the LDS church.[5]

In November 1899, David Patten Woodruff wrote from Burlington to Wyoming governor DeForest Richards for help in attracting Mormon settlers to the basin. David P. Woodruff would have known that Richards and Secretary of State Fennimore Chatterton had been elected in 1898, in large part for their campaign promise to develop 700,000 acres of Wyoming land through creating water diversion canals from "the Owl Creek, the Big Horn, the Shoshone and the Greybull Rivers." Naturally, the Wyoming officials were pleased at the prospect of having these campaign promises fulfilled. LDS church leaders acted prudently through the preapproval of Wyoming's top state officials before sending a substantial number of their members into a neighboring recently sovereign state to colonize, particularly appropriate in a time of widespread economic distress. Governor Richards answered David P. Woodruff on November 28, saying, "anything that shall reasonably lay in my power, shall be done to assist your friends in making a permanent settlement on the lands to be irrigated in the Big Horn Basin. I shall be pleased to hear from your brother, Mr. A. O. Woodruff, at any time."[6]

In a *Deseret Evening News* article in November 1899, Owen Woodruff touted the Big Horn Basin, mentioning 500,000 acres of land that can be irrigated by river water, a favorable climate, and that cattle were "able to winter-out every winter since our people have been there—from six to eight years." With soil of "good quality," farmers have "been able to produce for a succession of years, wheat, oats, barley, corn, potatoes, alfalfa, timothy and almost all kinds of vegetables." Woodruff summed his pitch: "I will take great pleasure in answering any inquires made personally or by mail, regarding this great country with its wonderful undeveloped resources."[7]

However, Owen Woodruff's assurance of "good quality" soil capable of producing a wide variety of grains and vegetables is troubling, when considering how the soil had been assessed. This was addressed by a son of a colonist schoolmaster, Melvin M. Fillerup, born in 1924 and raised among the early 1900–1901 settlers. After completing a high school education and law school, Fillerup returned to the basin to practice law in Cody and later represented the Sidon Canal District as their attorney. In his book *Sidon, the Canal that Faith Built*, Fillerup questioned the unanimity of the twelve Mormon men who evaluated the land, since it had been done inadequately and with haste. "It is most remarkable that these men on such a short visit and with probably no more soil testing than picking up a few handfuls of dirt and running [it] through their fingers would be unanimous ... [that the land was] suitable for colonization." The point of doubt is especially strong considering the evaluation took place in blizzard conditions with snow on the ground and wind-enhanced winter temperatures well below zero, freezing the soil, making analysis by any method—especially running dirt through one's fingers—inaccurate, if not ridiculous. "Nevertheless, this was their unanimous feeling in the report they returned."[8]

William Benona Graham, one of the twelve men who accompanied Owen Woodruff on his first visit, later suggested that at least some soil areas were or became less fertile than anticipated: "In the spring of 1901 my boys and I put in a good crop, and we hauled with us 3 seamless sacks of lucerne [alfalfa] and timothy seeds from Idaho, and planted that all in good faith that we would soon have a field of hay; but the mineral or something else destroyed the seed so it never came up. This gave us the 'blues.'"[9]

Roland Simmons, mayor of Cowley, wondered whether colonization originated as a formal church call or from Latter-day Saints seeking better land and more reward for their toil. He reasoned, like others, that both elements operated.[10] Simmons takes his first insight from Owen Woodruff's journal, where he cited Lorenzo Snow in a January 5, 1900, meeting: "The brethren who volunteer to go to the Big Horn Basin as colonizers can be set apart for this mission as I consider it *a sacred matter*. If there are not enough of the brethren [who] volunteer to go, we will call some to make up the requisite number."[11]

It is unclear, but no mention is made that the settlement plan was carefully formed—as was typical in earlier colonization efforts—with specifically chosen members whose range of skills and occupations would make the settlement self-sufficient, or nearly so.[12] However, a First Presidency meeting in January records the decision that individual letters of "calls from the pulpit" would not be given:

> President Snow explained to President [George Q.] Cannon that ... Elder Woodruff had been appointed to give his personal attention in the line of colonizing our people in good localities, and that Elder Woodruff was now endeavoring to get at least fifty heads of families to settle in Bighorn [*sic*] county, Wyoming, on an elegant tract of land with good resources and favorable climate and where land could be had for fifty cents an acre, with the privilege of the settlers working out canal interests. Therefore, Elder Woodruff felt that what ever [*sic*] Elder Rigby and the brethren did in the Snake River country should not be done at the expense of the settlement in the Big Horn country. It was therefore thought that it would be best for the Presidency not to give a letter to these brethren [Rigby in Snake River and Woodruff

in the basin] but that they be allowed to work on their own resources with the permission of the Presidency.[13]

In response to Owen Woodruff's *Deseret Evening News* article, numerous letters were sent by inquisitive church members to Woodruff requesting information about the Wyoming colonization. These letters clearly show that some members actively initiated their inclusion in the endeavor, rather than being passive recipients of a call. Author Charles Lindsay points out that Bear Lake County settlers may have volunteered because their farms had been devastated from a "scourge of squirrels that baffled every effort at eradication. For the period of several years it was next to impossible for them to harvest a crop. Many were ready to give up in despair." Lindsay also offers this assessment:

> The typical member of this colony was the man of middle age or younger, but a liberal sprinkling of these were accompanied by their parents. These older people were veterans, having made many such moves. A few had been converted to Mormonism in England, and some had drawn handcarts all the way from the Missouri river to the Salt Lake valley. Others had joined the Church in Kirtland, Ohio, Independence, Missouri or Nauvoo, Illinois. In any case, they had followed it from Council Bluffs, across the plains to Salt Lake City, and as the old South Pass was approached, this time from the opposite direction, they could join in the old plain's song at the regular evening prayer meeting with glowing enthusiasm.[14]

Historian Marshal Bowen's report provides additional significant data about the makeup of the migrants who settled in Cowley between 1900 and 1905. Bowen depicts the geographical relationships of several Mormon and non-Mormon communities that formed in the drainages of the Shoshone and Greybull Rivers. The area encompassed the drainages of rivers flowing from the Absaroka, Owl Creek, Big Horn, and Pryor Mountain ranges. Four-fifths of settlers came directly from Utah. However, the distribution of their origin was not random, nor did it correspond to population density across the twenty-seven counties then existing. The city of Parowan, Utah, only sixty miles north of the Arizona border, supplied forty-nine settlers, most recruited by Jesse W. Crosby Jr., appointed as an officer in the Big Horn Basin Colonization Company.

Bowen explains: "Most of [Crosby's] colonists did not begin arriving until late in 1900, the bulk of them arriving in 1902 and 1903, after a series of crop failures in the Parowan area." There were "fourteen adults and about a dozen children from Escalante, a small community east of Parowan," who moved to Cowley when LDS authorities called one [man] ... to transfer his sawmill from Escalante to a wooded area north of Cowley. Another group "arrived in 1903 when Escalante had a shortage of irrigation water. Combined with pioneers from Panguitch and Beaver, the settlers from Parowan and Escalante gave Cowley a distinctly southwestern Utah flavor." The Parowan migrants were closely interrelated. "Every adult settler from the Parowan area was accompanied by at least one other adult, in addition to his spouse, to whom he was related by birth or by marriage."[15]

An intriguing puzzle about an invited colonist with a distinctly southern Utah flavor is found in a November 1, 1903, letter to Owen Woodruff from St. Johns, Arizona, not far from Snowflake. It was written by seventy-year-old Nephi P. Johnson, who historians Will Bagley and Juanita Brooks have connected to the 1857 Mountain Meadows Massacre's horror. Cited prominently were Johnson's terrifying screams of "Blood! Blood! Blood!" in a troubled delirium preceding his death.[16] The letter was mailed to Salt Lake City, but Owen was likely in the basin at the time. It read:

> Dear Brother,
> According to promise, I now write you, will say I do not feel it necessary to write anything in regard to my family affairs, as I suppose you know all about it. Apostle Cowley also do, [sic] and I believe President Smith and Lund does to some extent, however if you desire further information I will be pleased to give it. B[isho]p. C. P. Anderson after returning from Snowflake told me you desired for me to go to Big Horn, Wy. Pres. [David King] Udall also had a talk with me and advised me to write you that I am willing to go. I will say that I am willing to go and labor where the servants of the Lord sees fit to send me, so if you still feel like sending me there, I will get ready and go as soon as possible, please advise me when to start, ect. [sic] Also if R.R. Ticket can be got through Bro. Spence, and if a stop over in S.L.C. for a few days can be permitted without much more expence [sic] than a through Ticket. Hoping this is satisfactory to you. I well [sic] close praying the Lord to bless you in all your labors. From your brother in the gospel. N. P. Johnson.[17]

In a follow-up letter of November 28, Johnson indicated that he had received no answer, making him "somewhat uneasy."

Pres. Udall had a talk with me and advised me to go, as he thought the way had opened for me to get my troubles fixed up. I am pleased to know that my brethren think as much of me as they do and feel to thank you for the interest that you seem to take in me. . . . PS. I will have $600 and a good set of carpenter tools.

In a third letter, on February 24, 1904, Johnson wrote to Woodruff:

Your kind letter came to hand. . . . I will be ready to leave here sometime in April or 1st of May. The reason for waiting untill [sic] then is . . . my Attorney who tried to get a divorce for me before, says the Judge here will give me a divorce now, and he will handle my case for nothing. . . . I kindly ask of you pray to the Lord in my behalf in this matter, also please ask Brother Cowley to pray for me that I may be relieved from my present condition. . . . I thank you for the interest you have taken in me.[18]

No evidence has been found, however, that Johnson migrated to the Big Horn. According to the 1910 federal census, he was that year in Mohave County, Arizona; he died in Mesquite, Clark County, Nevada, on June 21, 1919. However, the question remains: Why would the two most ardent, unyielding, pro–plural marriage apostles invite a seventy-year-old polygamist who was having wife trouble to join the Cowley colonists? The question of whether Cowley and Woodruff knew of his alleged ties to the 1857 Mountain Meadows mass murders is also intriguing.

In contrast to Cowley, its sister village of Byron was dominated by Latter-day Saints from northeastern Utah and adjacent Idaho. No matter where they came from, most had intimate acquaintance with being hungry, cash poor, and a harsh land that could wipe away the rewards of months of twelve-hour workdays, leaving them helpless.

One-sixth of Cowley settlers came from Morgan County, Utah, and the Wasatch mountain range; they were influenced by Charles A. Welch of Morgan and Byron Sessions, a northeastern Utah rancher. Most of these migrants settled in Byron, but a few trickled to Cowley to give it "an element of diversity that partially offset the dominance of families from Parowan, Escalante, Panguitch, and Beaver."

Settlers from Provo, Salt Lake City, Bountiful, and Ogden made up 22 percent of Cowley residents. They represented twelve towns and cities, and, with the exception of those from Bountiful, few knew each other before the move. They "lacked the solidarity of compact bands of friends and relatives from the smaller, more remote localities," according to Bowen. "People living in older, well-established communities near Salt Lake City, apparently satisfied with their location, were clearly more reluctant to leave solidly built homes, well-tended farms, good jobs, and friends of long standing for a fling at Wyoming pioneering."[19] Two dozen men, women, and children comprised a collection of cousins and in-laws from two neighboring families from Bennington, Idaho, near Bear Lake. The group included a widow, Emma Lindsay, and many of her twenty children and stepchildren; a few came as married adults. The group was recruited by Brigham L. Tippetts Sr.

Bowen wrote that the bulk of "Cowley's original settlers were youthful men and women, well-suited for pioneering by their vigor and exuberance, but perhaps lacking the stability and experience that older settlers might have possessed." Fewer than one-fourth had firsthand farming experience. Yet "at least 60 percent ... spurred by the need for survival, moved directly into farming occupations. By 1905 they were raising oats, wheat, alfalfa, garden vegetables, and a variety of barnyard livestock on the forty to eighty-acre irrigated plots surrounding the village of Cowley on what became known as the Cowley Flat."[20]

Progress in the field of labor began when Owen Woodruff led a party of Mormon faithful in the frigid midwinter to examine the lands named in his proposal. On February 2, 1900, Woodruff and thirteen men traveled by train from their meeting point in Ogden to Butte, Montana, where they held services with about seventy-five local Mormons, including the presiding elder Hiram Monson.[21] Woodruff spoke to the collected gathering: "Our people are very prolific, so much so that Utah is becoming overcrowded, and we are obliged to expand. We already have a colony of 400 in Wyoming and large colonies in Idaho, Arizona and Mexico." He continued, "The work we are now engaged in is in the nature of pioneering. The men who accompany me are pioneers in the work of colonization, and upon their judgement will rest the adoption or rejection of our colonization plan."[22]

From Butte, the Mormon party proceeded by train to Laurel then to Red Lodge, Montana, where on February 7 they were met by Henry Griffin, friend of William H. Packard, and Packard's son Amasa with wagon teams and mounts for their travel.[23] When Woodruff and his contingent camped at Eagles' Nest, they were met by Colonel William F. Cody, who entertained them with tales of his experiences in the west. Cody allegedly said:

I have secured a permit to irrigate nearly all land on the Shoshone River's north side, from Eagles-nest to the Big Horn River, but if the Mormons want to build a canal and irrigate the land down lower on the river I will relinquish both land and water to them, for if they will do this I know they are the kind of people who will do what they agree to do."[24]

In the group were two Big Horn Basin Colonization Company trustees, Charles Arthur Welch and Byron Sessions, with George Henry Taggart, John J. Simmons, John Croft and William George Simmons (of Morgan County), Hyrum King North (of Salt Lake County), Brigham Lewis Tippets and William Benoma Graham (of Bennington, Idaho), John Stevens and S. P. Sorenson (of Montpelier, Idaho), and Bishop W. P. Larson and Mr. Guernsay (of Bear Lake County, Idaho).[25]

The group arrived in the basin on the evening of February 11. Historian Mark N. Partridge, who had arrived in the basin as a five-year-old child, related the expedition's details in his 1967 book, *With Book and Plow*:

Figure 5. Mormon pathfinders to the Big Horn Basin, February 1900. *Front row, left to right*: George H. Taggart, Byron Sessions, A. Owen Woodruff, William B. Graham, Brigham L. Tippets Sr., S. P. Sorenson. *Back row, left to right*: Charles A. Welch, Hyrum K. North, John Stevens, William G. Simmons, John J. Simmons. Courtesy of LDS Church History Library.

Next morning, in weather ten degrees below zero, they crossed the Shoshone River on the ice. The ice broke and let one outfit into the water, but all three outfits reached the shore safely. The exploring party spent only two days on the proposed project. During those two days they drove teams approximately 30 miles. Since the days in early February are short, the investigation on the project could not have been very thorough.

Partridge added, "it was a bold venture to recommend that hundreds of families be sent to attempt such a project after only two days of investigation and that was done in below zero weather when it would have been difficult to take a soil sample. There is no evidence that any samples of the soil were taken."[26] Partridge's doubts of the adequacy of their soil examination match those outlined earlier by Melvin Fillerup.

On February 5, 1900, while the Mormon delegation explored the site, Wyoming Governor DeForest Richards, Secretary of State Fennimore Chatterton, Wyoming Supreme Court Judge Jesse Knight, and Utah's former territorial governor George W. Emery visited President Lorenzo Snow in Salt Lake City to ask that a colony of Mormons be sent to the Big Horn Basin.[27] Emery, while not a Mormon, had been an ally, which earned him the nickname "Elder Emery" from non-Mormons. In 1878 Emery infuriated Utah's non-Mormons for signing Mormon-sponsored territorial legislation that severely limited their voting rights. Emery's term as governor had ended in 1880, and this association with Chatterton, Richards, and Snow years later is unclear.

The underlying motivation to bring people to Wyoming came from legislation introduced by Wyoming's senator Joseph M. Carey, who had earned admiration from the post-Manifesto polygamist and apostle Abraham Hoagland Cannon for preventing anti-Mormon provisions from appearing in the Wyoming state charter.[28] The Carey Act of 1894, also known as the Federal Desert Land Act, permitted the federal government to transfer to a state up to one million acres of land that could be settled, irrigated, and farmed. Wyoming was the first to pass legislation enabling the act.[29]

On January 11, 1900, Owen Woodruff filed an application with the Wyoming State Board of Land Commissioners to construct a canal. Several years earlier, G. H. King and H. L. Earley of Cincinnati had been awarded a canal contract, but since they had not made progress, their claim was relinquished. First Presidency minutes from a January 23 meeting recorded that "Elder

Woodruff was now endeavoring to get at least fifty heads of families to settle in the Big Horn County, Wyoming, on an elegant tract of land with good resources and favorable climate and where land could be had for fifty cents an acre, with the privilege of the settlers working out canal interests."

On March 19, William Cody and his Wild West business partner Nate Salisbury signed a relinquishment to the Shoshone River waters, with approximately 21,000 acres of undeveloped land adjacent to the river, as described in the earlier Cincinnati canal permit, which they had acquired. Salisbury wanted to charge the Mormons, but Cody insisted that it would be provided without fee. Top-level church authorities, leading Wyoming civil officials, and entrepreneur William F. "Buffalo Bill" Cody were all involved with planning and implementing the basin's further settlement.

While in Cheyenne to finalize legal arrangements, Woodruff explained that "On May 1st, sixty or seventy families, numbering about 400 people will settle on the land paying 23 cents per acre when filed upon, and 23 cents more when the settlers prove up." To this unusual, even unique group of

Figure 6. Certificate for 75 shares of Big Horn Basin Colonization Company Stock, purchased by Edward Woolley Croft and signed by Charles A. Welch. Photo by the author.

principals in the history of Mormon colonization, another one, the Chicago, Burlington and Quincy Railroad, would be added within a year.[30]

In the office of President Lorenzo Snow in Salt Lake City on April 9,
1900, articles of incorporation were drawn for the Big Horn Basin Colonization Company. It was capitalized at $100,000, with 10,000 shares, and a par
value of $10 per share. Eight Mormons were named as corporation officers
and trustees: Abraham Owen Woodruff, president; Byron Sessions, vice
president; Charles Kingston, secretary; Charles Arthur Welch, treasurer;
along with Jesse Wentworth Crosby Jr., Hyrum King North, William Benona Graham, and Brigham Lewis Tippets.[31] A second meeting with Snow
took place three days later, in which the articles were amended and re-signed,
and Byron Sessions was selected as general manager and superintendent of
construction.[32]

In his account, Charles Welch indicated that each man could subscribe
for the amount of land he needed, but it is uncertain whether the mostly
impoverished colonizers knew that an assessment for purchase of tools
would be required. Each man was notified of his amount due, and each
was to purchase his own scraper. Welch explains that "it had been published
in the *Deseret News* . . . that all who contemplated going to the Big Horn to
settle should have sufficient money or supplies to care for themselves and
families for at least one year." These expectations were unrealistic, as economic distress was a major motivator that had led many colonizers. Not
surprisingly, it soon became obvious that "many were broke on arrival."[33]
It is also uncertain at what point the colonists learned that they would
purchase ownership of canal company stock through their physical labor,
and that their labor would be compensated by distribution of water, based
on the number of stock shares acquired during the work period of canal
construction.

CHAPTER 8

Treks, Trials, and Finances

All human plans are subject to ruthless revision by Nature or Fate or
whatever ... the powers behind the Universe.[1]

—Arthur C. Clarke

ABRAHAM OWEN WOODRUFF instructed all colonists—those called and
those volunteering—to meet on April 25, 1900, at the bridge at Ham's Fork
on the Green River, about three miles north of Kemmerer, Wyoming.[2] Starting from multiple locations in Utah and Idaho, they anticipated a spring
travel time, aiming for all to meet by that date and cross four significant
rivers—Green, Big Sandy, Wind, and Shoshone—before the high-water
runoff. Charles Welch gave the route he followed and the alternates:

> Salt Lake to Coalville, Echo, Wasatch, Evanston, Kemmerer Hams
> Fork, Slate Creek Ferry over Green River, up Big Sandy to Big Sandy
> Station, then up Little Sandy, which we will cross ten miles above the
> junction and then follow to Pacific Creek; to South Pass by way of
> Sweetwater and Atlantic City, up Burnt Grove Canyon, then north
> to Lander and Fort Washakie, the Shoshone Indian Reservation.
> Thence ford Wind River and over the Owl Creek Mountains, and
> from there go either way, to Meeteetse and Cody and down the Sho-
> shone River, or down the old Missouri Trail and Owl Creek to Ther-
> mopolis; thence down the Big Horn River to Basin and up to Bur-
> lington, across the hills to Foster Gulch to the Shoshone River and
> ford it.[3]

However, Welch explained, Woodruff's timetable "could not be carried out
as the weather was so bad that many of us could not get there by that date.
Some ... had left home to meet at Woodruff at an earlier date and could

Figure 7. Companies of organizing Latter-day Saints, bound for Wyoming, at Green River Crossing at Ham's Fort, May 1900. Courtesy of LDS Church History Library.

not wait for all to get together, so companies were organized as fast as teams arrived."[4] As this occurred, Woodruff organized them into seven companies, each with a captain, two assistants, and a chaplain. The company captains, in order, were Walker X. Pack, George Henry Taggart, John Jackson, Alfred Woodcock Nebeker, James Cowley Sessions, William Israel Stoddard, and James Alma Lee. A separate cattle company without migrants traveled separately with about two hundred head; they were placed in the charge of captain Hyrum K. North. In the seven companies were about 100 wagons, 124 men, 46 women, 94 children, and about 300 horses.[5]

These eight companies of colonists were the only units directly organized under Apostle Owen Woodruff's personal supervision. The first group started out of Utah and traveled into Wyoming in the spring, and after a 500-mile-long journey, they arrived on May 24 on the Shoshone River's northern side, near present-day Garland. The route followed by Charles Welch is clearly depicted in an account published in 1987 by his grandson Arthur Huff Welch, whose father, Frederick Arza Welch, was only a few

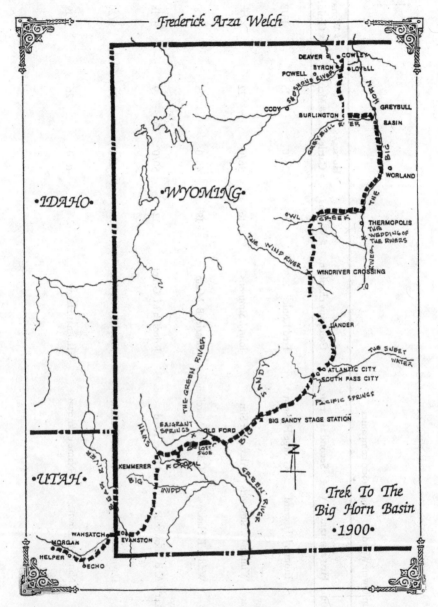

Map 3. Route of the Welch family from Morgan County, Utah, to Cowley, Wyoming. From the account by Arthur H. Welch, *Frederick Arza Welch*, vi.

Table 6. Abraham Owen Woodruff's eight 1900 companies

Company captain	First assistant	Second assistant	Company chaplain	# Wagons	# Horses/ # Cattle	# Men	# Women/ # Children
First Company Walker X. Pack[a]	Thomas J. Howard	George Harston	Fred Kohler	11	26/0	15	13/2
Second Company George H. Taggart[b]	William G. Simmons	Alexander Sim	John J. Simmons	16	36/0	22	6/27
Third Company John Jackson	Wilder T. Hatch	Gilbert J. Marchant	Charles B. Mann	19	45/0	25	6/8
Fourth Company Alfred W. Nebeker[c]	A. B. Snowball	Luther Reed	Jedediah M. Grant	12	50/0	9	3/18
Fifth Company James Sessions[d]	David Lewis	Walter Graham	Joseph H. NeVille	23	75–100/0	27	9/20
Sixth Company Israel Stoddard[e]	Name unknown	Name unknown	Thomas Heaps	20	48/0	26	9/19

Table 6 (*continued*). Abraham Owen Woodruff's eight 1900 companies

Company captain	First assistant	Second assistant	Company chaplain	# Wagons	# Horses/ # Cattle	# Men	# Women/ # Children
Seventh Company James A. Lee[f]	Name unknown	Name unknown	Name unknown	Unknown	Unknown / Unknown	Unknown	Unknown
Cattle Company Hyrum King North[g]		Dan Avis, Wells Davis, Lester Turnbow, Orlin Cox, Henry Herget		1	200	7	2/0
Totals				>100	>300	>124	Between 46 and 94

To move the companies more efficiently, all the cattle were congregated into one herd. Welch relates the difficulties when all the trail hands, except the cook "Herget," deserted. North hired several men to complete the drive. Welch, *History of Big Horn Basin*, 64–69, 72–75.

[a] He was from Davis County, Utah.

[b] He and his wife Jessie McNiven were from Morgan County, Utah.

[c] He and his wife Elizabeth Stowball were from Rich County, Utah.

[d] He and his wife Selena Holt were from Bountiful, Davis County, Utah.

[e] William Israel Stoddard was from Richmond, Cache County, Utah.

[f] James Alma Lee and wife Chloe Baird were from Davis County, Utah.

[g] Hyrum King North and wife Althea Conk Best were from Salt Lake County, Utah.

months old when he migrated with his father. At one point they passed the
site "where [Mormon cavalryman] Lot Smith burned provisions for Johnston's army on the Sandy," and they collected a few small remaining relics
of the 1857 Utah War attack. "Companies 2, 3, 4, were almost in the tops of
the mountains during a fearful blizzard."[6]

The three companies captained by George H. Taggart, John Jackson, and
Alfred W. Nebeker traveled from Ham's Fork upriver on Slate Creek into
the Fontanelle Mountains through which the Seeds-Kee-Dee-Agie or Green
River passes. As the group was preparing to camp for the night, "clouds
gathered thick and fast, the wind whistled a song of warning" to all hands.
Snow began to fall, while the wind rose to hurricane levels. By morning the
storm's intensity increased, whipping the tents, knocking down the stove's
pipes, and quickly forming deep snow drifts. It was impossible to keep the
camp's fires burning. The storm raged unabated through the second night's
darkness. Blankets and quilts were tied around horses and children to prevent their freezing. The horses were so hungry that they ate the ends of
fishing poles sticking out from the wagons and any exposed wood on or in
the wagon boxes not covered with iron strips. The two-year-old daughter
of John Henry Dickson and Avilda Diana Hickman Dickson had taken ill
at the storm's beginning. Her condition worsened as the storm increased.
"Suddenly the child had a convulsion. The mother, whose younger baby
boy was only six weeks old, picked up the little girl, jumped out of the sheep
wagon," and rushed with the child to the tent of Charles Welch, who they
knew from their home in Morgan County, Utah. But all efforts to aid the
child were futile. The grief of her sudden death was worsened, for there
was no material to fashion even a primitive coffin. Additionally, the parents
wanted the child to be buried in their family plot in Morgan. Although
strangers to the bereaved parents, William Passey from Bear Lake and his
son offered to return Avilda and the child's body to their Morgan home
and then return the mother to the traveling company.[7] After the storm, the
three companies had a comparatively uneventful remainder of their trip to
the intended site at the Shoshone River.

Edward C. Partridge, William C. Partridge, and Benjamin Salisbury
arrived with their company at the Green River, about thirty miles northeast
of Kemmerer, around April 25.[8] Although advised to go upstream twelve
miles and cross at the original Pony Express crossing site, they decided to
test the river's depth by walking their horses into the water. They were able
to find a shallow line in the shape of a half circle. One teamster, Orson
Frost, was nearly lost when he did not accurately mark the line of shallow.[9]

He and his sick passenger John F. Black were carried downstream, bobbing and pitching in the wagon for two hundred yards. William Dickson's experience in Company Two was similar when he attempted to find shallow water by riding his horse into the Wind River. Dickson was suddenly rushed downstream, clinging to his horse's mane; the animal finally found shallow footing, thus marking the site safe for crossing.[10] The Edward Partridge wagons again had difficulty at the Wind River crossing at a ford called Big Wind. When one wagon began drifting with the current, Partridge hooked its two-horse team and attached more horses to the wagon's tongue while he was standing shoulder deep in the swift, cold water. His actions allowed a safe crossing.[11]

After their safe crossing to the Shoshone's northern side, most colonists lived in tents, or in or under their wagons, pestered by wood ticks, rattlesnakes, coyotes, dust storms, and flies. Save for hay and grain they had purchased from a few ranchers along the Shoshone River, badly needed supplies were shipped in wagons over the forty-five miles from Bridger, Montana, by Charles A. Welch, whose commissary store sold them at retail to his fellow colonists.[12]

In the last part of April, the *Cheyenne Tribune* announced that about 450 people were en route to the Big Horn.[13] According to a database compiled from the accounts of Mark W. Partridge, Charles Arthur Welch, and others who wrote of this migration, there were at least 130 families.[14] Among them were many family heads of prominent LDS leadership.

On May 28, 1900, ground was broken to dig the Sidon Canal. Owen Woodruff held the plow for its first furrow as Byron Sessions drove the horse team of George Hartson.[15] Woodruff made "some great promises to the people, inasmuch as they would be faithful to the Lord and go forth and reclaim this country." He dedicated the land for the Latter-day Saints' abode, and the canal was blessed to carry the waters to make the land fruitful. Woodruff promised that the Lord would assist them if they would pay their tithes and offerings.[16]

By mid-June twenty acres of land were plowed and ready for planting as gardens; potatoes were already planted, and a small crop was anticipated. At the end of 1900, there were 1,018 Mormons in the three LDS branches. The Byron Branch had 325, with 350 in the Shoshone (Cowley) Branch and 343 at Burlington.[17] Historian Marshall Bowen gives slightly different numbers, that "by late summer of 1900, approximately 800 Mormon settlers had reached the Basin." Using LDS church statistics, Bowen claims "543 Mormons lived in Cowley and its immediate surroundings," and more than 1,700 pioneers lived

Figure 8 (*top*). A variety of scoop scrapers used in farming and canal construction in Wyoming and the West. Reproduced with permission from Jill Livingston, *Living Gold Press*, Klamath River, California.

Figure 9 (*bottom*). Four-horse team pulling an advanced-type scraper as the Sidon Canal is excavated. Reproduced with permission from California State University at Chico, Meriam Library Special Collections.

Figure 10. Horse or mule teams moving filled scrapers up a gradual incline to dump on the canal bank. Photo from http://seldomseensheep.tripod.com/morganfamilypioneerheritage /id53.html.

"within six miles of each other in and around Cowley, Byron, and Lovell."[18] The population arriving in Cowley was skewed by age. Nearly 90 percent were under fifty years of age, and their mean age at arrival was thirty-two years.

Only seventy-nine additional families arrived between 1901 to 1905. By the April–May 1910 federal census, there were 239 families in 236 dwellings in Cowley, and 216 families in 215 dwellings in the town of Byron.

Individual histories of many men, their wives, and families in the first group were extensively recorded by several colonizers, including Charles Lindsay, 1930; Charles A. Welch, 1940; Mark N. Partridge, 1967; Melvin M. Fillerup, 1988; and by historian Lawrence M. Woods, 1997. Partridge creatively asked his readers "to make an imaginary visit to a typical home in Cowley," the sort that would have been built as conditions improved for the colonists:

As we approach a dirt-roofed log cabin with one or two windows and a single door, we notice that there are no trees, shrubs, or lawn in sight. The only visible vegetation is salt sage, and that is not very luxuriant. A partly filled 40-gallon barrel [sits] near the ditch. Perhaps 50 yards from the house is a log stable covered with poles and

Table 7. Age distribution of 130 adult males who
moved to Cowley, Wyoming, 1900–1905[a]

Age Range	Percent
Over age 50	10.8
Under age 50	89
Under age 35	60
Under age 30	45
Under age 25	30
Between ages 21 and 25	20
Age 20 and younger	~10

Median age at arrival: 32 years

[a]Bowen, "Migration," 215.

dry willows. In front of the stable is a corral enclosed by a pole fence. Part ... is fenced off for a calf pen in which some calves are standing watching us. Nearby is a pig pen with hungry, squealing pigs. A small chicken coop, made of logs, has the door opened and chickens of various colors are around the dooryard picking up scraps of food that may have been thrown out of the house. ... As we knock ... we notice that the door is made of rough pine boards. There is no door knob. A buckskin string protrudes through a hole in the upper part of the door.... As we step inside and are greeted, we see the father, mother, and three or four children. The father wears a mustache and his whiskers have not been shaved since last Saturday night. He is busy mending a shoe with leather from an old discarded saddle or broken harness tug. The mother is cooking dinner.... The walls of the log room look just the same on the inside and on the outside. We notice the rough pine board floor and the cook stove.... We hear thunder. The lightning seems quite close, and the rain soon begins falling fast. Rain water starts leaking through the roof, running down the stove pipe, and little muddy streamlets start falling on the beds and splashing on the floor. Pans and buckets are hurriedly placed so as to catch the water.... Fortunately, the shower quickly passes, and when the water stops dripping, the pans and buckets are emptied, and life goes on as if nothing had happened.[19]

Some personal accounts have survived, recounting the specifics of companies, routes, individual experiences, and reminiscences regarding the 1901 or later groups. One illuminates the record of Martha Mae Maxwell, the author's aunt. She was sixteen years old when her family was called from Peoa, Summit County, Utah. Martha wrote:

> I didn't want to come. My uncle [and I] wanted Father to let me stay and attend Brigham Young College, but Father would not let me stay; therefore, I lost the only opportunity I ever had to realize my fondest hopes of going to "BY." We loaded our household goods in two covered wagons.... My brother Alvin [age 22] and [James] Guy Miles [age 16] drove a bunch of cattle all the way, taking turns riding the horse and donkey.... My sister Nellie [age 17] and I drove a four-horse team all the way. We helped to harness the horses, put the feed bags on their noses, hobble them, and turn them out to feed on the grass after they had finished their grain. It was fun for the young, but for my mother, it was a terrible experience. She was pregnant. I often wonder how she ever stood it all those long, weary days.[20]

Martha's brother Wallace Wright was born in Cowley that fall, and he tragically died in childhood. Martha continued:

> There were no bridges so we had to ford the rivers. When we reached Ham's Fork there was another outfit bound for the Big Horn. George Eyre and his family were from Southern Utah [Emery County] and alone. They were very glad to join us.... We hadn't come through a town since we left Kemmerer, Wyoming. When coming over South Pass, we saw the sign, "so many miles to Atlantic City." You can imagine our disappointment when we reach "the city"—just a little store and a place to post a letter. Anyway, we replenished our food supply and travelled toward Lander.... We were advised to take a shortcut.... It proved to be a long cut, and a terrible trip between Lander and Wind River Canyon. There was nothing but a barren Indian reservation.... When we reached Wind River Canyon ... the trail took us up a steep mountain, and I mean steep. We had to unload most everything and then put up extra teams on each wagon in order for the horses to pull them up. We then had to carry everything up to the wagons—now if you don't think that was a day! Then it was just as steep going down the other side. I thought any minute the wagon would tip over on top of the horses.... The next day we followed the Big Horn River down to the bridge at Thermopolis.

Martha Mae is incorrect, for this was the Wind River and does not become the Big Horn until its junction with the Owl creek (see map 3). She sums of the remainder of their journey:

> The river was very high and dangerous. We were plenty happy to find a bridge. We camped on the riverbank ... washed our clothes, and prepared to continue on. ... It was the 6th of July when we reached what was then Lovell. ... We camped that night on the river. ... Mother was feeling terribly sick and weary when a little red-haired lady came into our camp. After talking to Mother, she ... loaded us down with big loaves of wonderful bread. ... Next morning ... every team was ready to drive into the water. Father said to me, "Follow right behind me." Perhaps because of my fear of water, I didn't do as he told me. When they reached the other side, safely, there I was with [my sister] Grace [age 15], still sitting on the other side. They called me to drive in. ... The water was deep and swift; I became dizzy and I was pulling the horses into deeper water all the time. The water was then up to the horse's sides, almost to where they would have to swim. A man ... came back and led us across. Perhaps you don't think that was an experience! (Don't wonder why my hair turned grey so young.)[21]

Those arriving in the 1901 group could not count on help from the 1900 colonists, who were usually exhausted from canal digging, railroad building, and meeting their own needs. Those arriving after 1900 also missed out on drawing for homesite lots and cash payments for the project-redeeming railroad contract with the Chicago, Burlington and Quincy Railroad.

When the Mormon migrants began their Sidon Canal scraping on May 28, 1900, some had arrived only days before. With more than one hundred primitive horse-drawn slip scrapers, the excavation was to be fifteen to eighteen feet wide, in places thirty feet deep to accommodate the grade, and at one point requiring drilling in solid sandstone for a length of 940 feet.[22] From the canal's headgate on the Shoshone River, its waters flow windingly, but generally northeast, making thousands of acres productive on the river's north side. With the additional labor from the 1901 group and others arriving in the spring of 1902, the Sidon Canal reached Cowley on June 23, 1902, but it was not fully completed until April 1904.[23]

The underfunded endeavor and its cash-depleted settlers were repeatedly in crisis from the burden of buying supplies for canal construction and meeting daily needs. Enter the chief engineer for the Chicago, Burlington and Quincy Railroad, Mr. I. S. P. Weeks, who initially approached Jesse Wentworth Crosby Jr. as described in his letter to Owen Woodruff.

> Dear Brother,
> I. S. P. Weeks came to our camp on the 5th inst. [day of the month] & I walked with him over the Mortenson works & on the 6th I went with him over the new work sections.... While we were traveling he expressed himself as being highly pleased with our work, etc., and said he would like to hire 65 young men of our people & asked if we would work for them laying track.... I met him at Bridger [Montana] again yesterday ... & he again renewed the talk of the employment of 65 Mormon boys, not less than 20 years of age. Said he would pay from $1.75 to $2.25 per day & would board the men for $4.00 per week.... They would arrange cheap rates to Denver and ... to Toluca & would return the men by the same route. He said they must be good, sober men, as there is [*sic*] joints along the line ... at Bowler and at Browns & Gardners, one at Piney ... one at Section 10 where our people will have to camp while doing the work on Section 10.... I would like to know what your views are about our boys working on track laying. Kind regards, your Bro.[24]

Mr. Weeks offered an initial contract of $80,000 to construct more than twenty-seven miles of railroad grade from Pryor Gap in Montana to and beyond the Jack Morris ranch, now the community of Frannie, Wyoming.[25] This permitted one crew to work the railroad, giving half their pay to purchase shares in the canal company. Approximately 90 percent "of the men of the colony took their families and moved their tents and wagons to various camps along the right-of-way where the railroad grade was to be constructed." The 10 percent not working on the railroad bed made up a second crew, who continued digging the canal. They were led by construction superintendent Byron Sessions. They were not paid in cash, but teams were credited with $4.00 worth of canal company stock for working ten hours each day.[26] Single hands were credited with $2.25 in stock per day. Stock began at $6.00 per share and was later increased to $10.00, with one share of stock required for each acre to be irrigated.

No one was to receive cash for canal work. "In fact, each man was required to pay cash for two percent of his canal stock. This money was used to buy plows, scrapers, and other equipment" from the Welch Commissary. The labor colonists were cash poor, purchasing provisions from the commissary largely on credit. By January 1901, "more than $4,000 was due the Company for goods." To pay this, a 2 percent assessment was laid on the subscribed stock and a 75 percent assessment followed, to be paid before August.[27] Neither Partridge nor Lindsay address the issue of any workers too cash-strapped to pay the assessments; presumably their canal company shares were reduced or transferred to Welch.[28]

An April letter from Crosby, supervising the railroad workers and opening the tunnel at Camp Bowler, reported to Owen Woodruff of "about 50 cases of smallpox in the camp, but no deaths." Sessions was reported to have "stirred his men" at Byron, saying the Cowley colonists "were doing them two to one [i.e., working twice as hard]."[29]

Seemingly approved by Woodruff, Crosby wanted the $80,000 contract to be in the name of Bishop William H. Packard, giving his bond for its performance. But Packard did not sign, for he would not accept personal responsibility for its payment.[30] Packard's wife, Cynthia, left her account, noting "Will didn't dare to let any person have the whole contract as he was under heavy bonds to have that road through in a certain length of time." She added that "Crosby was sore because Will didn't turn the whole contract over to the Stake President [Crosby] and his counselors." When camp cooks stopped serving meat to the workers, Packard found that Crosby had told them they "had better stop bringing beef, as Packard was likely to fail and not be able to pay him. Will assured him he would get his pay so they had no more trouble.... Will told me that before he left the railroad, all of his bills were fully paid, that the only man that was short of what was due was him."[31]

Owen Woodruff appointed Jesse Wentworth Crosby Jr. to oversee the work, and Charles Arthur Welch to keep the books and run the commissary. The Chicago, Burlington and Quincy Railroad contract stipulated payment of 13.5 cents for each cubic yard of earth moved, 24 cents for gravel, 36 cents for loose rock, and 80 cents for solid rock. Welch and Crosby made profitable subcontracts with individuals, including Edward C. Partridge and David Lewis, at lesser amounts, 11 to 13 cents per cubic yard moved. Welch noted that "all the men selected to look after any part of the work of colonizing were never told what wages they should receive, and were not granted any special favors."[32] The contract's work terms were completed on August 22, 1901, and at the final settlement, $90,100—or $1,413,000 in 2010 dollars—was paid. This was more than $10,000 greater—$157,000 in 2010 dollars—than the original contract required.[33] "We paid off every person who had worked on the job and had a surplus of about ten thousand dollars."[34]

Welch claimed that "numbers of people had died during the winter on account of hardships endured and for lack of proper shelter as tents and sheep wagons were the only thing that stood between freezing death and living."[35] By these enterprises, Charles Arthur Welch and Jesse Wentworth Crosby Jr. apparently added significantly to their existing wealth. As Welch modestly admitted, Crosby was already the wealthiest man to come to the Shoshone River Project. Formerly an LDS leader in Panguitch, Utah, a bishop's agent, stake president, or counselor, he had also accumulated wealth from stock raising and mercantile business. "His checks were good in all of southern Utah ... and were always honored at banks."[36] Crosby brought 600 head of cattle and 250 horses in forty-five railroad cars when he arrived via Bridger, Montana, in 1900, and thereafter he continued in the livestock business.[37] After their arrival in the basin, both men profited from the Chicago, Burlington and Quincy Railroad contract as noted. Additionally, Welch operated the commissary, selling hardware and domestic goods shipped from the nearest rail hub at Bridger to the working colonists.

Together, Crosby and Welch opened a store in Cowley in 1901, enlarged it significantly in 1909, and by 1911 it was a substantial hardware, merchandise, and clothing store.[38] Both Welch and Crosby built homes that were elaborate and impressive for the time.[39] Welch, Lemuel J. Willis, and Crosby also owned a railroad company, and in 1900 they subcontracted building four miles of its spur—from the Pryor Gap line to Scribner—to Neils Otto Mortensen, a Mormon recently arrived from Parowan, Utah. Others, not named, took up lengths of one to two miles.[40] The Toluca Line, through the Crow Reservation, covered a distance of 130 miles and saved 60 to 100 miles of hauling freight to the basin.

The first station was named Ronald, a siding holding twenty-six cars; then came Mifflin, then Coburn, where passengers from Billings could connect; then Moran, Keyser, Pryor, Chicopee, Oswald, Crockett, Bowler, Scribner, Frannie, Mantua, Garland, Ralston, Corbett, and finally, Cody.[41] Only four stations—Coburn, Pryor, Frannie, and Garland—"had telegraph connections so when a train was stalled or broken down between these stations no one knew where the train was, except the crew and its passengers." Because of weather and steep grades, the train was rarely on time.[42]

While the majority of Woodruff's settlers struggled financially for many years, the early religious and civic leadership prospered financially. Among these, Byron Sessions was a notable exception. He was by some accounts broken physically and poverty-stricken from the drain of work demanded by digging the Sidon Canal. Rich County Stake President John M. Baxter recalled that Sessions found the canal construction far more difficult than expected. He had sold his Rich County land and stock at a great loss, and he used up what remained of his savings on the new settlement to support his family. Baxter recalled of Sessions, "it was not long until the funds he had at his command were exhausted. His horses got poisoned, and he lost all but two or three head. His [first] wife [Idella Winn Twombly, mother to ten children] took seriously ill and he was at her bedside for fourteen years.... He was, therefore, reduced to extreme poverty."[43]

As the end of Owen Woodruff's first year of the Big Horn Basin efforts, his accomplishments were significant. He had brought hundreds of colonists, they had begun digging a thirty-seven-mile-long canal for irrigation, and they had constructed a twenty-seven-mile-long railroad track, which had brought them desperately needed financial relief.

CHAPTER 9

Promises and Accomplishments

In all probability, the whole project would have failed.[1]

—Mark N. Partridge

IN HIS 1904 REPORT of matters in Wyoming, Governor Fennimore Chatterton used the cities of Cowley and Byron as examples of success resulting from the Carey Act. He wrote proudly that on land with "scarcely enough vegetation to support a jack rabbit," the colonists had—by the second year's end—raised sugar beets with better sugar content than those of European farms. The oat yield was seventy-five bushels to the acre; cherry trees had climbed to four feet high; and sugar cane and peanuts were being raised. Chatterton continued: "The water rights for this tract and land cost these people only eight dollars and fifty cents per acre. The land today could not be purchased for twenty-five dollars per acre, and in three years it will be sought for at one hundred dollars per acre." Chatterton correctly perceived progress, but his political mindset stretched reality. He omitted mention of the extraordinary problems the colonists had faced, simply claiming there were in the settlements twelve hundred "prosperous people in happy and comfortable homes."[2]

As noted, the settlers had finished digging a thirty-seven-mile-long canal, including 900 feet hollowed through a solid rock tunnel.[3] Colonist Ariel Rabannah Doty's personal journal gives a small glimpse into the daily details of what was faced in accomplishing this project:

> Nov 17 1903. minus 12 degrees. Very cold. gloves + rubber boots, river, ground is frozen.
> Dec. 1903. Great disappointment in camp tonight. The boys have just learned that their ditch has got to be 14 feet [wide] in bottom which they had figured as a 12 foot [wide] ditch.

Dec 5 1903. John Black had a little accident by blowing up 34 sticks
of donemite [sic]
Dec 17 1903. Maxwell [first name not given] lost a horse today (sick)
Jan 4 1904. Worked all day in frozen dirt and nearly pulled our teams
to death.
Jan 16 1904 Worked all day on the approach to tunnel.
Feb 1 Worked all day on Tunnel with team.
Feb 15 Excitement ran high in camp this morning when R[obert]
Maxwell challenged Birt [Gilbert] Marchant for a scrap.
Feb 25 1904 worked in Tunnel last night.[4]

Owen Woodruff urged the colonists to complete the tunnel, promising
that their difficult labor and obedience to the church's admonitions would
be rewarded: "It will take a united effort to perform this gigantic task, for
we are few in number. I urge you to pay your tithes and offerings. Keep the
Sabbath Day. Do not profane the name of duty. Be honest with all men, and
if you do all these things this will be a land of Zion to you and your children
and children's children throughout the generations to come."[5]
     However, not long after beginning the Sidon Canal, the colonists real-
ized the project's enormity, and they along with their local leaders became
seriously concerned. A special prayer service was convened, and "they
beseeched the Lord for help." Woodruff "officially called all those in the
camp on a mission to complete the canal and establish homes." Many times
thereafter, Woodruff and other church officials continued to admonish their
disheartened people to build homes and reside in the valley permanently.
"If it had not been for such counsel and encouragement, in all probability,
the whole project would have failed," records historian Mark Partridge.[6]
Charles Welch adds that at one low point, conditions were so difficult that
"a check for two thousand dollars was sent from Salt Lake."[7] According to
Melvin Fillerup, the check was made out to Byron Sessions, but he did not
cash it immediately. When Woodruff next visited Cowley, he threatened
to resign as an apostle and don worker's clothes and return to Wyoming to
finish the canal by himself. Humbled, perhaps embarrassed by this rebuke,
fresh resolve arose among the discouraged Latter-day Saints. The $2,000
check was returned to LDS church leaders in Salt Lake City.[8]
     Economic conditions were still gloomy at the Big Horn Stake Confer-
ence on September 12, 1903, when the Mormons of Cowley and other cities
were visited by their prophet, President Joseph F. Smith. With him were
the three polygamist apostles: Owen Woodruff, John Whittaker Taylor,

and Matthias F. Cowley. The group's only monogamist was Smith's second counselor, Anthon H. Lund. President Smith promised his listeners: "God bless this people and remove the barrenness of the land. The day will come that *prosperity and riches* will come unto this land and people." More cautiously, Lund added, "The Lord will prosper and bless and before long you will have plenty."[9]

Similar promises of prosperity had been made by Apostle John W. Taylor to polygamist with three wives Charles Ora Card and the Latter-day Saints settling in Canada in 1889. Taylor "rose and spoke and bore a powerful testimony, stating he had beheld the Savior. He predicted that this would become a fruitful land and yet in time of need, it would be a haven of rest for those people who desired to serve God."[10] Unlike the Big Horn project, Card's efforts to settle Alberta were not in answer to a call. "Card had lobbied hard [to move to Canada] among plural families in Cache Stake. Some men accepted his request as a call; others felt it would be a good way to escape the pressures of U.S. marshals." In January 1887, Card had submitted a list to Taylor of forty men all "desiring refuge in the north." However, in the end only ten agreed to make the trip. In a letter to Canada's prime minister John F. MacDonald, polygamists Francis M. Lyman, John W. Taylor, and Charles Card explained that "they were not asking Canada to legalize polygamy or to sanction plural marriage but simply to accept existing families."[11]

A major impediment to farming in the Big Horn was alkali in the soil; it remained a problem, even as late as 1935, as noted in that year's agricultural report:

> The surface soils in this area were generally free from harmful concentrations of alkali salts in their virgin state. The application of irrigation water, however, upset this natural condition. At first, abundant crop yields were produced under practically all methods of farming, but as the years passed by, white crusts of alkali salts began to appear on the surface of some of the soils, which inhibited the growth of plants.... The prevention of further accumulation of the salts and the reclaiming of lands which have become unproductive because of alkali, is, at present, one of the important problems."[12]

University of Wyoming historian Phil Roberts holds that almost all the Mormon projects were irrigated only for subsistence crops and did not reach the level of commercial agriculture.[13]

Owen Woodruff apparently questioned whether the basin's soil and rocky surface might contain valuable chemicals or ores. He submitted samples to Professor John A. Widtsoe in Logan, Utah, where Widtsoe was a director at Utah State Agricultural College. Widtsoe's report suggested the potential value of pursuing further samples of sulfur and nitrate:

> You will observe that the alum sample contained 52.05 percent of pure-water free alum, making it a most excellent specimen. One of the sulfur samples contained 64.61 percent sulfur; two of the others contained over 40 percent and the fourth, over 30 percent. If these deposits are extensive, they ought to be very valuable for the production of sulfur.... I have mentioned to you before that if our people would be on the look-out for nitrate deposits, they might discover something that would be worth fortunes to the discoverers, and be of great benefit to the agriculturists of this region. The only nitrate deposits of the world are located in South America, but our climatic conditions in the western part of the United States are such that it is very likely that large nitrate beds exist here also, although they have not yet been uncovered.[14]

It is uncertain whether Woodruff sent additional soil or rock samples for analysis.[15]

Historian Marshall Bowen establishes that Cowley migrants were relatively young, with 89 percent under age fifty and 30 percent under age twenty-five. Only fourteen men who arrived were over age fifty, and half were elderly who came with their children or grandchildren (See table 7 in chapter 8).

Bowen also explains that a large proportion of arrivals from 1900 to 1905 were families from the southern Utah colonies of Parowan, Escalante, and Cedar City. The next most-numerous Utah area was Wasatch and Summit Counties.

Many farmers came to the basin having learned to survive despite years of water scarcity, and they had assumed that "abundant Shoshone River water would result in outstanding yields." From their former experience, they believed that the more water given, the more plentiful the crop. Therefore, they permitted "water to flow into their field for as long as thirty-six successive hours." At this time, they were not yet aware of a heavy clay hardpan that lay not far under the surface that obstructed deeper seepage. With time and overwatering, alkali migrated upward and accumulated near the

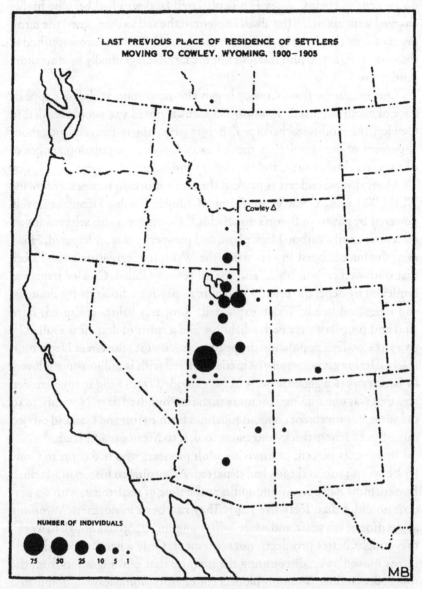

Figure 11. Origins of 1900 Big Horn Basin colonizers. Reproduced with permission from Marshall Bowen, "Migration to and from a Northern Wyoming Mormon Community, 1900 to 1925," *Pioneer America* 9, no. 2 (1977).

surface. There were "serious crop failures in 1905, 1910, and 1912. By 1920 over 60 percent of their Cowley Flat's cultivated land area had become highly charged with alkali."[16] The alkali content in the soil so threatened the farming economy that by 1924 drainage was required. This was accomplished at the cost of $212,000 plus interest, but the farmland gradually became more productive.[17]

Out-migration from Cowley began almost as soon as the first appearance of alkali occurred. The 1910 US Census noted 574 people resided in Cowley. The exodus reached a peak in 1912 when ninety-five residents, about 15 percent of the population, moved away. Cowley's population apogee of 687 was reached in 1920, and its nadir of 366 occurred in 1970.

Many diverse endeavors marked the area's efforts to prosper. Following World War I, the Great Western Sugar Company built a factory at Lovell, powered by gas from Byron's minefields.[18] Cowley was also selected for an oil refinery and a carbon black plant, and prosperity was anticipated. However, the bubble burst in 1923 when the Wyoming legislature passed a bill that outlawed carbon black, and the oil refinery failed. Cowley remained burdened by debt; the town was unable to pay for schools or for drainage and irrigation needs. Welch explained, "property values collapsed; farm land and property were each a liability, and a spirit of despair prevailed."[19] By 1930 Cowley's population dropped to 526. By 1933 the Great Depression reached its lowest point; all of America suffered with 15 million unemployed. In January 1936 a gigantic burst of gas exploded from a dig in the Tensleep area that was uncontained for more than four hundred days. Not until 1940 did some improvement come, as pipelines from Byron and Garland carried oil to Lovell where trucks and trains took it to Montana and Utah.[20]

By 1925, 41 percent of surviving adult pioneers who had come to Cowley between 1900 and 1905 had departed. According to historian Marshall Bowen, most had been young adults at the time of settlement, with 60 percent no older than forty-five years. They had been in northern Wyoming about nine or ten years, and while "still young and vigorous enough to work," they sought better prospects, not retirement. Only a handful of older residents moved away, discounting the premise that out-migration from the rough, demanding Wyoming pioneer community would leave it "dominated by feeble old-timers" planning to live "out their last years in more comfortable, settled circumstances."[21] The destinations of those leaving Cowley were primarily southwestward to Mormon communities in Utah, Idaho, and California. Salt Lake City received 9 percent; the Wasatch Mountains' west slope along Bountiful to Murray, 12 percent; and about 30 percent to

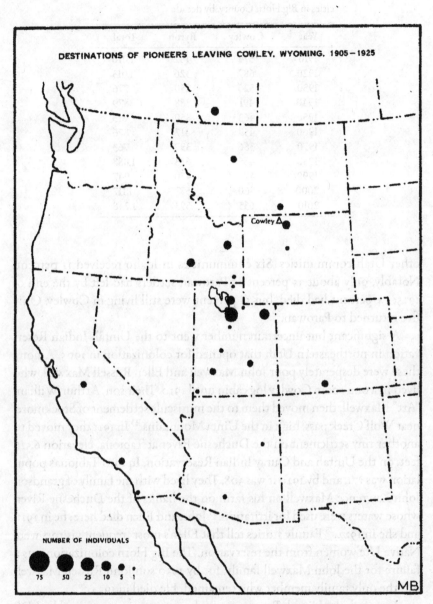

Figure 12. Destinations of 1900 colonizers who left Cowley, 1905–1925. Reprinted with permission from Bowen, "Migration," 219.

Table 8. Population change in two LDS-founded
cities in Big Horn County, by decade

Year	Cowley	Byron	Total
1910	574	442	1,016
1920	687	326	1,013
1930	526	250	776
1940	491	388	879
1950	463	350	813
1960	459	417	876
1970	366	397	763
1980	455	633	1,088
1990	477	470	947
2000	560	557	1,117
2010	655	593	1,248

other Utah communities. Six communities in Idaho received 11 percent. Notably, only about 35 percent of Parowan settlers had left by the end of 1925; 14 percent had died, but 51 percent were still living in Cowley. Only five returned to Parowan.[22]

A significant but uncertain number went to the Uintah Indian Reservation in northeastern Utah that opened for colonization in 1905. Among these were desperately poor John Maxwell and Ellen Russell Maxwell, who lived in a one-room Cowley log cabin until 1910. Their son, Arthur William "Att" Maxwell, then moved them to the miniscule settlement of Stockmore, near Wolf Creek pass, high in the Uinta Mountains.[23] In 1911 they moved to another tiny settlement on the Duchesne River at Tabiona, elevation 6,516 feet, on the Uintah and Ouray Indian Reservation. In 1910 Tabiona's population was 171, and by 1920 it was 308. They lived with the family of grandson John Lawrence Maxwell on his farm on the banks of the Duchesne River, whose waters were used for irritation.[24] John and Ellen died here; he in 1911, and she in 1922.[25] Family stories tell that Ellen's most frequent visitors were Native Ute women from the reservation. The Big Horn colonization was a failure for the John Maxwell family, for by 1930 son John Russell Maxwell was the only family member who remained. He died in 1934.[26]

As noted, the Uintah Reservation colonization was supported by LDS church leadership in Salt Lake City and managed by local leaders William H. Smart and Joseph White Musser. The devastating impact of this forced colonization on the Utes, and their ensuing 1906 failed flight to join the Lakotas, are treated elsewhere in this work.[27]

Table 9. Religious makeup of Big Horn and Park Counties, Wyoming

Big Horn County, Wyoming		
Category	Percent	Number of congregations
Catholic	3.9	3
Mainline Protestant	4.4	9
Evangelical Protestant	7.5	11
Other	33.4	13
None	50.7	N/A

Source: http://www.city-data.com/county/Big_Horn_County-WY.html

Park County, Wyoming		
Category	Percent	Number of congregations
Catholic	10.6	4
Mainline Protestant	9.7	9
Evangelical Protestant	12.5	37
Other	11.3	13
None	55.9	N/A

Source: http://www.city-data.com/county/Park_County-WY.html

Judged by population increase and other economic parameters, prosperity and wealth have been elusive for the cities founded by the Big Horn colonists. Combined data for Cowley and Byron show an increase of only 232 people over the 100-year span from 1910 to 2010, with Cowley's increasing by only 81. Cowley's population has been greater than that of Byron at each decade measured except the 1970s and 1980s. In comparing the 2010 population for the cities in neighboring Park County against those in Big Horn County, the data show that Park is more populous than the more Mormon Big Horn.

One measure of Mormon settlers' longevity is the LDS population size relative to other religious affiliations. Data regarding the religious makeup of Big Horn and Park Counties, the two major counties in northern Wyoming, shows that both have more than 50 percent claiming no religious affiliation. However, Big Horn has 33 percent whose religious affiliation is listed as other, which would presumably include LDS church members. Park County has only 11 percent in this category. Historian Darcee D. Barnes notes that Lovell was already 69 percent Mormon when the first colonizing companies arrived in 1900, but its Mormon population increased to 83 percent by 1910, as more colonists arrived during that decade.[28]

Table 10: Population comparison by perceived
"Mormon-ness"[a]

Park County, Wyoming	
	City
9,520	Cody
6,314	Powell
327	Meeteetse
115	Garland
16,275	

Big Horn County, Wyoming	
	City
2,360	Lovell
1,847	Greybull
1,285	Basin
655	Cowley
593	Byron
288	Burlington
178	Deaver
157	Frannie
114	Manderson
50	Otto
7,528	
23,803	**Total**

[a]US Census data for 2010.

Both Big Horn and Park Counties similarly voted Republican in the 2012 presidential election—81 and 78 percent, respectively. But they are dissimilar in that Big Horn remains 100 percent rural, with 18 percent of people over age twenty-five holding a graduate degree, compared to Park as only 44 percent rural, with 24 percent of those over twenty-five with a graduate degree.[29]

Economic measures of household income also confirm that wealth has not come to Wyoming's Big Horn County. The farming and ranching cities of Cowley, Byron, Lovell, and Burlington—adjacent to the thriving tourist area of Cody—have not fared as well as a control group from the farming and ranching cities of Oakley, Coalville, and Kamas, Utah—all adjacent to the resort area of Park City. Cody has numerous tourist attractions of its own and is linked economically to Yellowstone National Park, fifty miles away, that receives more than four million tourists a year and contributes some part of $680 million to surrounding communities in Wyoming, Montana, and Idaho. Park City is thirty miles from Salt Lake City, and its six hundred thousand tourists-per-year economy is tied to skiing, biking, hiking, and cultural festivals at an estimated $529 million per year. Racial disparities across the seven cities does not explain the economic and population differences, since they remain strikingly uniform, with a very high percentage of white residents.

After the area saw nearly a decade of medical care by John Maxwell, who did not hold a medical degree, the first qualified medical doctor came to Cowley and Lovell around 1907 or 1908, Edward Woolley Croft. He was born in Tooele County, Utah, in 1872, the son of Thomas Woolley Croft, who had immigrated with his wife as LDS converts from London. Thomas had one child with her before she died. Edward and four siblings were born to Thomas and his second wife, Elizabeth Richardson Croft. After a time living in Salt Lake City, then in Tooele County, the family moved to Bear Lake County, Idaho. Edward attended public schools in Paris, Idaho, and graduated from the Bear Lake Academy.[30] The death of his father in 1881 at age fifty-eight left Edward supporting his mother and siblings, and he began working as a millwright. Edward later worked in the newspaper business; in 1895 and 1896 he was publisher and editor of the Republican-leaning *Paris Post*.

Edward Croft and Helen Brown were married in September 1896; from 1897 to 1910, they had seven children. In fall of 1896, Croft was called on an LDS church mission and served twenty-eight months in Wisconsin. Upon

Table 11. Comparison of rural cities in Big Horn County, Wyoming, and Summit County, Utah, by race and income

	Year 2000			
City	Population	Household income	Family income	Percent white
Burlington, Wyoming	250	$28,281	$31,875	91.3
Byron, Wyoming	557	$34,375	$37,045	90.8
Cowley, Wyoming	560	$38,759	$39,722	97.2
Lovell, Wyoming	2,281	$30,745	$35,815	90.9
Oakley, Utah	948	$61,250	$62,059	96.4
Kamas, Utah	1,274	$41,667	$46,750	96.3
Coalville, Utah	1,382	$39,342	$43,929	93.1

his return, he joined Salt Lake City's Consolidated Wagon and Machine Company, owned by Heber J. Grant,[31] with Croft soon becoming the manager of a branch at Afton, Wyoming. He remained here until 1903, when he was admitted to Northwestern University in Illinois where he studied medicine. When Croft graduated in June 1907, he earned election to the medical school honorary society of Alpha Omega Alpha.

Dr. Edward Croft returned to Wyoming and opened a general practice as a physician and surgeon in Cowley, where for many years he was the only certified doctor practicing in that part of Wyoming. Croft is credited with delivering around three thousand babies. He moved to Lovell, Wyoming, and in 1923 he and Harvard-trained William Watts Horsley—a gifted, caring physician and skilled surgeon—built a hospital there. In 1931 Dr. Thomas Brown Croft, Edward's son, joined the two doctors. Around 1965 Dr. Horsley moved to private practice.[32] Personally, Dr. Edward Croft was loved and respected; professionally, he was a member of Wyoming's State Medical Society, the American Medical Association, and Northwestern Wyoming Medical Society. He served for five years as a board of trustees member at the University of Wyoming in Laramie. For fifteen years Croft was president of Big Horn Stake and remained active in LDS religious affairs. Dr. Croft died August 8, 1936, in Lovell, and he was buried in the Lovell Cemetery.

In questioning whether the settlement of Cowley was worth the cost paid by her ancestors, Elizabeth Shaw Smith notes that her great-grandfather William Clayton Partridge Sr. and wife Sara Jane "Sadie" Stott had "very little money, and were never able to retire or relax." Smith reports that for two decades the Partridges wished they could return to Utah. She polled her extended family, and they concluded that the Partridges would have fared far better had they remained in Provo, Utah, and none felt their Wyoming colonization move improved the family economically. Yet Smith judges her Partridge great-grandfather as "good clay" and his Cowley experiences "fire-fixed a remarkable man."[33]

The 1906 appearance of Cowley's first newspaper *The Cowley Weekly Progress* was evidence of maturation, but it also reveals that the region's Mormon influence experienced external criticisms. Its first issue of one thousand copies was published on June 15 by a thirty-seven-year-old Swedish convert—editor and manager—Emil Veterlaus, who claimed eighteen years of experience in commercial printing. Even though Veterlaus had been in Cowley only about a year, he announced that his local newspaper would supply a "long felt want in the Mormon Colony" as "a defender of their rights." He promised that malicious insinuations and slurs "hurled at the Mormon people by unscrupulous editors and writers" would be challenged by the *Progress*. This promise stands as evidence that the Mormon's presence in the area experienced some level of political or social opposition. The inaugural issue's front page covered the details of applications for the pending drawing for Shoshone Reservation land, including dates for filing, and that an appearance in person was required except for those "who served for at least 90 days in the army and navy ... during the Civil War, the Spanish-American War, or the Phillippine [*sic*] insurrection." Veterlaus added that the "Government Plan of Disposing Crow Reservation lands" in Montana was the same as those for the Shoshone. A *Cowley Weekly Progress* annual subscription price was $2.00.[34]

Veterlaus described the *Progress* to be "uncompromisingly Republican," espousing protection of American industries and labor as well as unmasking graft and corruption in public servants. He had invested $1,500 in a Diamond Cylinder hand press and planned for the *Cowley Weekly Progress* to become a permanent fixture, the best periodical in the Big Horn Basin. He hoped to see his paper in the home of every married man in Cowley and Byron, especially in those of Latter-day Saints.[35] This newspaper, later called *Cowley Progress*, was still in circulation in 1920 and focused on its base of predominantly Mormon readership, with reports and articles such as the LDS ward reunion. "The Annual Ward Reunion last evening was by far the greatest event of its kind ever staged in Cowley's entire history... [as] the crowning climax of them all." This report suggests that disparities in income and social standing created ill will within the community, for it added that the church parties did more "to create good fellowship and to eliminate hateful class distinction than any one of a dozen other things can do."[36]

Since evidence suggests that present-day polygamy is still ongoing in Big Horn Basin communities, the case can be made that its colonization was partially successful for having created a persisting "cultural region," as described by Yorgason and Meinig.[37]

What did President Joseph F. Smith and other LDS leaders have in mind with their promises of "prosperity and riches" to the Big Horn Latter-day Saints? Was it a comfortable income, a luxurious home, an absence of debt, three-piece suits, club memberships, chauffeured travel, and thousands of dollars in retirement monies? While some obedient, high-ranking members lived in such circumstances, by and large the promised blessings neither came to the 1900–1901 colonists nor have they come to the descendants who remained.

Distinguished writer Wallace Stegner wrote of his formative boyhood years in the small town of Eastend, a frontier settlement like those in the

Big Horn, on the northern plains of Canada not far from the Montana-Saskatchewan border. In his novel *Wolf Willow*, Stegner disguised the town's name as Whitemud. If he had visited such places as Cowley and Byron along the Shoshone River, he might have judged them favorably—as he had Whitemud—as having good seedbeds, and as good places to just be.[38] These are good places for boy or man, girl or woman, if open spaces, sunrises, sunsets, and the soft sounds of early morning rain falling outside your window bring joy, and if you take pride in conquering tasks demanding physical labor. If being independent from rules imposed by urban living are your yardstick for prosperity, as well as having an enduring relationship with your religious roots, extended family, and neighbors; hunting game and fishing for the family table; watching the seasons change outside your door; and smelling rain as it comes across fields. If these are among your criteria, then it might be that Joseph F. Smith and Owen Woodruff's prophecies of reward might have proved partially true, at least for some 1900–1901 colonists or their descendants remaining in the Big Horn Basin.

CHAPTER 10

An Innocent in the Big Horn Basin?

The Mormons on the Shoshone found themselves ill-equipped to func-
tion in the emerging world. They did not understand the world of big
money or the politics of development.[1]

—Robert E. Bonner

THE NIGHT WAS FRIGID at the Eagle's Nest stage station on February 20, 1900, where Abraham Owen Woodruff and the eleven men who
had come with him stopped for rest and shelter. They braved Wyoming's
winter to examine the Big Horn Basin's land for colonization. Shortly, they
were joined by William F. Cody, who arrived well supplied with potions
of expensive antifreeze—but he found no takers among the alcohol-averse
Mormons. Cody's close friend and partner in the Shoshone Land and Irri-
gating Company, Nate Salsbury, did not accompany Cody. Ever the con-
summate storyteller, Buffalo Bill "spun tales far into the night," speaking of
such things as his respect for Brigham Young and the Utah pioneers' accomplishments. As conversation moved to serious matters at hand—of land and
irrigation—Cody announced he would relinquish part of his water rights
on the Shoshone River's north side so that the Mormons could build their
canal and establish settlements there.

Cody spoke truth. Barely two weeks later, on March 9, 1900, the relinquishment was signed by Salsbury and Cody to release water rights and
land formerly held by eastern investors in a project known as the Cincinnati
Canal, on which no work of improvement had been done.[2] The conversa-
tions at the Eagle's Nest gathering in February did not make it clear that
Mormon High Priest Charles Kingston had filed an application with the
state engineer for the Cincinnati Canal's water rights, which were transferred to him as agent for the Mormon colonists.[3]

The journals of Owen Woodruff lack treatment of Buffalo Bill Cody,
even though by 1895 Buffalo Bill was perhaps the most famous American

alive. Cody had been a youthful teamster with the 1857 supply train for Albert Sidney Johnston's Utah Expedition, and he was among those captured by the Mormon raider and Nauvoo Legion's cavalry, Major Lot Smith. During the Civil War, Cody served for a time with the Kansas volunteer infantry. Later, as a western hunting guide, he filled a contract with the Kansas Pacific Railroad to slaughter more than four thousand buffalo to feed railroad workers. Ned Buntline's 1869 book, *Buffalo Bill, King of the Border Men*, chronicled Cody's time with the Fifth Cavalry and General George Sheridan and the Department of the Platte. Cody's stage career began in 1873, and in 1883 he partnered with Salsbury to create the Wild West shows of theatrical self-presentation that made Cody rich, while others critically named him as a "frontier impostor."[4]

Cody's arrival in the Big Horn Basin began by way of an aspiring Sheridan businessman, George Thornton Beck, son of Kentucky senator James Beck, who had unsuccessfully sought Grover Cleveland's appointment in 1886 as governor of Wyoming Territory. After the 1894 Carey Act was passed, George T. Beck assembled a survey party of eighteen that included Elwood Mead, Wyoming's territorial engineer, and Cody's son-in-law, Horton S. Boal. That summer they crossed the Big Horn Mountains and passed along the Big Horn River, to the Stinking Water River, as far as Sage Creek. They laid out survey lines, including what would become the sites for Cody and Cowley. On return to Sheridan, Beck reported his findings and shared Mead's technical engineering report with Omaha banker, friend, and real estate man, Horace C. Alger. After Cody heard the trip's report from his son-in-law, he approached Beck and Alger, asking to join their partnership.[5] Alger quickly agreed since they would thereby acquire "the best advertised name in the world."[6] The Shoshone Land and Irrigation Company's formation followed. Under Beck's supervision, the company started construction on the Cody Canal on the Shoshone River's south fork in summer 1895.

The name of Charles Kingston, a Mormon convert from England, like Cody's name is also not found in Owen Woodruff's journals. Much of what transpired in Wyoming regarding water, irrigation, and railroad lines from 1897 to 1904 was likely known to this Mormon and conveyed to Owen and church leadership. Charles Kingston was born to Frederick Kingston and Mary Anne Hunter in Northampton, England, in 1856. Family tradition claims that Charles's father Frederick was present at a meeting where Orson Pratt was preaching the LDS gospel, and the assembled crowd became agitated and determined to tar and feather the apostle. Although he was not an LDS believer, Frederick engaged the mob leaders in a fight, allowing

Pratt to escape from the hall through an open window. Not long afterward, Frederick was converted and baptized, but in 1858 he experienced serious financial reverses and was not able to pay off his creditors, who sought his arrest and prosecution. Forewarned of a warrant for his arrest, he stowed away in a ship bound for the United States and somehow found his way to Utah by 1860.

After Frederick was able to find employment, he sent money to his wife for her passage. However, Mary Anne was determined she would not leave until his debts were paid. Neither she nor son Charles had accepted the Mormon gospel; they lived in an environment still hostile to the Latter-day Saint Church and their beliefs. Nearly twenty years later, Charles emigrated to Utah without his mother. Arriving at his father's home in Morgan County, Utah, Charles was still holding a negative view of Mormonism. Out of curiosity he read his father's books regarding this peculiar faith; he became curious and attended a church meeting where he heard two speakers, apostle and polygamist John Henry Smith and Junius Free Wells. Both were secret Council of Fifty members.[7]

From these pulpit addresses and from further study, Charles became a believer and was baptized. It was not long before he claimed experiencing a night visitation where heavenly beings appeared, saving him from a profound darkness. Much affected, he was ordained an Elder in 1883, and five months later he was married to Mary Pricilla Lovell Tucker in the Endowment House by Council of Fifty member Daniel H. Wells, father of Junius Wells. There followed Charles's ordination as a Seventy, a mission to Great Britain, a move to Rock Springs on his return, and then to Star Valley, Wyoming. There he was ordained a High Priest and Stake High Council member, and the Young Men's Mutual Improvement Association was placed under his charge. From 1884 to 1903 eleven children were born to Charles and Mary Pricilla.

Two events in 1897 brought Charles Kingston into the affairs of Owen Woodruff. President Lorenzo Snow appointed Kingston to a special mission for the church as a railroad agent, to travel and care for "the scattered Saints located along the line of the Union Pacific in Wyoming at whatever times and places he should be able to visit." In June 1897 US President William McKinley appointed Kingston to the Land Office Register in Evanston, Wyoming.[8] Kingston went to the Big Horn in November 1898 and met Cody, who had developed an irrigation project including a canal and considerable land that he offered for sale. Charles inspected the Cody land package and determined that it was not in the church's best interest to purchase it.

Instead, he located another area, checked the irrigation potential and found it satisfactory, and upon returning reported to Snow, with eight apostles present. At the meeting a colonization company was organized, with Owen Woodruff as president and Charles Kingston as secretary.[9]

Owen Woodruff and Charles Kingston visited the colony at Burlington in July 1899 while assessing the basin for further settlement. In August 1900 it was Kingston who saw the plight of Woodruff's colonists and who contacted Wyoming Congressman Frank M. Mondell, who was also a Burlington railroad director, to use his influence to get the contract resumed. Otherwise, the canal project would have had to be abandoned.[10]

Throughout his steady upward mobility and associations with several Council of Fifty members, and despite his tenure in the polygamist haven of Star Valley, Charles Kingston appears to have remained a monogamist. Claims are made that he married a second wife, Mary Ann Wass, eleven years after the Manifesto, on November 14, 1901, in Salt Lake City. However, no official documentation of this marriage has been found. Federal census records from 1910 to 1930 provide no corroboration of her presence apart from or near Charles, Mary Pricilla, or their family.[11] The question of Charles Kingston's participation in plural marriage takes importance because his firstborn son, Charles William Kingston, and grandson Charles Elden Kingston became ardent polygamists, who founded the fundamentalist United Order Law of Consecration polygamy sect within the Davis County Cooperative Society in Utah.[12] If Charles William's father, Charles, had been valiant in defending plural marriage for Latter-day Saints, it would be relevant to further explain his helpful association with Owen Woodruff's purposes within and outside the Big Horn Basin.

Even before water carried by the Sidon Canal reached the townsite of Cowley on June 23, 1902, Owen Woodruff had been concerned that more water rights and land would be needed by the basin's Mormon colonists. Still working toward that goal, he wrote a letter on September 17, 1903, to Wyoming Congressman Frank Mondell in Washington on the subject. Mondell answered:

> I do wish it were possible to make some arrangements whereby your people could secure the land which you desire. I have talked with the Governor about it a number of times.... He seems firmly of the opinion that there is no way in which he can arrange the matter, unless Messrs. Wiley, Guernsey, and their people [Cody and Salsbury] voluntarily relinquish their rights to the tract in question.

I also talked with Mr. Wiley about the matter.... [and] he claimed that the tract ... was quite an important feature of their enterprise and that their people were very much averse to giving it up. In fact he seemed to think they had not been entirely well treated in that he claimed some land above your original survey had been granted to your people which he thought they were entitled to.... They could not think of giving up any of this land, as the success of their enterprise depended on keeping it.... It would seem as though the only hope lay in changing the opinion of those controlling the other ditch proposition; and I would suggest ... that personal interviews be had with a view of coming to an understanding if possible.... I regret to say that my efforts do not seem to have been crowned with success.... I like the way your people have developed the Cowley and Byron settlements. We need more of that kind of enterprise, and my very best wishes are with you, and I am at your command whenever I can serve you.[13]

On New Year's Day 1904, Owen Woodruff was in Salt Lake City. He selected a sheet of Big Horn Basin Colonization Company stationery, whose letterhead listed him as its president, and began typing a lengthy letter to one of Utah's senators, Thomas Kearns Jr. The letter was a plea for help with his senatorial colleagues from Wyoming in obtaining further water rights. Woodruff stressed that the colonists had successfully excavated the Sidon Canal, water was flowing to Big Horn County soil, and the canal would shortly be completed to the end of its thirty-seven-mile-long line. He emphasized that they had tried unsuccessfully for three years to acquire additional Shoshone River water rights.

On this day Utah's other senator Reed Smoot, a monogamist Mormon elected by Utah's legislature in 1903, was under fire over the LDS church's continuing plural marriages. Hearings to investigate not him but the church were set to begin in the senate, and much of Smoot's time was devoted to eagerly preparing a defense. This might explain in part Woodruff's choice to write to the Utah senator who was not Mormon. However, Kearns was an influential, uber-wealthy silver mine entrepreneur, elected by the Mormon-dominated state legislature. Kearns was at this time the *Salt Lake Tribune*'s shadow owner.[14] Woodruff wrote to Kearns:

As you already know I spend most of my time in the interest of colonization and irrigation work in Big Horn County, Wyoming.

I desire at this time to ask you to kindly aid me in the accomplishment of a matter I have had in mind for a long time. About three and a half years ago Governor DeForrest Richards of Wyoming, with then Sec. of State Fennimore Chatterton (the present Governor) and Supreme Judge Jesse Knight paid a visit to this city for the purpose of interesting our people in the development of northern Wyoming. This visit was very a pleasant one and these gentlemen assured us that in the event of our undertaking to establish some colonies . . . we could count on their support and hearty cooperation in this work. As a result of this friendly visit . . . the Big Horn Colonization Company was incorporated and I was chosen as President of the Company. This company has within the past three and a half years located about three thousand people in Big Horn County. . . . We have succeeded in the completion of the Sidon Canal at a cost of $125,000, and the people are demonstrating what the soil and climate are capable of producing.[15]

Woodruff explained that the Mormon colonists' land acreage was less than the available river water could irrigate, and that he and Governor Richards had worked for years to secure "what is known as the Whistle Creek or Wilwood tract of land . . . on the south side of the Shoshone River," a little upstream "from where our new colonies are located."[16] At Governor Richards's suggestion, the Mormons performed an engineering survey in 1903, sending completed maps and their application for the land they desired to irrigate to the state engineer Fred Bond and the state land board. Inexplicably, no reply came from Bond, and two months later the papers, among others of Bond's, were found by another board member. Also found was an unsent letter written by Bond, alleging that four days before Woodruff's submission was received, he had granted an application to the Oregon Basin Irrigation Company for a large tract of land that included the ten thousand acres cited in Elwood Mead's survey.[17] Woodruff continued his letter to Kearns:

Governor Richards learned of the State Engineers Action in this case and was very much exercised over it and the last meeting which he attended before his last sickness was on this subject, at which he declared that something must be done to remove the obstacles out of the way of our enterprise. . . . It was not long [when] the Governor died . . . and Mr. Bond the State Engineer took sick and died also. The matter is now in the hands of the new Governor, Mr. Chatterton and the new State Engineer Mr. Johnston with whom I have but a slight acquaintance.[18]

Woodruff named Wyoming's state senator Charles A. Guernsey as one principal interested in the Cody-Wiley project, but he called on Kearns to "reach" Guernsey by contacting him through Wyoming's US senators, Francis E. Warren and Clarence D. Clark, as well as the state's US congressman, Frank W. Mondell. All of "whom have treated me with kindness when I have called on them or when I have solicited their aid in our behalf," wrote Owen. He claimed their support was due because "Our Company has completed the largest canal in Wyoming and has actually made more homes and laid the foundation for more production than all the Companies in Big Horn County combined." Further, Woodruff argued, "This tract of land ... [that] I want to get the Oregon Basin people to relinquish is not vital to their proposition while it is to ours," for they would retain "more than one hundred thousand acres" for their canal, which "is more than they would ever have water sufficient to irrigate." Woodruff suggested that "assurances" existed from parties with money for a sugar refinery factory to be built if the Mormons obtained the land and planted sugar beets. He also recommended that Kearns ask the Wyoming senators and representatives to meet with the Burlington & Missouri's George W. Holdrege to discuss the potential factory as a significant attraction for railroad business.[19]

A series of letters back and forth followed, resulting in little progress. Kearns answered Woodruff on January 8, indicating he had sent Woodruff's letter to Senators Warren and Clark and Representative Mondell and that he would supplement with personal interviews. Mondell answered Kearns on January 9, 1904, indicating he believed that Wiley's enterprise would benefit by allowing the land to Woodruff, but he could find no legal support to force it. On January 14, Kearns forwarded a letter received from Senator Warren with several suggestions for Woodruff.[20]

While Owen Woodruff's five-page letter to Senator Kearns laid out well the Mormon colonists' case for adding water rights and irrigation acreage, it did not contain functionally important matters of background and relevant events already transpired. Woodruff described the personal assurances of Governor Richards and Wyoming senators and congressmen who had previously treated him with kindness. He added the Mormon colonists deserved what they asked for because they had been successful despite great challenges that threatened failure and demanded much expense and sacrifice from his people. He implored Kearns to deal with the Big Horn Basin

Development Company's influential leaders to relinquish a small portion of water and land under contract. By logic and fact, it was of little to no value to the Oregon Basin project but of critical importance to the Mormons.

That Woodruff did not provide Kearns with the name of Solon L. Wiley, a development company officer, and the involvement of Congressmen Frank Mondell and Charles Guernsey, might have been for brevity's sake. Woodruff may not have been fully aware of these individuals and corporations of wealth and power competing in the field of Wyoming water and land development. Woodruff did not copy nor approach the US Reclamation Service, Elwood Mead, William F. Cody, Nate Salsbury, Solon Wiley, nor George T. Beck.

George T. Beck, as noted, was a Kentuckian who traveled west as a prospector in Colorado, then he moved to Wyoming Territory as a surveyor for the Northern Pacific. By 1889 he became a sheepman on the Big Horn Mountain's east slopes. Beck's modest success with sheep was followed by an interest in politics, but he failed in his House of Representatives bid in 1890. Beck was in Sheridan when the railroad arrived in 1892, and William Cody was pushing for the construction of the Sheridan Inn, a hotel for railroad-delivered wealthy sportsmen hunting in the Big Horn mountains.[21]

Around 1893 several businessmen from Sheridan, including Beck, became interested in canals and acreage for irrigation. Hearing of an irrigation reclamation project of 400,000 acres from the 1894 Carey Act, Cody asked Beck to include him, and Cody was accepted for his promotional value. Thus on March 20, 1895, the Shoshone Land and Irrigation Company came into existence with Cody as president, George T. Beck as manager, and Elwood Mead as surveyor. A week later the company submitted a request for 26,000 acres to the Wyoming state land board, which was accepted in September. Construction began that fall.[22]

Initially Cody and Beck were equal partners, but with time Cody and partner Nate Salsbury became the larger shareholders. The SL&I Company was one of three initial Carey Act projects submitted to the state land board, but Mead, who was the Wyoming state engineer, cut the total acreage to 25,000. In 1899 it was Cody who formally offered free right-of-way across the SL&I Company lands to influence the Burlington & Missouri to build its line connecting Toluca with Cody. During the visit of Governor Richards to Latter-day Saints in Salt Lake City in January 1900, it became apparent that the water rights he promised them "conflicted to some extent with the Cody-Salsbury permit." But Richards brokered an agreement whereby Cody gave up some rights to the Mormons. The land relinquished was at the far eastern end of Cody's project.

From the time of their first efforts the Mormons judged their allotment too small, and in the fall of 1900 they again approached Governor Richards for aid in getting more water rights from Cody and Salsbury's SL&I Company. This time the colonel was less pliable, claiming the parcel was the heart of his project with the Burlington and fearing it would fail if the second piece were relinquished. Woodruff countered with legal arguments that Cody's contract was violated in 1903 by his failure to begin construction. However, state administrators were influenced by Cody's celebrity and "did not risk frightening off private money by enforcing laws or requirements too strictly."[23] Probably unknown to Woodruff, despite letters with them, were the positions of Mondell and Warren. They were capitalists and politically aligned to support whatever industries or for-profit opportunities might come to the state by Burlington's rail service.

Woodruff knew the Carey Act gave each public land state one million acres on which the state would control developing irrigation projects. It is less certain whether he was aware that the 1902 Newlands Act put the federal government—in this case the US Reclamation Service—directly into irrigation development in competition with the state for control. Warren at first supported the state, but after the Newlands Act, he soon recognized that only the federal government could bring the massive amounts of money into Wyoming that would be needed. He began supporting the US Reclamation Service position. Popular opinion in Big Horn County favored Mondell's view and the Reclamation Service. Not only did federal efforts bring big money, they also brought technical expertise, quality, organization, and permanence. This brought an impressive contrast to what had previously been primitive scraping operations that were human and animal labor intensive, technologically wanting, impermanent, and repeatedly underfunded.

Chatterton did not support the Mormons but favored the Cody-Salsbury-Wiley project that ultimately collapsed, as did Chatterton's attempt to be elected governor from acting governor after Richards's death. The C-S-W project suffered a lingering death, finally going into receivership in 1908. Cody was, in historian Bonner's view, a man for whom the processes of political manipulation and making money were interpersonal. Cody nurtured direct, warm relations with Warren and Chatterton, with President Theodore Roosevelt and Secretary of Interior James Garfield, but such practical men did not confuse friendship with government, political, and financial imperatives.

Bonner emphatically asserts that not only Cody but also the Mormon leaders failed, for they "did not understand the world of big money or the politics of development," and they were marginalized by a developing "twentieth-century model for western water development."[24] That the political expertise of Owen Woodruff and church presidents Wilford Woodruff and Lorenzo Snow was insufficient in dealing with Wyoming's governors, state senators, reclamation experts, and railroad capitalists can also be appreciated from a recent study by historian David Walker. This 2019 work lays out how the capitalist skills of Mormons such as businessman William Godbe, Brigham Young, George Q. Cannon, and John Willard Young utilized the capitalistic skills of national railroad leadership to the end of expansion of Mormon industry. Railroads made Utah resources and products available west and east, brought tourism dollars to Utah, and facilitated the access of distant investors to its expanding economy.[25] But by 1904 these stalwarts at using political skills to enhance the financial standing of themselves and their church were long gone, save John Willard Young, and he had fallen from grace for misuse of church funds.[26]

Conversely, railroad agents such as the Union Pacific's president Sidney Dillon urged lawyers to work with pro-railroad congressmen, requesting some lenience on antipolygamy acts, for "the Mormons are our friends." Western historian Robert G. Athearn devotes two full chapters to the complicated story of Utah's Mormons attempts to involve the Union Pacific's leadership in benefitting their economy. It tells of efforts beginning in 1871 of Brigham Young, his sons Joseph A. Young and John W. Young, together with George A. Smith, Daniel H. Wells, Albert Carrington, and the Youngs' attorney Bishop John Sharp to influence the Utah Central and Utah Southern and other lines. Athearn writes, "In case after case the Union Pacific was called upon for aid, frequently at times when such assistance was difficult to provide. Without the partnership between the Mormons and the Union Pacific, rail service to Utah might never have materialized."[27]

Even if the politically astute among top church leadership could have been convinced, the financial peril experienced by the LDS church would have prevented their involvement with the political struggles over water rights and distribution. Additionally, the threatening and expensive imbroglio playing out in the senate chambers from 1904 over continuing polygamy would take precedence for their attention—and their money—over the Mormon irrigation problems in the Big Horn.

Owen Woodruff's earnest January 1904 efforts were only months before his untimely and unforeseeable death in June. No other noble leaders among the Latter-day Saints who might have been better equipped in the Wyoming world of big money took up the cudgel.

CHAPTER 11

Polygamy Among the Colonists and Its Residue

There is nothing more difficult to take in hand, more perilous to conduct, or more uncertain in its success, than to take the lead in the introduction of a new order of things.[1]

—Machiavelli

WYOMING'S SMALL TOWN of Cowley was named for one apostle among the four most persistent defenders of polygamy. However, polygamy was of very little concern to Wyoming's first governors after statehood was achieved in 1890. These civic leaders merely wanted good farmers and were not inclined to enter disputes about their marriage practices. In fact, Wyoming's US senator Joseph M. Carey had been influential in keeping anti-Mormon provisions out of Wyoming's statehood charter.[2] The state's sitting governor from 1899 to 1903, DeForest Richards, and his secretary of state, Fennimore Chatterton, championed the 1900 colonization by Mormons without comment on polygamous unions.

If Abraham Owen Woodruff left any specific, written record of intent to secretly preserve plural marriage in the new Big Horn communities, it might exist in the LDS Church History Library records or possibly as unreleased material in a secret file or vault.[3] His surprisingly brief autobiography contains neither mention of any 1900–1901 colonization efforts in the basin, nor his performing the many illegal plural marriages that are documented elsewhere and that had a fateful impact on his final decade of life.

Nonetheless, at least five men among the 1900–1901 colonists were publicly known polygamists. These were Jesse Wentworth Crosby Jr., with three wives; George Henry Crosby, Haskell Shurtliff Jolley, Gilbert Johnson Marchant, and Warren Marshal Johnson, with two wives each. More than fifty children were born to these five men. The first three were ecclesiastically and financially accomplished before their arrival in the basin and became more so after their relocation. Jolley became president of the Big Horn

Basin Clay Products Company. Welch owned the only retail store where colonists could purchase needed supplies for their families. He also sold the required equipment—scrapers, shovels, boots, and tools that frequently needed replacement—to the workers digging the Sidon Canal. With ample capital Welch was able to purchase these at wholesale from companies in Red Lodge or Bridger. Crosby and Welch prospered financially through owning the highly successful Crosby-Welch Department Store in Cowley.

Jesse Wentworth Crosby Jr. married sixteen-year-old Sarah Pauline Clark in 1867 and twenty-one-year-old Sarah Francis Jacobs ("Aunt Sarah") in 1878. Ten children in total were born to these two women. Crosby's third marriage was to thirty-four-year-old Sarah Ann Meeks in a post-Manifesto union in 1894. All three marriages were performed in Washington County, Utah. When one of the women protested to President Woodruff about her husband's plan to marry a new wife after the Manifesto, "the First Presidency not only approved the new marriage in April 1894 but also instructed the complaining plural wife to also give her husband written permission to also marry the new wife under civil law, which he did. Crosby subsequently fathered children by both the pre-Manifesto and post-Manifesto plural wives."[4]

Crosby was president of Utah's Panguitch Stake in 1882 and was active there in the mercantile business and stock raising. His wealth became so widely acknowledged that his "checks were good in all of southern Utah; they floated around for months at a time and were always honored."[5] Presumably, Crosby's marriage to three wives placed him in a favorable light with Owen Woodruff and Matthias Cowley. With this approval, the strong financial position he brought from Panguitch, and his leadership skills, Crosby readily became "the most wealthy man in the Colony which came to the Shoshone River Valley," according to historian Mark N. Partridge.[6] With cattle and sheep endeavors, Crosby and business associate Charles Welch were visibly prosperous among the basin's Mormon society. Polygamy had also been a prominent, recurring, interconnecting element within Panguitch's Mormon leadership. In 1882 Mahonri Moriancumer Steele Sr. was ordained as Crosby's first counselor by John Henry Smith. On August 26, 1900, Owen Woodruff ordained David Cameron as second counselor in the Panguitch Stake. Cameron was the only monogamist.[7]

George Henry Crosby, the older brother of Jesse Wentworth Crosby Jr., married eighteen-year-old Sarah Brown in 1869 and twenty-seven-year-old Amelia Leany in 1885; both took place in Washington County, Utah. He had been a bishop in Nutrioso, Arizona, served in the Arizona legislature, was appointed the first patriarch in the Big Horn Stake, and served as a bishop for thirty-two years. The Crosby brothers might have judged it less likely to be pursued by US marshals after their move from southern Utah to distant, rural, and isolated Big Horn County.

Haskell Shurtliff Jolley married Effie S. Liethead in 1881. Apostle Anthony W. Ivins performed Jolley's marriage to twenty-eight-year-old Ellen E. Harrison from Pinto, Utah, in 1898, three years before Jolley arrived in the basin in 1901.[8] Five children were born to this union. In 1902 he purchased the townsite of Lovell and subdivided it for settlement. Jolley contracted for railroad construction south from Frannie, Wyoming, and obtained contracts for canal construction in the area.[9] In his 1911 report of polygamy's revival, journalist Burton Hendrick claimed "another notable case in which the Mormon Church advanced a new polygamist is that of Haskell S. Jolley, Bishop of Lovell Ward in Wyoming. For several years Jolley occupied a bishopric [position] in a much less important Stake in southern Utah." Referring to Jolley's marriage to Ellen, Hendrick wrote, "since this marriage Jolley has steadily advanced ecclesiastically and financially. He has been placed in charge of many church irrigation schemes in Wyoming and is rapidly accumulating a fortune."[10]

Gilbert Johnson Marchant, from Salt Lake City and Peoa, Utah, was the third known polygamist. He married fifteen-year-old Elizabeth Wright in 1876 and two years later married her sixteen-year-old sister, Louisa Ann Wright. He fathered twenty-one children with them. Marchant was hunted by US marshals and eventually arrested. He spent three months of 1892 in Utah's territorial penitentiary. While there Marchant learned the trade of butchering, and he later worked at buying and slaughtering cattle to feed the prisoners.[11] Since Elizabeth died in Peoa in 1899, shortly after birthing her tenth child, Marchant was not by strict definition a polygamist at the time he joined the 1901 Wyoming colonization. However, the functional result at her death was that her nine surviving children were added to nine surviving children among eleven born to Louisa Ann. Following Louisa Ann Marchant's death in 1919, Gilbert Marchant's third marriage was sequential to Anna Matilda Martin, in 1921.

The colonists' genealogical records yield other interesting instances of late polygamy in the Big Horn. William Wesley Willis, the second son of John Henry Willis and Francis Reeves, was born two years after his father participated as a perpetrator in the 1857 massacre of at least 120 Arkansas migrants at Mountain Meadows. According to historian Will Bagley, one surviving migrant child, Nancy Huff, described John Willis—into whose home she was placed for the winter after the massacre—as publicly executing an older child deemed by Willis too old to be spared.[12]

William Willis was born in Toquerville, Washington County, Utah, and married Dicy Ray Perkins of Iron County, Utah, on March 3, 1884. They had five children in southern Utah before moving with William's younger brother, Lemuel Josiah Willis, and other Latter-day Saints from that area in 1900. Dicy died on September 18, 1910, and William married Elizabeth Malvena Clark Leithead sometime between April 1910 and 1912. Their daughter Francis was born in May 1913. It appears that William Willis was polygamously married for at least five months of 1910.[13]

One Big Horn polygamist, Warren Marshal Johnson, experienced a pioneer life that was unusually difficult, abounded in tragedy, and repeatedly challenged his faith, even during his short time in the Big Horn. Johnson was an outlier to the general condition of polygamist men as mostly robust, wealthy, and leaders of their community. Born in 1838 in Bridgewater, New Hampshire, poor health at the age of twenty-six sent Johnson west to find warmer climes. Due to illness along the way, he was left in Utah at the home of Dr. Jonathan Smith. Smith's daughter, Permelia Jane, nursed Johnson to recovery. Convinced of Mormonism's certainty from reading the Book of Mormon, Warren was baptized into the LDS faith in 1866.

After ordination as an elder in 1867, Johnson was sent with others to the "Muddy Mission" in southeastern Nevada, considered "one of the roughest that confronted the Mormon pioneers." Warren married Permelia in Salt Lake City in October 1868, and he married a second wife, Samantha Nelson, three years later in Glendale, Utah.[14] Under extraordinarily difficult frontier circumstances, seventeen children were born to the family, eight to Permelia and nine to Samantha. In 1875 Brigham Young called Johnson, Permelia, and Samantha to take over Lee's Ferry on the Colorado River's desolate banks. Johnson replaced John D. Lee, who had been evading federal arrest for his role in the 1857 Mountain Meadows Massacre.

In 1891 four of Warren Johnson's offspring died tragically in a matter of days from diphtheria. They were buried in a row next to one another.[15] Warren and his wives operated the ferry until 1895. In December Johnson with fellow polygamist and a stake president Edwin D. Woolley Jr. were returning from inspecting and pricing some property near Fredonia, Arizona, that was comparable to what Johnson was preparing to leave at Lee's Ferry.[16] After taking on a load of hay, their wagon wheel went into a deep rut, the loaded rack tipped, and both men were thrown off; Woolley was unharmed but Johnson sustained a serious injury that rendered him permanently paraplegic.

Though bedridden, Warren still made the decisions for his family. It is difficult to fathom how a man of his judgment, knowing he was crippled for life, would choose to pioneer in the rugged northland, but in January of 1900 he decided to sell all Johnson holdings and migrate to Canada. During a stopover in Salt Lake City and consultation with church authorities, the family's objective was changed to the Big Horn Basin in Wyoming. They arrived at Camp Shoshone late in July, and in September Owen Woodruff directed the drawing of land by lot.[17]

By trading some stock, Johnson obtained a ranch about thirty-five miles from Byron near the Greybull and Big Horn River's confluence. His older sons built their homes in Byron and Coburn. The winter of 1901–1902 was severe "even for that country," and most of Johnson's cattle perished. His health continued to fail, and Warren Johnson died on his ranch in March 1902.[18]

At least one post-Manifesto plural marriage was performed in the Big Horn Basin among the Latter-day Saints who arrived in 1900–1901. On August 13, 1903, fifty-two-year-old Byron Sessions was married in the community of his name by Matthias Cowley to twenty-one-year-old Janet Easton, the daughter of coal miner and Scottish emigrant George Easton and Janet Cupples. In 1900 the Easton family lived next door to the ten-children family of Byron and his wife Idella ("Ida") Winn Twombly Sessions in Lovell.[19] It is uncertain where Janet Easton Sessions lived after the 1903 marriage, but a daughter, Helen, was born to her in Salt Lake City in 1905.[20] In his history, Welch notes that Byron's first wife Ida, who married Byron in 1870 and bore ten living children, suffered from chronic ill health and was bedfast for long periods of time.[21]

At the time of his marriage to Janet, Byron Sessions was the Lovell stake president with co-polygamist Jesse W. Crosby Jr. as first counselor. It is uncertain whether Sessions publicly acknowledged the plural marriage or Helen as his daughter.[22] Rich County historians claimed that by this time, Byron and Ida lived in "extreme poverty."[23] If this or Ida's ill health were operational in Byron's decision to marry a second wife is speculation.

In the present day, fundamentalist religious organizations still exist, formed around their belief in the essential nature of plural marriage, developed from early Mormon leaders during Utah's pre-1900 era, including John Wickersham Woolley and Lorin Calvin Woolley. Also important in their history—as previously noted—is polygamist Mormon Joseph White Musser, who served with post-Manifesto polygamist William H. Smart in Utah's Uinta Basin colonization. Years later, Musser was called the "'father of the Fundamentalist movement' because of his prolific writings that articulated their doctrine and their Fundamentalist position in relation to the LDS Church." Musser was excommunicated from The Church of Jesus Christ of Latter-day Saints in 1921 for pursuing additional plural marriages.[24]

The organization descending from the two Woolley men and Joseph White Musser is the Apostolic United Brethren (AUB), totaling approximately eight thousand members throughout the world. One of their colonies presently exists in Lovell, Wyoming. Headquartered in Bluffdale, Utah, they have there a chapel, an endowment house, a school, archives, and a sports field. The AUB also has known branches in Santaquin, Utah (Rocky Ridge); Eagle Mountain, Utah (Harvest Haven); Cedar City, Lehi, Granite, and Mount Pleasant, Utah; Pinesdale, Montana; Mesa, Arizona; Humansville, Missouri; and Ozumba, Mexico.[25] AUB members also live in Germany, the Netherlands, and England.[26]

The Apostolic United Brethren is sometimes called the Allred Group for Rulon C. Allred and his brother Owen A. Allred, who served as its president. Joseph Musser was influential in Rulon's rise in the sect in southern Utah. Its sordid history is marked by the 1988 murder of Rulon Allred by Rena Chynoweth, allegedly under the direction of another member, Ervil LeBaron.[27] The AUB has received widespread publicity from television coverage of Kody Brown and at least three "sister wives." While the AUB openly promotes polygamy, it is not connected to the mainstream Latter-day Saints, whom they consider doctrinally mistaken for failing to continue practicing plural marriage. The AUB is without known historical connections to Owen Woodruff, Matthias Cowley, John W. Taylor, Marriner Merrill, George Q. Cannon, or Joseph F. Smith.

In November and December 2015, the author queried by mail more than fifty civic leaders, city and county officials, police, and a variety of non-Mormon religious leaders regarding the presence of open or covert polygamy in Big Horn and Park Counties. From the anonymous survey responses, there is evidence that some mainstream Latter-day Saint polygamists reside in Lovell and nearby areas, where wives live in separate locations and marriages are allegedly performed in secret.[28] Respondents from Powell estimate that at least six women are in plural marriages in that area, and a Greybull respondent claims knowledge of three men, each with two wives, with estimates of men involved as high as twenty. Burlington is also named as having polygamist families. Clearly, this survey does not qualify as scientifically valid, but it does suggest that some mainstream Latter-day Saint polygamists presently live in Big Horn and Park Counties. Insufficient data prevents meaningful evaluation of total numbers of participants, their demographics, or of any causative relationship with the efforts of early area polygamists more than 118 years ago.

If the basin was not intended to be a platform for expansion of plural marriages, other objectives could have added fuel to LDS efforts to colonize rural, isolated Wyoming. There is a modicum of evidence that intrafamily competition or rivalry between Wilford Woodruff's sons, David Patten Woodruff and Abraham Owen Woodruff, might have played a significant role. Colonization may also have been viewed as a potential opportunity for the financially troubled LDS church to profit from a water company partnership with the flamboyant William F. Cody, using irrigation of potentially fertile land and with nearly free labor supplied by LDS church members.

Some colonists requested their assignment in order to leave failed farms, hoping for newfound success. Undoubtedly some were leaving the pressures of economic depression described by Arrington: the dearth of arable land and relative overpopulation of Utah. Some—as with the author's own family—believed they went in answer to the traditional call by LDS church authorities.[29] It might be that the leadership's motivation was nothing obtuse, but simply the church's organized, late, formal effort to enlarge its geographical footprint, to plant yet another community of faithful tithe-paying believers, as it had done in hundreds of instances since 1830.

Whatever private objectives and instructions might have been given to Owen Woodruff regarding colonization, they have not been found in public records. An opportunity to make such a record might have ended with his untimely death, which was only eleven weeks after Joseph F. Smith's Second Manifesto, in which it was affirmed that no plural marriages "have been solemnized with the sanction, consent, or knowledge of the Church of Jesus Christ of Latter-day Saints." Smith's affirmation was untrue, of course. But Owen never gave up his work for the success of his Big Horn Basin project. The LDS leadership and the cause of plural marriage without end lost one of their brightest stars when Owen Woodruff died from smallpox on June 20, 1904, in El Paso, Texas.

Charles Welch, with whom Owen had worked closely, said of him: "Our leader loved the people of the Big Horn, and thoughts of their welfare were ever upmost in his mind. In his letters to the local authorities on the ground he would say, 'I love you as I love my own brothers in the flesh, and want you to succeed in redeeming this land.'" Welch continued, "He was our dearest friend, and we loved him dearly." On his visits to the Big Horn, Owen would "go from tent to tent and call every man and grown up boy by name without the least hesitation." He would "meet men in all walks of life in a pleasant and friendly way."[30] Another observer left this appraisal of Owen Woodruff: "His was an affectionate disposition. He was loving and lovable. The ice of reserve always melted before the warmth of his nature. He was like a brother to all his associates. In whatever relationship of business or social life he stood to them, they knew him first and foremost as a friend. In the Big Horn colony, that feeling of love for him was most intense."[31]

It is a sad irony that by avoiding service of subpoenas with his journey to Mexico in 1904, Owen missed the Sidon Canal's completion.

A measure of appreciation of Owen Woodruff's standing with his leadership contemporaries is found in the memorial penned by his post-Manifesto polygamist friend, Benjamin Erastus Rich:

> Apostle Abraham Owen Woodruff is dead. An Apostle of the Lord Jesus Christ for eight years and his mortal career ended when only 31 years of age. . . . No man on earth was more beloved by those who knew him than was Brother Woodruff. He was the very embodiment of gentleness, kindness, and Godly charity. His aim in life was to be a true representative of the divine Master, a special witness for Him to Gods children on earth. We doubt if there be a member of the Church who was personally acquainted with this young Apostle who would not willingly have died in his stead had it met with God's approval. He was so much beloved by all he seemed so much more capable of doing good than the majority of us who have been spared for a season. God's ways are indeed not as man's ways or Brother Woodruff would still be with us.[32]

Eighty-nine years after his death, Owen's remains and his wife Helen's were brought back from the distant soil of Texas and Mexico where they had been placed. In July 1993 they were reinterred in the Salt Lake City Cemetery.

During the basin's colonization planning period, Matthias Cowley married Harriet Bennion, his third wife, in the Logan Temple in 1899. He then married Mary Lenora Taylor, fourth wife and second post-Manifesto marriage, on September 16, 1905, in Canada.[33] Another area family committed to plural marriage after the Manifesto was the Clarks. Hyrum Don Carlos Clark, first counselor in Star Valley's Auburn Ward and Eliza Avery Clark's father, had professed complete surprise when hearing from Owen Woodruff of plans for continued sub rosa marriages. On December 27, 1903, he entered a polygamous marriage with Mary Alice Robinson in Salt Lake City. Mary

Figure 13. Apostles and friends, Abraham Owen Woodruff and Matthias F. Cowley. Fox and Symons Photography Studio, Courtesy of LDS Church History Library.

Minerva Clark, sister of Eliza Avery Clark, entered a polygamous union with Edwin Turpin Bennion in 1903.[34]

The intent of a secret nidus for expanding polygamy within the Big Horn colonization while it was dying elsewhere is a perplexing, intriguing question. As noted, the evidence is strong but circumstantial, stemming from its timing within an era of intense national criticism of plural marriage and of those adamant in preserving the practice they were absolutely certain was given by immutable revelation. John W. Taylor, Marriner Wood Merrill, Abraham Owen Woodruff, and Matthias Foss Cowley were all participants and unyielding in polygamy's defense. According to Hendrick, Merrill was

> probably the most influential Mormon in the northern part of Utah, and deserves a special niche . . . for his devotion to the new and everlasting covenant. With him polygamy was a lifelong conviction. He always asserted that when he was a boy of nine years before he had ever heard of Joseph Smith or the Mormons, God had revealed to him in a vision the principle of plural marriage. Merrill clearly acted upon this belief from that to his death in 1907; he had seven wives, forty-five children, and one hundred and twenty-seven grandchildren.[35]

Hendrick expounded that Merrill paid not "the slightest attention to the manifesto" but "regarded it as his highest duty to ignore it. In March 1891 . . . Merrill himself performed the marriage which united his son Charles E. Merrill in polygamous marriage to Chloe Hendricks," and he "showed his contempt of the manifesto by taking a new plural wife himself."[36]

It is noteworthy that several men performing and abetting polygamous colonies in Mexico were involved, directly or indirectly, in Wyoming's Big Horn settlements. On-the-ground leaders—Jesse Wentworth Crosby Jr., George Henry Crosby, and Haskell Shurtliff Jolley—were also known adherents, and two were post-Manifesto violators. As noted, even Byron Sessions joined the post-Manifesto ranks with his plural marriage in 1903 to Janet Easton. Relatives of Owen Woodruff in the Clark family were also lawbreaking participants, keeping the principle alive in the hinterland.

Historian Kenneth Cannon II noted that not only did plural marriages persist, but the "eleven General Authorities guilty of unlawful co-habitation in the years 1890–1905 had a total of twenty-seven wives bearing . . . seventy-six children," illustrating "a high disregard for the illegal co-habitation clauses of the anti-bigamy acts by a majority of those who made up the highest echelons of church hierarchy."[37]

Owen Woodruff's death marked a turning point, as church leadership ceased their centralized control over colonization. The strongest colonization supporter was gone, and this coincided with the breakup of his fellow apostles who were committed to continuing plural marriage. Marriner Merrill's death followed in 1906. John W. Taylor was disgraced by excommunication and died from stomach cancer in 1916. Repentant Matthias F. Cowley's fall was somewhat less severe than Taylor's.[38] Had their lives not been derailed by sacrificial actions, two lived long enough to have been candidates, by priesthood status and their fervent beliefs, to become key figures in potentially growing polygamy within the Big Horn colony, just as Apostle Moses Thatcher had been in Star Valley until his death in 1909.[39]

The Big Horn Basin colonization scheme not only featured the efforts of four LDS apostles obsessed with advancing polygamy, it also serves as an unusually clear early-twentieth-century example of a Mormon syndicate operating at the intersection of religious conformity, polygamy, nepotism, kinship, corporate business ventures, and high priesthood status. As historian Kathleen Flake wrote, "plural marriage . . . comprised another layer of patriarchy" and "was designed to monopolize power (and resources) by creating dynastic alliances among Mormonism's ruling class."[40] Within this admixture, LDS church leaders could almost be assured of financial success through interconnected laissez-faire capitalism.

Save for the overt practice of polygamy, all these readily identified variables continue to be operative within the present-day LDS church's vast multibillion-dollar empire of commercial, real estate, and retail complexes; for-profit enterprises; and diverse stock and investment holdings. Historian D. Michael Quinn notes that the LDS church is "an organization that earns billions in annual revenue." It "has long maintained that it operates without paid clergy, which is true at the local level. However, for those at the top who are called general authorities, there is an annual living allowance that in 2014, according to available documents, amounted to $120,000 each." General authorities serve "as directors and board members of church-owned and church-affiliated businesses, giving them additional personal income over what they receive directly from the church."[41] Their positions may also provide access to insider investment information.

In late 2019 the *Washington Post* announced that the LDS church had amassed about $100 billion in accounts intended for charitable purposes. David A. Nielsen, a Mormon and former investment manager at Ensign Peak Advisors, submitted a whistleblower report to the Internal Revenue Service on November 21. He accused the LDS church of stockpiling their financial donations instead of using them for charitable works. Nielsen said the Ensign firm created on behalf of the church a system of more than a dozen shell companies to make its stock investments harder to track. According to the complaint, the LDS church collects about $7 billion each year in tithing.[42] Historian John Turner reports: "If the numbers are accurate, Ensign is the nation's largest charitable endowment, with as much money as Harvard University and the Bill and Melinda Gates Foundation have at their disposal, combined, if not more."[43] The Nielsen report also alleges that Ensign Peak Advisors diverted $1.4 billion in tithing funds to pay for the development of LDS church–owned City Creek Center. This city-center enterprise—directly across the street from the church's downtown mecca Temple Square—includes a large upscale shopping mall and houses many retail businesses. The whistleblower's allegations were quickly answered in the church-owned *Deseret News:*

> We take seriously the responsibility to care for the tithes and donations received from members. The vast majority of these funds are used immediately to meet the needs of the growing church including more meetinghouses, temples, education, humanitarian work and missionary efforts throughout the world. Over many years, a portion is methodically safeguarded through wise financial management and the building of a prudent reserve for the future. This is a sound doctrinal and financial principle taught by the Savior in the Parable of the Talents and lived by the church and its members. All church funds exist for no other reason than to support the church's divinely appointed mission.[44]

A follow-up financial report in the *Salt Lake Tribune* describes an additional $37.8 billion that Ensign invested for the LDS church. Among the traded stocks include Apple, $1.68 billion; Microsoft, $1.5 billion; Google, $930 million; Amazon, $856 million; Johnson and Johnson, $646 million; Intel, $604 million; and Facebook, $538 million, according to this report.[45] Regardless of whether "all church funds exist for no other reason than to support the church's divinely appointed mission," or allegations of tax fraud are true, or whether tithing money has been diverted, the *Washington Post, Salt Lake Tribune*, and Turner articles provide ample evidence of the immensity and complexity of the LDS church's obscure financial empire.

CHAPTER 12

A Platform for Polygamy's Survival

No year will ever pass ... in this country [Mexico] ... or wherever, from
now until the coming of the Savior, when children will not be born in
plural marriage.[1]

—Abraham Owen Woodruff

PRESIDENT WILFORD WOODRUFF'S promised abandonment of polygamy
in his 1890 Manifesto was issued only after a series of punitive federal laws
had passed against plural marriage: the 1862 Morrill Act, the 1874 Poland
Act, the 1882 Edmunds Act, and the financially penalizing 1887 Edmunds-
Tucker Act. After the Manifesto was published, the nationwide public
protests against Mormons diminished for a time; however, polygamy was
neither a dead issue with the LDS church nor with the American people.

Almost immediately, questions about the Manifesto's meaning surfaced
inside and outside the church. Would the cessation of plural marriage apply
only to those in the United States? Was it allowed if performed outside
the nation's boundaries; or if the ceremony was performed while sailing on
international water; or riding in a closed carriage; or sitting on a moving
train in Oregon?

As early as 1874–1875, colonies had been established in Mexico specifically to avoid detection and punishment for Latter-day Saints who participated in plural marriage.[2] After the Edmunds Act passage, public pressure
increased, resulting in the church moving even more polygamous "sealings"
to Mexico and Canada, outside US federal jurisdiction.

In a secret meeting in June 1885, Apostle John Henry Smith, himself a
polygamist, recorded a gathering of LDS church President John Taylor with
other leaders. At midnight in George Q. Cannon's farmhouse, they decided
they "would form a colony in Old Mexico by unanimous vote ... that delega-
tions should go to the city of Mexico and also to our brethren on [Arizona's]

Casa Grande River." Outside, several men stood guard, on the lookout for spies. The men did not adjourn the meeting until well after midnight.[3]

John Taylor was involved in a far more significant move to maintain polygamy about fifteen months later. On September 26–27, 1886, another secret meeting, this one accompanied by "otherworldly events," took place at the home of John Wickersham Woolley in Centerville, Utah. Taylor was in hiding there—fearing arrest by US marshals. According to materials furnished by historian Michael Quinn, "the [long-deceased] Prophet Joseph Smith stood by, directing the proceedings." It was witnessed by Charles H. Barrell, Daniel R. Bateman, Hiram B. Clawson, George Earl, Leonard John Nuttall, and Lorin Woolley's mother and sister. Taylor "allegedly ordained Samuel Bateman, the First Presidency's First Counselor George Q. Cannon, Charles Henry Wilcken, John W. Woolley, and Lorin [Woolley] as 'high priest apostles,' . . . commissioning them to keep plural marriage alive, even if the LDS Church gave it up." Wilcken and John Woolley were "introduced to him [Joseph Smith] and shook hands with him."[4] The next year, "upon the return of the First Presidency's Second Counselor, Joseph F. Smith, from Hawaii to Utah in 1887, he was likewise ordained and commissioned" him, but "without the presence of a *resurrected* personage."[5]

President Taylor recorded a handwritten account of the revelation and had his secretary, Leonard John Nuttall, make copies for John and Lorin Woolley, Charles Wilcken, Samuel Bateman, and George Q. Cannon. Taylor then laid his hands on each man's head and gave them the authority to perform marriages and to call others, when needed, to ensure the work of plural marriage would continue. Lorin Woolley named the seven men (including Taylor) who had been given this secret responsibility the Council of Friends. Taylor put the "men under covenant to ensure that no year passed without children being born in the covenant of plural marriage, and said they were to accomplish their missions apart from the LDS Church if necessary, as it appeared the church would go 'monogamous.'"[6]

According to historians Craig Foster and Marianne Watson, Lorin C. Woolley filed a signed affidavit with the Church Historian Office in 1912 with a brief account describing the 1886 revelation at the home of John Taylor's father.[7] In 1929 Lorin C. Woolley formed a group called the "Council of Seven," claiming they held the true priesthood authority that had existed in secret in Nauvoo.[8] The other six Woolley named were John Yeates Barlow, Joseph Leslie Broadbent, Charles Zitting, Joseph White Musser, LeGrand Woolley, and Louis Alma Kelsch. They held that the mainstream LDS church had lost its authority to receive revelation from God by discontinuing plural marriage.[9]

To their deaths, all remained ardent fundamentalists, and several were excommunicated from the LDS church. President Heber J. Grant issued stern warnings denouncing their teachings and practices in 1925, 1926, and 1931. The 1886 revelation was never accepted by LDS leadership, and in June 1933 the First Presidency denied the revelation. An "Official Statement" was published in the *Deseret News*, warning members not to be misled by the corrupt, adulterous practices of this secret oathbound organization, the Council of Seven.[10]

In May 1890 the Edmunds-Tucker Act's constitutionality was upheld by the US Supreme Court. In the thirty-seven days from September 24, 1890—the day the Manifesto was issued—to November 1, the First Presidency authorized seven members to go to Mexico for plural marriage ceremonies. Two were authorized there each year in 1891, 1892, and 1893. By 1894 one marriage occurred in Canada, six in Mexico, and two in Utah temples, with a similar pattern in 1895 and 1896.

In June 1897, the First Presidency authorized the Juarez stake president, monogamist Anthony W. Ivins, to perform plural marriage ceremonies in Mexico. During 1898 mounting pressure from church membership by polygamy supplicants resulted in even more permissiveness in Mexico. While critics were told that plural marriages in Mexico had ceased in 1899, it is clear that this was not the case. Leaders merely "turned a blind eye to those still occurring in Utah and Idaho."[11] Although the data is likely incomplete, it appears that Ivins performed almost as many plural marriages as Matthias F. Cowley (see Table 12). Most by Ivins were after 1899 and almost certainly in Mexico, although only two are documented (see Table 11).

LDS church President Lorenzo Snow spoke to the St. George congregation on May 8, 1899, assuring them, "I will say now before this people, that the principle of plural marriage is not practiced. I have never, in one single instance, allowed any person to have that ceremony performed, and there are no such marriages at the present time, nor has there been during the time of my presidency over this church.... No man or woman can ever say that any such thing as this has been done."[12] However, in the 237 days between September 13, 1898, to May 8, 1899, when Snow made this declaration, at least seven polygamist marriages were performed and at least one by Apostle Cowley.[13]

In the latter part of 1899, more than seven million Americans signed a petition directing the US House of Representatives to deny Utah's B. H. Roberts his elected seat. Roberts was the stepson of John W. Woolley.[14] Roberts was widely known in Utah as having two wives, with one

Table 12. Post-Manifesto plural marriages by Anthony W. Ivins, by date performed[a]

Husband	Wife	Date of marriage	Place of marriage
Byron Harvey Allred Sr.	Mary Eliza Tracy	November 21, 1890	
Bryant Stringham Jr.	Sabrina Smith	June 22, 1897	
Walter William Steed	Alice Belle Clark	June 22, 1897	
Samuel Frederick Ball	Margaret Brown	September 16, 1897	
Arthur Riley	Sarah Lydia Davis	September 16, 1897	
William D. Hendricks	Eleanor A. Maybine	December 3, 1897	
Joseph Askie Silver	Elizabeth Farnes	January 24, 1898	
Joseph Henry Dean	Amanda W. Petterson	May 10, 1898	
Haskell S. Jolley	Ellen E. Harrison	June 1, 1898	
Helaman Pratt	Bertha C. Wilcken	July 14, 1898	
James Hood	Jamina J. Russell	August 10, 1898	
William Cole Ockey	Ovena Jorgensen	September 14, 1898[b]	
Miles Archibald Romney	Lilly Burrell	October 23, 1898	
Heber Manassah Cluff	Susan Caroline Sims	October 30, 1898	
Winslow Farr Jr.	Sarah Mitchell	January 10, 1899	
George Conrad Nagle	Maggie Romney	July 23, 1899	
Charles Frederick Gardner	Sarah Ellen Cox	March 9, 1902	
Guy Carlton Wilson	Agnes M. Stevens	March 13, 1902	
Walter Beers Lewis	Esther D. Wilson	May 17, 1902	
Willard Call	Leah Pratt	August 18, 1902	Colonia Juarez, Mexico
Orson Pratt Brown	Eliza Skousen	September 7, 1902	
Samuel Walter Jarvis	Pearley Taylor	October 28, 1902	
Henry Eyring Bowman	Wilhelmina Walser	November 27, 1902	

Table 12 (*continued*). Post-Manifesto plural marriages by Anthony W. Ivins, by date performed[a]

Husband	Wife	Date of marriage	Place of marriage
James Franklin Carroll	Annie Eliza Burrell	January 19, 1903	Colonia Juarez, Mexico
John Jacob Walser II	Elizabeth Braithwaite	January 19, 1903	
Jens Christian Breinholt	Margarethe L. Hansen	January 20, 1903	
Edward William Payne	Rosalia Tenny	March 1, 1903	
Daniel Brooks Jones	Rhoda Ann Merrill	March 10, 1903	
Guy Carlton Wilson	Anna Lowrie Ivins	May 13, 1903	
Abraham Done	Ellen P. Moffett	June 5, 1903	
William Albert Morton	Josephine Erickson	June 13, 1903	
Byron Harvey Allred Jr.	Mary Evelyn Clark	July 15, 1903	
Warren Longhurst	Eva Allred	July 15, 1903	
Benjamin B. Brown	Mary Vilate Hansen	August 26, 1903	
Arthur Benjamin Clark	Ethel A. Shirley	September 29, 1903	
Edward Christian Eyring	Emma Romney	November 3, 1903	
Jorgen S. Jorgensen	Johanna L. Iborg	November 25, 1903	
John Askie Silver	Nell Young Clawson	January 31, 1904	
Frederick W. Jones Jr.	Laura Ann Moffett	March 1, 1904	
James Thompson	Bertha J. Nielsen	March 3, 1904	
Brigham Horace Pierce	Sarah Ellen Harris	March 11, 1904	
Charles Edmund Richardson	Daisie Stout	March 13, 1904	
Heber Erastus Farr	Rangmilda Bluth	March 25, 1904	

[a]In June 1897, the First Presidency authorized Juarez Stake President Anthony W. Ivins to perform polygamous ceremonies in Mexico.

[b]Ivins performed only five marriages during Lorenzo Snow's presidency, from September 13, 1888, to October 10, 1901.

marriage, to Margaret Shipp in 1894, performed post-Manifesto. Roberts also refused to cease cohabiting with his wives.[15] This evoked President Lorenzo Snow to publish in the *Deseret News* on January 8, 1900, a signed letter on polygamist marriages and cohabitation. Again, he falsely claimed—as President Woodruff had done ten years earlier—that "the church has positively abandoned the practice of polygamy, or the solemnization of plural marriages, in this and every other state.... Nor does the church advise or encourage unlawful cohabitation on the part of any of its members."[16]

This statement could be called the 1900 Snow Manifesto. The declaration repeated an earlier warning that should "any member disobey the [civil] law either as to polygamy or cohabitation he must bear his own burden; or, in other words, be answerable to the [governmental] tribunals for his own action pertaining hereto."[17] Note that cohabitation was not declared abandoned by doctrine or that any change in quotidian marital practices had been advised or ordered. At least four disingenuous denials were made by three LDS church presidents: in 1890 by Woodruff, in 1900 by Snow, and in 1904 and 1906 by Joseph F. Smith.

Despite these words from Presidents Woodruff and Snow, Apostle Matthias Cowley gave his own message to the LDS people gathered at the Uintah Stake conference on August 12, 1900: "The law of plural marriage is God-given and as eternal as any ever given by the Father, and they who disbelieve it or seek to hide behind the government restrictions of the manifesto or are afraid to advocate its principles *are not Latter Day Saints*."[18] Apostle Owen Woodruff had earned a churchwide reputation before 1901 as a polygamy supporter. Byron H. Allred, with the family of that name later known as fundamentalists, wrote to Woodruff from Chihuahua, Mexico. Allred was concerned that his twenty-year-old daughter, Alta, was not yet married, and that she had selected Owen to marry, for "of all she has seen you are her choice."[19]

Up until 1904, the apostles John W. Taylor, Matthias Cowley, and Owen Woodruff passionately insisted that polygamy was still a divine, unchangeable commandment, not to be delayed, and to be obeyed in action. Their beliefs were reinforced by recurring referrals and permissions given unofficially by high-ranking LDS leaders to conduct such marriages. Up to his death in 1901, George Q. Cannon, first counselor to Wilford Woodruff, was considered chiefly responsible. In Cowley's trial, Cowley stated, "President Cannon told me he had the authority from President Woodruff and Brother Joseph F. Smith told me on two occasions that Brother Cannon had the authority and Brother Woodruff didn't want to be known in it."[20]

Of note is that Cannon's son Frank J. Cannon insisted that Joseph F. Smith was the responsible leader issuing marriage permissions throughout this period, not his father.[21]

After George Cannon's death, Joseph F. Smith was indeed likely responsible, for he performed the plural marriage of Lillian Hamlin on June 17, 1896, in the Salt Lake Temple to the deceased David Hoagland Cannon, with Abraham H. Cannon as proxy.[22] During their honeymoon in California, Abraham acquired an ear infection that proved fatal, but in the six weeks after his marriage and before his untimely death, he fathered a child.[23] To this post-Manifesto marriage—performed by the church's highest leader—a child was born nine months later, proving it was beyond mere paper proxy of marriage for deceased David Hoagland Cannon. A daughter, named Marba—Abram spelled backwards—was born to Lillian in Pennsylvania on March 22, 1897.[24] Later that year Lillian was in Lake Oswego, New York. She returned to Utah, and during a period beginning in June 1898 Lillian held a position at Brigham Young Academy.[25] However, by June 1900 Lillian and her four-year-old daughter were living 150 miles from Salt Lake City, in Castle Dale, boarding with Kathinka Anderson, a Norwegian woman and her five children.[26] Lillian Hamlin Cannon was married to bishop Lewis Mousley Cannon in 1902, and their child, Matthew, was born in Mexico in 1903.[27]

After 1895, some plural marriage referrals, like those to the three apostles, were sent to Anthony W. Ivins in Mexico. Victor Jorgensen and Carmon Hardy set out the details: "Woodruff said he would have nothing to do with the matter but referred them to George Q. Cannon. Cannon then gave the couple a letter addressed to Anthony W. Ivins who, when contacted, was said to have performed the marriage" (See Table 3). In some cases a form letter was used, which "would appraise Ivins that they had previously obtained consent."[28]

Historian Martha Bradley lists two Wyoming "asylums" for polygamists: Afton, Star Valley, in Lincoln County, by 1885; and Lovell, in Big Horn County, by 1900–1901. Also an asylum was Lyman, in Uintah County, Utah, date not specified. Two sites are listed for Idaho: Franklin in 1860 and Rexburg in 1883; one site in Oregon—Summerville—in 1892.[29] While Mormon faithful had attempted settlement in Star Valley as early as 1879, historian Dan Erickson clarifies 1885 as when this western slope of the Rockies became a haven for polygamists fleeing federal legislation and law enforcement. Bradley explains that "even though bounty hunters pursued polygamists into Wyoming... the risk was minimal compared to the danger in Utah and Idaho."[30]

Owen Woodruff and Matthias Cowley deserve the label of fundamentalists, as they, along with John W. Taylor, were foremost among the ardent proponents of contemporary polygamy as essential rites within what they considered unchangeable Mormon doctrine.[31] Cowley refused to accept the Manifesto as the word of God; had Latter-day Saints only persisted, he believed, God would have brought them victory. In a Logan Tabernacle meeting in January 1901, Cowley explained what he believed about John Taylor's unpublished revelation:

> None of the revelations of the prophets either past or present have been repealed. . . . I wish to remind you of a certain revelation given you through President Taylor. The command was given to set our quorums and houses in order, and the promise was that if we should obey the command God would fight our battles for us; but we did not obey the command, so God did not fight our battles for us. If we had obeyed that command given through President Taylor there would have been no manifesto."[32]

In a Twelve Apostles meeting that preceded the April 1904 spring conference, Owen Woodruff spoke in opposition to the prospect of President Joseph F. Smith making a statement against plural marriage in the upcoming meeting. Nonetheless, others were in favor, including church attorney Franklin S. Richards. In Smith's second Manifesto he stated, I "do hereby affirm and declare that no such marriages have been entered into, contrary to the official declaration that plural marriages have been solemnized with the sanction, consent, or knowledge of the Church of Jesus Christ of Latter-day Saints." He added that "if any officer or member of the church shall assume to solemnize or enter into any such marriage he will be deemed in transgression against the church, and will be liable to be dealt with according to the rules and regulations thereof and excommunication therefrom."[33]

Notably missing from the Manifesto was mention of marriages performed outside US jurisdiction, nor cohabitation, nor did it recognize the penalties of fines and imprisonment already existing under federal law. Also not addressed was what the Senate was investigating: why had Utah's theocratic government that controlled all things political and civil not officially ended illegal marriages or acted against cohabitation? Smith's reluctance to speak against cohabiting is understandable, given that his wives gave birth to eleven children after the Manifesto was published. Yet no action had been taken against him by any legal authority in Utah.

This changed in November 1906 when a citizen, Charles Mostyn Owen, brought a charge of polygamy against Smith based on the birth of a son— Royal Grant Young—to Smith's wife Mary Taylor Swartz on May 21, 1906, in Salt Lake City. The complaint was altered to a charge of "un-lawful cohabitation," and in District Court Judge Ritchie could have imposed a maximum sentence of both jail time and a fine. He chose a reduced sentence of no jail but with the maximum fine of $300, which Smith paid immediately.[34] In concluding the court session Smith briefly said, "I have appreciated the magnanimity of the American people in not enforcing a policy that in their minds was unnecessarily harsh. . . . When I accepted the manifesto, issued by President Wilford Woodruff, I did not understand that I would be expected to abandon and discard my wives. . . . I have conscientiously tried to discharge the responsibilities attending them, without being offensive to anyone. I have never flaunted my family relations before the public, nor have I felt a spirit of defiance against the law."[35]

In violation of his father's widely publicized 1890 Manifesto, Owen Woodruff married a second wife, Eliza Avery Clark, a Utah-born daughter of a Mormon bishop, Hyrum Don Carlos Clark. Eliza was a recent graduate of Logan's Agricultural College of Utah. At the time Owen was

Table 13. Children born after the 1890 Manifesto by the wives of Joseph F. Smith[a]

Child number	Date of birth	Child's name	Wife's name	Wife's age at child's birth[b]
1	8-25-1891	Jeanetta	Sarah Ellen Richards	41
2	10-26-1892	Samuel Swartz	Mary Taylor Swartz	27
3	1-6-1893	Andrew Kimball	Alice Kimball	35
4	12-21-1893	Ruth	Edna Lambson	42
5	1-3-1894	Edith Eleanor	Julina Lambson	45
6	11-13-1894	James Swartz	Mary Taylor Swartz	29
7	12-28-1896	Asenath	Sarah Ellen Richards	46
8	5-12-1897	Martha	Edna Lambson	46
9	1-3-1900	Silas Swartz	Mary Taylor Swartz	34
10	4-9-1900	Fielding Kimball	Alice Kimball	42
11	5-21-1906	Royal Grant	Mary Taylor Swartz	41
N/A	12-7-1906	Marjorie Virginia (adopted)	Julia Lambson	N/A

[a]Joseph F. Smith's first marriage was to his cousin, Levira Smith, in 1859. This ended in divorce and no children were born.
[b]In seven of the eleven pregnancies, the mother was in her fourth decade at the time of birth. Scientific evidence shows that pregnancies for women beyond age thirty-five are considered high risk, with an increased chance of miscarriage, fetal abnormality such as Down's Syndrome, and abnormal chromosome defects.

engaged overseeing the Big Horn Colonization project. The marriage was performed by Owen's boyhood friend and fellow apostle, Matthias Cowley, in Preston, Idaho, in January 1901.[36]

In May 1903, Star Valley resident Wiley Nebeker wrote Apostle John Henry Smith, reporting the rumor that there were men in the church, some called as apostles, continuing polygamy. He identified Cowley, and he might have also referred to Woodruff, as among those specifically chosen to continue the principle in secret.[37]

Eliza Avery Clark's autobiography relates the conversation in which Owen Woodruff approached her father to ask his opinion of her marriage to him. Hyrum Don Carlos Clark was initially shocked. Clark related that Owen "pointed out how several of the brethren in high positions had been advised to take plural wives."[38] Carlos Ashby Badger, a Utah lawyer who assisted Reed Smoot in his federal investigation, entered into his diary a 1904 note that Alonzo Blair Irvine—who had married Rosannah Jenne Cannon in 1898—claimed that Owen Woodruff had told him "certain worthy individuals were being chosen to continue the principle."[39]

Arthur William Hart, a Preston lawyer whose second post-Manifesto, post-statehood plural marriage was performed by Cowley in Salt Lake City in 1903, claimed that Apostle Cowley "told him he [Cowley] was instructed to choose a 'few select people' to carry on the work [of polygamy]."[40] Preston, Idaho—only about thirty miles from Logan, Utah—was a favored location for Cowley, for he performed at least eight marriages there from 1898 to 1903 (See Tables 1A and 1B).[41]

Coming into the Big Horn Basin from Wayne County, Utah, Joseph Eckersley had become well acquainted with David Patten Woodruff from his time with the Midland Mail Company and his service as Big Horn County's assessor. Eckersley was made second counselor in a stake presidency in 1903 when Matthias Cowley said to him that "'it was not the policy of Pres[iden]t. Joseph F. Smith to censure any man for entertaining the order of plural marriage since the days of the Manifesto, provided he act wisely and does so with the sanction and by the authority of the proper authority.'" In meetings of the Twelve Apostles and First Presidency, as late as "September and October, 1903 . . . John W. Taylor and Marriner W. Merrill were still urging that some plural marriages ought to be solemnized to keep the institution alive."[42] As late as 1903, Woodruff performed three plural marriages, probably in Mexico (See Tables 1A and 1B).

Woodruff and Cowley were well-known principal LDS authority figures in the 1900–1901 Big Horn Basin colonization. Both also participated in the Logan Knitting Factory, along with other high-ranking Mormon officers Joseph Merrill, Melvin J. Ballard, and Joseph E. Cardon.[43] Apostle Ballard was also interested in the Mexican colonies for many years, and he was enigmatically described as their "chief sponsor" up to 1938, when Mormon colonists there still looked to him "for advice in matters spiritual as well as material."[44]

Another instance of high-ranking polygamists advancing business interests was the founding of a sugar factory in Lewiston, Idaho, in midsummer 1903. Polygamists Owen Woodruff, Joseph F. Smith, Marriner Merrill, and George Chandler Parkinson joined polygamists Charles Wilson Nibley, William Hendricks Lewis Jr., and monogamist Anthon H. Lund at the principals meeting in Logan; $200,000 was raised in capital stock.[45] According to a report in the *Deseret News*, "The company has obtained an option on about 1,700 acres of land in Lewiston and will probably purchase this acreage and more."[46]

In November 1902 Reed Smoot was elected by Utah's state legislature as state senator. Smoot was handsome, educated, wealthy, well connected, and politically astute. He had been ordained an apostle two years earlier and was to represent Utah's predominantly Mormon population in Washington. Smoot was not a polygamist and was said to have lived an unblemished life. He had been given the personal approval to run for political office from the theocracy's topmost officer, President Joseph F. Smith. Smoot's arrival in Washington, DC in February 1903 ignited a firestorm of criticism and vehement opposition due to mounting evidence that LDS church members and leadership had neither abandoned plural marriages nor ceased living in marital union with multiple wives. The Senate hearing's chair made it clear that Smoot was not on trial, but the object "was to investigate the Mormon Church."[47]

Within a year the senate was investigating many aspects of Mormon declarations about polygamy along with venues wherein the alleged law of God was given precedent over federal law. This included secret temple oaths to destroy the United States government for being against the Lord's reestablished church and for shedding the blood of its prophets, Joseph and Hyrum Smith.[48] On February 24, 1904, a Senate subpoena arrived in Salt Lake City that ordered President Smith and seven apostles to appear for testimony. Included were three men active in the Big Horn Basin colonization: John W. Taylor, Matthias Cowley, and Marriner W. Merrill.[49] On the same date, Anthon H. Lund wrote in a semicode to Owen Woodruff in Byron warning of a subpoena intended for him, and urging that he flee:

This afternoon we had a surprise sprung upon us. F. M. Lyman and John Henry Smith were summoned to go to Washington, we hear of fifteen more that are to be summoned; of these six are apostles making eight in all, and President Smith. Whether my fellow sufferer among the fleas at Frankfort is among the number is uncertain, but we are told he can easily get a free trip to the Capital! I know he is too busy to indulge in this pleasure, and I wish him a pleasant journey. Tell him this is urgent.[50]

Owen Woodruff almost certainly would have been served a subpoena had he not gone secretly to Mexico, where he planned to then travel to Germany to avoid federal authorities. Fearing their mail would be opened by US marshals, Owen and his wives used code names for people and places to obscure their plans.[51]

While they were in Mexico, Owen's first and legal wife, Helen May Winters Woodruff, contracted a virulent case of smallpox from which she died on June 7. Word of her death traveled to Liverpool, where the three-wife apostle Heber J. Grant had traveled to avoid congressional subpoenas.[52] Helen's death was especially troubling for Grant's second wife, Hulda Augusta "Gusta" Winters, who was Helen's older sister. Grant wrote to Owen, "when you married Helen ... it was a day of rejoicing and ... we felt to thank the Lord." Grant added a note that "not one single act of your life since your marriage to Helen has decreased my love or respect for you."[53]

Within days of Helen's death, Owen was also stricken. He succumbed on June 20, 1904, in El Paso, Texas, where he had been moved in the faint hope of receiving better medical care. Some sources indicate that Owen and Helen Woodruff had earlier been vaccinated for smallpox, but they declined the advice of revaccination by Anthony Ivins and Joseph F. Smith.[54] There is evidence that Helen had acquired some immunity to smallpox from an earlier mild case. While Owen and Helen were in Burlington on August 10, 1901, Owen recorded, "We drove to Byron and stopped at the house of Pres[iden]t. Sessions. The day was hot and the journey tiresome. Helen was taken very ill with fever and every symptom of Smallpox. Pres[iden]t. Byron Sessions and I administered to her and she was healed."[55]

The family's decision against vaccination might have been more complicated than merely a cavalier dismissal of science, instead trusting in God for protection. At the time, vaccination for smallpox was a complicated issue, subject to impassioned public disagreement, especially among Salt Lake City residents. Intense debate and discussion involving officials of the

Education Board and Health Board, Mayor Ezra Thompson, and the city council took place regarding its effectiveness and safety as well as compulsory participation. While many local doctors favored prophylaxis, even to the point of mandatory vaccination of all school children, other doctors, church officials such as Brigham Young Jr., and various citizens were outspoken in opposition. Immunization coverage in the media competed with the extensive coverage of B. H. Roberts's seating in congress and the Boer and Spanish-American Wars. Yet at least twenty-eight lengthy articles appeared in the *Deseret News* in January 1900 issues, arguing the points of vaccination effectiveness, safety, forced compulsion, and who held jurisdiction for approval. Schools were closed for twelve thousand students for several weeks, and the issue was finally sent to the state's supreme court.[56]

Moving frequently to avoid capture by US marshals and bounty hunters, Matthias Cowley did not respond until June 28, eight days following the death of Owen Woodruff. Cowley poured out his sorrow and loss in a letter from Sterling, Canada, about thirty-nine miles north of the Montana border:

> I have lost, so far as the present life is concerned, the very best friend I had among the Twelve. We were born to the Apostleship the same day and have enjoyed unbounded love and confidence in each other ever since. He has done more to endear his name and memory in the hearts of the Saints than most of us would be able to do in twenty-five years and yet he has done it all in the less than 7 years since our call came. How the Saints of the Big Horn Basin will miss him.[57]

Having been vaccinated against smallpox in 1901, Eliza Avery Clark Woodruff moved to Mexico in the fall of 1903 with little smallpox risk. She lived in the home of Anthony W. Ivins and taught at the Juarez Stake Academy during her pregnancy.[58] A daughter was born to her and her late husband Owen Woodruff in April 1904. Eliza had cared for both Owen and Helen through their final illness, while also caring for their combined family's four children, including her two-month-old daughter, Ruth Clark. Following the death of Owen and Helen, Eliza Avery remained in the Woodruff home in Colonia Juarez until May 1905 and rented rooms to a Dr. and Mrs. Farr.[59]

Owen and Helen's four children lived for several years with their grandmother Emma Smith Woodruff in Salt Lake City. The youngest, Rhoda, unexpectedly died at age three. At Emma's death, Heber J. Grant and his wife Augusta, Helen's sister, adopted the children, where they remained until adulthood.

In an apostle's meeting on January 11, 1899, only eighteen months after his first marriage, Owen Woodruff expressed concern that he had not yet had children born to him, and then he "expressed great delight with the promise of the Lord through Pres[iden]t. Richards to Bro. Grant yesterday that he shall live to have sons."[60] While Owen did have one son, Wilford Owen Woodruff, born October 31, 1899, Wilford Owen had a "contentious existence" as a child and adult that raised considerable anxiety for Heber and Augusta. They had cared for him and his sisters for years. While Wilford served a mission and married a wife in the temple, he felt very compelled to enter plural marriage. He was later excommunicated, and his first wife, Evelyn Ballif, divorced him. Wilford was later rebaptized and remained with his second wife, Anna LaRetta Hansen, who bore seven children.

Historians Lu Ann Taylor Synder and Phillip A. Synder assert that Wilford Owen almost completely abandoned his first family of five.[61] In Grant's diary for October 27, 1940, he recorded that Wilford Owen had said, "My father had two wives and I am going to have two. My grandfather had five." Grant added, "It alarmed me very much. I think Owen's head hasn't worked just right ever since the serious automobile accident he had." In multiple diary entries through the 1930s and 1940s, Grant expressed concern that Wilford Owen was publishing a paper "almost Communistic in nature," and that Wilford's "mind is affected . . . on account of the terrible auto accident he had some time ago." Grant also wrote of Wilford that "some of his friends feel that his mind has gone wrong and that he ought to be sent to the asylum instead of being cut off the Church. I hope and pray they are right."[62] Wilford Owen Woodruff died in Las Vegas, Nevada, in 1986 at age eighty-six and was buried in the Salt Lake City Cemetery.[63]

Marriner W. Merrill, at age seventy-two, received several subpoenas to testify at the Smoot hearings, but Merrill declined, truthfully citing health issues that prevented his appearance in Washington. This left Taylor and Cowley as the most promising witnesses for the prosecution. However, both traveled, separately, around the western states in secrecy to avoid subpoenas; furthermore, they refused to testify. President Joseph F. Smith's statement was entered into the Smoot hearing records that Smith "had communicated to Messrs. John W. Taylor and Cowley my earnest desire that they should appear and testify before the committee, and am in receipt of letters from them stating, in substance, that they are unwilling, voluntarily, to testify. . . . As this is a political matter, and not a religious duty devolving upon them or me, I am powerless to exert more than moral suasion in the premises."[64] Had Smith honestly admitted that his considerable authority could readily require their compliance, it would have provided prima facie evidence for critics that the LDS church leaders did, in fact, "exercise secular power in all matters."[65]

In late April the Smoot hearings were suspended due to fall elections. Cowley and Taylor remained absent. From the remainder of 1904 to the time hearings resumed in 1905, many senators became increasingly irritated over Cowley and Taylor's recalcitrance to appear or testify. Smith was vigorously queried regarding his failure to discipline them, for senators firmly believed Smith held authority in all areas—religious and civil. Smith was forced to admit that during the entire forty-three years that polygamy had been illegal by federal law, not a single LDS church member had been disciplined, even while Smith singularly held the power to do so both civilly and ecclesiastically. Smith's dilemma was that Taylor and Cowley could claim they had only followed church doctrine and had not lost their apostolic appointment. Most Twelve members agreed. Senator Smoot wrote that he would "rather be expelled from the Senate, go home and resign from the Quorum, than have it said ... that Taylor or Cowley was sacrificed or resigned to save me."[66]

Yet historian Michael Quinn records a different story regarding Smoot's position: "In 1904, Apostle Smoot advised the First Presidency to have post-Manifesto plural wives hide in order to avoid being arrested. Then from 1905 onward, Reed Smoot pressured President Joseph F. Smith to excommunicate all post-Manifesto polygamists, no matter who performed or authorized their marriages." Smoot "failed at this but succeeded in getting John W. Taylor and Matthias F. Cowley released, by threatening himself to resign from the Apostleship, if they were not released."[67]

In a letter to Owen Woodruff in late January 1904 Smoot wrote:

I am not worrying about the investigation of myself, the only thing that is troubling me is the inclination of many, and the determination of some, to go into a never-ending investigation of the Mormon Church, and charge me with being responsible for the sayings of every man, and the actions of every member of the Church.... Nothing will be left undone to stop this unfair procedure, and I sincerely hope and pray that we will be able to do so. Give my love to your mother and Helen and all of the brethren, and may success ever attend you is the wish of your brother.[68]

While Smoot awaited word of action against Taylor and Cowley, Smith spent several months in 1904 "seeking alternatives to dropping" them from apostleship, then additional months "trying to convince the quorum that there was no alternative."[69] It was a given that Smith's most fundamental obligation was to defend the church at all costs. Thus, Cowley and Taylor reluctantly signed letters of resignation on October 28, 1905. Both were told that the resignations would not be acted upon "unless matters came to the last ditch of necessity."[70] Nonetheless, both were sacrificed and released from the Quorum of Twelve, though they retained their church membership, which was announced at the April 1906 general conference. Being "out of harmony" with the church was the simplified public explanation.[71] However, unrelenting pressure was placed on Smith to do more to convince not only the church's enemies but its own membership of their leadership's earnestness in ending plural marriage.

Throughout the Smoot hearings, Anthony W. Ivins remained in Mexico. Despite having performed as many or more illegal plural marriages than Cowley, Ivins was not called for testimony, and he declined President Smith's request to appear and perjure himself before the committee. Polygamist marriages by Ivins in Mexico had the leadership's approval, but unlike Taylor and Cowley, Ivins received no public criticism for performing them.[72]

In 1900 Joseph F. Smith authorized Alexander F. MacDonald to perform plural marriages in Mexico without informing President Lorenzo Snow, and in 1901 Snow—without this knowledge—threatened to excommunicate MacDonald for performing the marriages.[73] MacDonald officiated at least sixteen marriages in Mexico, but he was not called to testify in the Smoot hearings. George Teasdale, with a large number of wives, had only performed three marriages, yet he was summoned. Teasdale remained in Mexico and did not appear (See Table 3).

Owen Woodruff had been dead for less than a year when Taylor and Cowley were sacrificially removed from the Quorum of Twelve Apostles. Owen very likely would have been deeply troubled had he lived to 1911, when the two were summoned by mail on First Presidency letterhead to appear in Salt Lake City. While the First Presidency consisted of Joseph F. Smith as president, John Henry Smith as first counselor, and Anthon H. Lund as second counselor, none were present at either's excommunication trial. Both Taylor and Cowley requested that they be allowed five minutes to talk—face to face—with Smith, but this was denied. Indirect testimony from Joseph F. Smith—the alleged source of many verbal permissions for plural marriages and who seemingly subscribed to John Taylor's September 1886 revelation—does not appear in trial records.

Taylor and Cowley were unanimously excommunicated from the LDS church by the Council of Twelve Apostles, under the solitary signature of

Francis M. Lyman.[74] Quinn points out that in January 1905, Lyman had gone
to Canada to persuade John W. Taylor to testify before the senate. Taylor
reluctantly agreed, though he added, "I will tell the truth. I warn you, I'm
going to tell the truth."[75] That night, Lyman had a dream of a disaster that
would result from Taylor truthfully testifying in Washington, DC. The next
morning as Taylor was en route to the railroad, Lyman rode his horse and
buggy quickly through the snow and intercepted Taylor, telling him not
to go.[76]

Trial records of both excommunications in 1911 were not publicly
available until 1976, when they were published anonymously by the Mormon
Underground Press. The record noted that John W. Taylor was summoned
to appear before the Twelve on February 22, 1911. He was charged with
marrying a plural wife, that "she was his typewriter [sic]," and "the girl had
a baby," and he had married the mother. Taylor (and Cowley) were named
as giving others authorization to perform marriages in Canada. In his complicated response, Taylor objected to being asked about his personal family
matters and emphasized that "I accept as true *all the revelations received
by the Prophets* of the Lord on this subject."[77] He then read a revelation
recorded by his father, John Taylor, while church president, dated September 27, 1886, noting that it had never been presented publicly.[78] It said:

You have asked me concerning the new and everlasting covenant and
how far is it binding upon my people.

Thus sayeth the Lord. All commandments that I have given must
be obeyed by those calling themselves by my name, unless they are
revoked by me, or by my authority, and how can I revoke an everlasting covenant? For I, the Lord, am everlasting and my everlasting
covenant cannot be abrogated nor done away with, but they stand
forever. Have I not given my word in great plainness on this subject?
Yet have not great numbers of my people been negligent in the obser-
vance of my law and the keeping of my commandments? and yet I
have borne with them these many years, and this because of their
weakness because of the perilous times.

And furthermore, it is now pleasing to me that men should use
their free agency in regard to these matters, nevertheless I, the Lord
do not change, and my word and my law, and my covenants do not.
And as I have heretofore said by my servant Joseph: All those who
would enter into my glory must and shall obey my law and have I
not commanded men, that if they were Abraham's seed and would

enter into my glory they must do the works of Abraham? I have
not revoked this law, nor will I, for it is everlasting and those who
will enter into my glory must obey the conditions thereof. Even
so Amen.[79]

Asked how extensively this revelation had been circulated, Taylor answered
that copies had gone to [Colonia Juarez Bishop] Joseph Robinson, to Cowley from Rodney Badger, and to President Joseph F. Smith, who claimed he
placed a copy in the Church Historian's office.[80]

A photograph of a revelation—purported to be the same revelation in
John Taylor's handwriting—appears in Briney's *Apostles on Trial*.[81] Quinn
cites Mormon Apostle Melvin J. Ballard as authenticating the handwriting
as "undoubtedly" that of John Taylor. Also confirming the handwriting was
Reed C. Durham Jr., the LDS Coordinator of Seminaries and Institutes.
Speaking to a group of Mormon high priests on February 24, 1974, in Salt
Lake City's Foothill Stake, Durham said, "We've analyzed the handwriting.
It is John Taylor's handwriting."[82] It read:

Sept. 27 1886
My son John. you have asked me concerning the new & everlasti[n]g
covenant [and] how far it is binding upon my people. Thus saiath
[*sic*] the Lord all commandments that I give must be obeyed by those,
calling themselves by my name unless they are revoked by my [*sic*]
or by my authority, and how can I revoke an everlasting covenant;
for I the Lord am everlasting & my everlasting covenants cannot
be abrogated nor done away with; but they stand for ever. Have I
not given my word in great plainness on this subject? Yet have not
great members [numbers] of my people been negligent in the obser-
vance of my law & the keeping of my commandment and yet have I
borne with them these many years & this because of their weakness
because of the perilous times & furthermore, it is more pleasing to
me that men should use their free agency in regard to these matters. Nevertheless I the Lord do not change & my word & my covenants & my law do not. & as I have heretofore said by my servant
Joseph ale [all] those who would enter into my glory must & shall
obey my law & have I not commanded men that if they were Abraham's seed & would enter into my glory, they must do the works of
Abraham. I have not revoked this law nor will I for it is everlasty

[*sic*] & those who will enter into my glory must obey the conditions thereof, even so amen.[83]

During his trial, Taylor said, "I have never married any one without the endorsement and authority of the President of the Church."[84] This statement covers the tenures of Presidents Wilford Woodruff, Lorenzo Snow, and Joseph F. Smith.

John W. Taylor was excommunicated for his 1909 marriage, for relying on his father's purported revelations that had never been presented to the church body or published by its leadership, for cursing Apostle George Albert Smith, and for his lack of penitent spirit.[85]

The John Taylor revelation of September 27, 1886, was neither formally presented to the Quorum of Twelve Apostles for acceptance by the church, nor has it been officially published. On July 15, 1933, the First Presidency accepted custody of the 1886 original text, but they denied its authenticity. Photocopies have been unofficially published, and it was from one of these that Ballard affirmed Taylor's handwriting. John W. Taylor had discussed the revelation in meetings of the Twelve Apostles on October 2, 1889; September 30, 1890; and February 22, 1911—only twenty-nine days before his excommunication.[86]

Cowley's trial was about twelve weeks after Taylor's, on May 10, 1911. Present was George Albert Smith, who had not appeared for John W. Taylor's trial. Heber J. Grant, who was a jurist in the first day of Taylor's trial, was absent on Cowley's second day. Grant also did not appear in the session when Cowley was accused of being "at the forefront and . . . the cause of more people entering into this condition of plural marriage than anyone else."[87]

A letter had been sent to Cowley in May 1904, emphasizing the public message against plural marriage given by President Joseph F. Smith in April that year. Cowley answered repeatedly that most marriages he had performed had been before 1904; that most had been with implied consent of George Q. Cannon after clearance from Presidents Woodruff or Smith; and that he thought the 1904 Manifesto did not apply to foreign countries.[88] Joseph F. Smith privately, secretly, and through others gave permission to Cowley and Taylor to perform plural marriages, yet his silence tacitly berated their actions. It appears that Taylor and Cowley were profoundly disappointed that Smith refused to meet them vis à vis, as they pleaded for him to do.

Cowley admitted that he believed that President Wilford Woodruff had married a plural wife a very short time before he died. Cowley's last comment was penitent:

If there is anything I can do to make good our honor to the nation
and to the saints I am willing to do it. I want you to know that I am
not rebellious and never have been and if I have erred it has been
because of the circumstances and the example of my brethren. I am
in harmony with you and I would like you to put me upon my honor
to make that good in the future. I would rather die than be cut off
from the Church.[89]

While Carmon Hardy records that only two among the jury wished to see
punishment inflicted, the verdict was identical to Taylor's: a unanimous vote
for excommunication.[90]

While Cowley and Taylor received a monthly salary during Joseph F.
Smith's presidency, it was discontinued by Heber J. Grant at his appointment.[91] Both men struggled to support their large families. Cowley reported
spending "about $7,000 supporting his sons and others in the mission
field" while working at "the County Assessor's Office, selling church books,
life insurance, real estate."[92] Samuel W. Taylor reported that he rode his
bicycle to deposit his father's monthly church check at the Farmers and
Merchants Bank.[93]

Both Cowley and Taylor continued to exercise some aspect of their
lost priesthood authority, for they remained in high regard and popular as
church speakers. Sadly, Taylor died at age fifty-eight from gastric carcinoma
at the Salt Lake City home of his wife, Nellie. Of note—but uncertain of
fact or meaning—President Joseph F. Smith reportedly went privately to
the home on the evening of Taylor's death, giving Nellie the needed LDS
temple robes for his burial.[94] In August 1916, rumor circulated that Taylor
was posthumously baptized by proxy and reinstated into the church by two
different stake presidents. However, this was followed by a sharp statement
from the First Presidency and senior member of the Twelve:

> It is a matter of public knowledge that the late John W. Taylor, once
> a member of the Council of Twelve Apostles, was excommunicated
> from the Church of Jesus Christ of Latter-day Saints by the solemn
> and official action of the Council. Notwithstanding all the reports to
> the contrary, we hereby certify that the excommunication has never
> been revoked, rescinded, nor in any way modified, and that the said
> John W. Taylor has not been restored to membership in the Church
> of Jesus Christ of Latter-day Saints. [Signed]

Joseph F. Smith, Anthon H. Lund, Charles W. Penrose, First Presidency. Heber J. Grant, In behalf of the Council of the Twelve, Salt Lake City, Utah, August 25, 1917.[95]

John W. Taylor's descendants, particularly Raymond Woolley Taylor, worked fifty-four years for Taylor's reinstatement. With the aid of Hugh B. Brown, first counselor in the First Presidency, this finally occurred on May 21, 1965, under the hand of Joseph Fielding Smith, then president of the Quorum of Twelve Apostles.[96] It was not until 1993, twenty-eight years later, that the act was reported in the LDS church Almanac.[97] Cowley's readmission was more prompt. He was restored to full membership in 1936, nearly four years before his death.[98] In October 1938, Cowley had recently returned from missionary service for the church in Great Britain and was invited to be the featured speaker in the Salt Lake Tabernacle. His text was announced as "The Gospel."[99]

Whether Owen Woodruff was aware of his father's secret 1897 marriage to Lydia Mary von Finkelstein Mountford remains a question.[100] However, it was known to Cowley and almost certainly known to Marriner Merrill and John W. Taylor. All four may have considered Wilford Woodruff's final marriage a thinly disguised coded message that contributed significantly to their unyielding support of continuing plural marriage.

The actions in 1911 against Cowley and Taylor did not mark the end of plural marriage, nor the attempts by LDS leadership to punish those who continued it. Living in Kaysville, Utah, in 1913, John Wickersham Woolley was called as a church patriarch, "a trusted position of honor and spiritual importance." Yet less than a year later, he was "'honorably released' from his stake's high council," and by January 1914 "the 82-year-old was under scrutiny by LDS headquarters for recently performing polygamous marriages."[101] Visited by two Quorum of Twelve members, Woolley signed an affidavit naming four men for whom he had performed plural marriages, believing he had authority from President Joseph F. Smith through Matthias F. Cowley.[102] On April 1, 1914, the *Salt Lake Tribune* carried an announcement of "Excommunication of John W. Woolley," according to an "official notice in the *Deseret News* yesterday evening." It read: "By unanimous vote of the council of twelve apostles, John W. Woolley was excommunicated from the Church of Jesus Christ of Latter-day Saints for insubordination to the discipline and government of the church. Signed by Francis W. Lyman in the church's behalf. Salt Lake City, March 30, 1914."[103] Lyman had also signed the excommunication notices for Cowley and Taylor.

Was a future site for disguised polygamy the secret motivation behind the highest of LDS leaders to call hundreds to leave more mature counties and situations to start over in the Big Horn Basin's frontier? The personal, historical records by Charles Welch, Mark N. Partridge, and Melvin M. Fillerup give no hint or suspicion that Owen Woodruff shared such a secret charge. The widespread economic deterioration in 1890s United States included the LDS church as well as Utah with its diminishing water-available land and relative overpopulation. Regardless of plural marriage, these were undeniable motivators for church authorities to continue issuing calls for colonization. Whether this last colonization by Latter-day Saints to the isolated area of Wyoming is another expression of an adamantine refusal to abandon plural marriage remains a conundrum.

It was 1935 when the attorney Hugh B. Brown wrote a law for Utah's legislature that unlawful cohabitation was no longer a misdemeanor, but a felony. Eighty-five years later, in February 2020 a bill was introduced by Republican Senator Deidre Henderson of Spanish Fork to remove polygamy from Utah law as an illegal act. Rather than deterring or eliminating polygamy, the state's threats of harsh punishments had "driven polygamous communities underground; cut families off from jobs, education and health care; and given rise to a subculture that gives predators free rein to prey upon vulnerable people," according to Henderson. Lawmakers were asked to support a bill to reclassify bigamy and codify the Utah attorney general's office to not prosecute otherwise law-abiding polygamists, among consenting adults.

Senate Bill 102 passed the Senate and House unanimously. Under Utah law, polygamy remains a crime but as a minor infraction, which may be lower in severity than some traffic tickets. Polygamy may remain a felony if in connection to criminal homicide, kidnapping, trafficking, smuggling, sexual offenses, child abuse or abandonment, neglect or exploitation of a vulnerable adult, or sexual battery. Another lawmaker said in "the twin polygamist communities of Hildale [Utah], and Colorado City [Arizona], progress has been made there to reopen public schools and legitimize local law enforcement, but more needs to be done."[104] In November 2020, Deidre Henderson was elected as Utah's Lieutenant Governor.

Abraham Owen Woodruff's promise by prophecy—that "no year will ever pass, from now until the coming of the Savior, when children will not be born in plural marriage"—remains unbroken, both by mainstream Latter-day Saints and by several fundamentalist offshoots.

Chronology

ABRAHAM OWEN WOODRUFF (AOW) AND WYOMING'S COLONIZATION TIMELINE

From at least 1807

| | Mountain ranges circumscribing the Big Horn Basin are explored by many fur-trading mountain men. |

1871

| | First Euro-American—non-Indigenous—settlement in Big Horn Basin by John DwightWoodruff. |

1882

| | The Edmunds Act, an antipolygamy bill directed at LDS church, is enacted by Congress. |
| October 13 | Revelation concerning polygamy as an unchanged doctrine is alleged by President John Taylor. As with a very similar revelation in 1886, it was not officially published by the LDS church. |

1884

| March | First LDS colonizing efforts in northern Mexico, with some investigation of New Mexico and Arizona. |
| | John Henry Smith—a two-wife polygamist also sealed to three women and nineteen children—visits Mexico on |

LDS church business to oversee the Mexican Colonization and Agricultural Company's affairs.

1886

September
26–27

LDS Church President John Taylor claims a revelation
emphasizing that plural marriage, like all other commandments, is everlasting and cannot be undone. Taylor
ordains Samuel Bateman as first counselor in First Presidency and George Q. Cannon, Charles H. Wilcken, John
Wickersham Woolley, and Lorin Calvin Woolley as "high
priest apostles" and members of a "Council of Friends"
commissioned to keep plural marriage alive even if the
LDS church gives it up. They purport to experience the
presence of long-dead Joseph Smith Jr.

1887

Federal officials through the Edmunds-Tucker Act seize
money, financial assets, and property of the LDS church.

US marshals search communities across Utah and southern Idaho in search of "cohabs"—polygamists cohabiting
with plural wives.

July 18

President John Taylor ordains Joseph F. Smith to the
same appointment as the Council of Friends to sustain
plural marriage.

1890

May

US Supreme Court upholds Edmunds-Tucker Act's
constitutionality.

July 3

Idaho granted statehood, with a population of 88,548.

July 10

Wyoming granted statehood, with a population of 62,555.

October 6

With the Cullom Bill nearing passage in the US Senate,
Wilford Woodruff issues "Official Declaration" or Manifesto renouncing plural marriage.

1892

May	David Patten Woodruff, William Henry Packard, Henry Griffin, and James Shaffer make exploratory trip into Big Horn Basin, Wyoming.

1893

Spring	D. P. Woodruff and Packard, with 300 Mormons, migrate and form settlement at Burlington, Wyoming.
	Nationwide economic depression encompasses entire United States.

1894

	Massive influx of California's unemployed men overwhelms Salt Lake City and Ogden, Utah.
August 18	Carey Act passage, allowing private companies to erect irrigation systems in arid western states and profit from the sale of water.

1896

	Colonization Committee of LDS church organized with appointment of AOW and John Henry Smith.
January 4	Utah granted statehood, population approximately 276,000, after assurances from LDS leaders of relinquishing polygamy.

1897

February 5	President Wilford Woodruff meets Lydia Mary Finkelstein Mountford.
June	US President William McKinley appoints Charles Kingston as Register in the US Land Office in Evanston, Wyoming.
	LDS Church President Lorenzo Snow appoints Charles Kingston on a special mission as railroad travel agent to

look after needs of Mormons along the Union Pacific's line.

June 30   AOW is married to first wife Helen May Winters by his father, President Woodruff, in the Salt Lake Temple. Four children are born in Salt Lake City to this union: Wilford Owen Woodruff (1899–1986) Helen Woodruff Anderson (1901–1990) June Woodruff Stewart (1902–1995) Rhoda W. Woodruff (1903–1907).

September 25–26   President Wilford Woodruff secretly marries Lydia Mary Finkelstein Mountford, a married woman, as a plural wife.

October 7   AOW ordained an apostle by his father. He is only twenty-four years old.

1898

May 8   Lorenzo Snow categorically denies plural marriages taking place.

September 2   President Wilford Woodruff dies at age ninety-one.

September 13   Lorenzo Snow ordained as LDS church president.

LDS church debt estimated at $2 million ($366 million in 2010 dollars).

1899

July 6   Big Horn Basin colonization discussed by Twelve Apostles, and AOW is authorized to begin efforts.

July 30   AOW and Charles Kingston visit Burlington, Wyoming, and organize it as a ward of Woodruff Stake.

November 8   AOW sustained as Colonization Agent for LDS church.

November 26   AOW performs marriage of Lucy Alice Farr to Edward William Payne in Colonia Juarez, Mexico.

December 29   AOW reports to the First Presidency that at Colonia Oaxaca, Mexico, he sealed couples unable to afford to travel to nearest temple.

1900

January 8	LDS Church President Lorenzo Snow issues letter (the Snow Manifesto) to church members proclaiming the church had abandoned polygamy and warning that living in unlawful cohabitation would endanger them in civil law.
January 11	AOW and Charles Kingston file a canal application with the Wyoming State Board of Land Commissioners.
January 13 or 18	AOW secretly marries a second wife, Eliza Avery Clark, performed by Matthias Cowley in Preston, Idaho. Eliza's tentative engagement to Fred Dixon of Star Valley, Wyoming, was broken when he was approached by AOW or his agents.
February	Under LDS church sponsorship, thirteen men brave a severe winter storm to investigate the Shoshone River valley for colonization.
February 5	Wyoming's governor, secretary of state, supreme court judge, and former Utah Governor George W. Emery meet with President Lorenzo Snow.
March 9	William F. Cody and partner Nate Salsbury sign relinquishment papers for the Shoshone River's waters, formerly the Cincinnati Canal, and the 21,000 acres to be irrigated.
April 9	Big Horn Colonization Company capitalized for $100,000.
April 24	AOW meets colonists at Ham's Fork in Wyoming and organizes eight companies for trek to Big Horn Basin area.
May 20	First company of colonists arrive at destination on the Stinking Water River, soon renamed the Shoshone River.
May 28	Mormons break ground for creation of Sidon Canal.
June 7	Eliza Avery Clark and younger sister, Mary Minerva, attend Agricultural College of Utah in Logan.

| October 15 | Work begun on $80,000 contract with Chicago, Burlington and Quincy (CBQ) Railroad to grade and lay twenty-seven miles of track. |
| November 1 | Eliza Avery Clark receives endowments in Logan Temple. |

1901

April 12	George Q. Cannon dies in Monterey, California, after an extended period of failing health.
May and June	John Henry Smith travels to Mexico and with Anthony Ivins meets Mexican President Porfirio Diaz regarding Mormon colonies in Mexico.
August 22	Grading for CBQ railroad contract completed. Payment about $10,000 above $80,000 contract, aiding Latter-day Saints and saving the colonization project.
October 10	Lorenzo Snow dies; Joseph F. Smith ordained LDS church president on October 17.
November 11	Burlington and Missouri's first Toluca–Cody line train arrives in Cody, with William F. Cody as most famous passenger.
Winter	Winter 1901–1902 is severe "even for that country."

1902

May 5	AOW and Helen May Winters Woodruff start for Mexico City.
June 23	Water carried by Sidon Canal reaches townsite of Cowley.
August	Eliza Avery Clark Woodruff has miscarriage in Colonia Juarez.
Winter	Eighteen log houses are built in Big Horn Basin colonization area.

1903

| July | AOW visits Big Horn Basin. |

August 13	Byron Sessions married to Janet Easton by Apostle Matthias Cowley.
September 17	AOW writes letter to Wyoming Congressman Frank Mondell asking help in procuring additional water rights and land for Big Horn Basin colonists.
November 11	AOW performs plural marriage of Louis Paul Cardon to Mary Irene Platt.

1904

January 1	Owen Woodruff mails long petition to Utah Senator Thomas Kearns asking for aid in securing additional water rights and land to be irrigated on the Shoshone River's south side, slightly upstream from established Mormon colonies.
February 24	Anthon H. Lund writes Owen Woodruff of pending Washington subpoenas and cautions him to flee.
	AOW and family stopover in Mexico on trip to Europe to avoid subpoena from US Senate's Smoot Committee.
April	Sidon Canal completed over thirty-seven miles and water reaches end of line.
	Second Manifesto denying continued polygamy issued by President Joseph F. Smith.
April 11	Ruth Clark Woodruff, child of Eliza Avery and AOW, is born in Colonia Juarez, Mexico.
June 7	Helen May Winters Woodruff dies of virulent smallpox in Colonia Juarez, Mexico.
June 20	After days of illness at bedside of his stricken wife, AOW dies of smallpox in El Paso, Texas. Both may have disregarded advice of LDS church and health officials to be (re)vaccinated.
July 7	Charles W. Penrose appointed to fill AOW's post in Council of Twelve Apostles.

1905

February– March	John Henry Smith visits lands of Utah Mexican Rubber Company in Mexico.
October 28	Matthias F. Cowley and John W. Taylor removed as apostles.

1906

April	Cowley's and Taylor's apostleship removal for being "out of harmony" with the church is announced at General Conference in Salt Lake City.
May 21	Birth of Royal Grant Smith, the final post-Manifesto child born to President Joseph F. Smith and his fifth wife, Mary Taylor Swartz Smith.
November	President Joseph F. Smith is convicted on reduced charge of cohabitation and fined $300 in Utah's District Court following Royal Grant's birth.

1907

January	Joseph F. Smith announces the LDS church free of debt caused by the Edmunds-Tucker Act.

1909

June 15	*The Cowley Weekly Progress's* first newspaper issued.
September 16	Matthias Cowley married to fourth wife, Lenora Taylor.
November	Big Horn Basin's judicial era of "Judge Lynch" ends with legal conviction of five cattlemen for the murders of three sheepmen. Jury composed of several Mormons, including jury foreman William Henry Packard.

1910

September	Big Horn Academy, the area's first high school, is opened in Cowley.
	President Joseph F. Smith performs civil marriage in the Salt Lake Temple for John Wickersham Woolley.

October	First Presidency order adopted in fall conference for stake presidents to investigate and excommunicate officiators and husbands of post-1904 plural marriages.
	Patriarch Judson Tolman excommunicated for not relinquishing plural marriage, despite being commissioned by Joseph F. Smith to perform such marriages from 1906 to 1910.

1911

March 28	John Whittaker Taylor excommunicated from LDS church by unanimous vote.
May 11	Matthias Foss Cowley excommunicated from LDS church by unanimous vote.

1914

March	Apostle and Patriarch John Wickersham Woolley excommunicated from LDS church for performing polygamous marriages.

1916

September 1	Eliza Avery Clark Woodruff marries George Cannon Lambert.
October 10	John Whittaker Taylor dies from stomach cancer at Salt Lake City home of second wife, Nellie Eva Todd.

1928

	Lorin C. Woolley forms Council of Seven, claiming mainstream LDS church lost authority to receive revelation by discontinuing plural marriages.

1935

	Utah Legislature elevates crime of unlawful cohabitation from a misdemeanor to a felony.

1936

| March or April | Matthias F. Cowley reinstated to LDS church membership. |

1940

| June 16 | Death of Matthias F. Cowley in Salt Lake City. |

1965

| May 21 | Quiet reinstatement of John W. Taylor to LDS church membership performed in President Joseph Fielding Smith Jr.'s office. Not until 1993, twenty-eight years later, is act reported in LDS church almanac. |

1993

| July 17 | Earthly remains of AOW and wife Helen May Winters Woodruff exhumed and reburied in Salt Lake City Cemetery. |

2019

| December 17 | Investment manager for LDS firm becomes a whistle-blower, revealing LDS church has amassed $138 billion and uses massive funds for profit rather than charitable purposes. LDS church spokesperson denies misuse of funds. |

2020

| February | Utah Legislature's SB102 unanimously passes in both houses to reduce polygamy from felony to misdemeanor, with punishment lower in severity than some traffic tickets. |

Notes

PREFACE

1. Fillerup, *Sidon, The Canal that Faith Built*, 55–59.
2. Welch, *History of the Big Horn Basin*, 142–43.
3. Traxel, *1898, The Birth of the American Century*, xi–xiii.
4. Smart, *Last Colonizer*, 4.
5. Ibid., 120.
6. Journal of Abraham Owen Woodruff, February 11, 1901, p. 27, book 1, fd. 1. Francis Marion Lyman had three wives: Rhoda Ann Taylor, Clara Caroline Callister, and Susan Delilah Callister.
7. Journal of Abraham Owen Woodruff, January 6, 1901, p. 3 book 1, fd. 1. See also Smart, *Last Colonizer*, 112, 132–33.
8. John E. Jones, secretary to Senator Kearns, to Owen Woodruff, April 23, 1901, typescript; box 4, fd. 17, A. O. Woodruff papers.
9. Ibid., April 30, 1901. In 1904 Herrman was charged with participating in an Oregon land fraud scandal. He was tried but not convicted.
10. Smart, *Last Colonizer*, 54.
11. Merrill became an apostle on October 7, 1889.
12. By early 1903 the US Supreme Court ruled that Congress could abrogate all existing Indian treaties; in June the land was opened for allotment regardless of consequences for its Indigenous peoples. *Lone Wolf v. Hitchcock*, January 1902; MacKay, "Opening of the Uintah Indian Reservation," 68–89.
13. Report of James McLaughlin from a meeting with the Utes in 1905, cited in "Indian-White Relations and the Opening of the Reservation: 1905," O'Neil and Sylvester, eds., *Ute People: An Historical Study*, 49.
14. Smart, *Last Colonizer*, 157.
15. The multiple noncoincidental interconnections among these men is also noteworthy. After Rudger Clawson converted Joseph White Musser to enter polygamy, it was Matthias F. Cowley who married Musser to Mary Caroline Hill on March 13, 1902. Musser became a three-wife post-Manifesto

polygamist when he married Ellis R. Shipp on July 24, 1907. Hardy, *Solemn Covenant*, Appendix. Musser was later called the "father of the Mormon fundamentalist movement" and associated with Lorin C. Woolley and others in their preservation of polygamy. Foster and Watson, *American Polygamy*, 66.

16. Italics in original.

17. Smart, *Last Colonizer*, 164. At this time Smoot was the subject of an intense US Senate investigation of polygamy and LDS leadership control of both civil and ecclesiastical matters in Utah (see chapter 10).

18. "To Colonize the Uintah Reserve, Hierarch Wants the Earth," *Salt Lake Tribune*, July 2, 1905.

19. Smart, *Last Colonizer*, 170–71.

20. This little-published tragedy was first treated by historian Floyd O'Neil in "An Anguished Odyssey," 315. See chapter 11.

21. Ibid., 52.

22. Ibid., 316.

INTRODUCTION

1. Campbell, *Establishing Zion*, 59. Sailing from San Francisco, the Honolulu-bound missionaries arrived December 12, 1850. Prominent among this first Sandwich Island contingent was George Q. Cannon, who would later become highly involved with plural marriages through participation, verbal approval, and indirect support. For his own polygamy he was arrested, jumped bail, and on recapture served time in Utah's territorial prison.

2. Sherlock, "Mormon Migration and Settlement After 1875," 53–54.

3. Ibid.

4. Ibid.

5. Arrington, "Utah and the Depression of the 1890s," 3–18. The author acknowledges the recent request that "The Church of Jesus Christ of Latter-day Saints" is preferred over "LDS church," "Mormons," and "Mormon church," but economy of space and concern for reader fatigue led the author to commonly use the shorter terms.

6. Sherlock, "Mormon Migration and Settlement After 1875," 53–54.

7. Peterson, "The Americanization of Utah's Agriculture," 109, 111, 116.

8. One sample of this concept comes from Lorenzo Snow's couplet of June 1840: "As man is, God once was; as God is, man may become."

9. This analogy overlooks the South's immense financial investment in the ownership of millions of human bodies as profit-producing property. It is noteworthy that most Mormon polygamous men, while doctrinally directed to follow polygamy, benefited directly from their wives' labors. By doctrine, women were inferior to men; beyond denial is that some were treated little better than property.

10. As noted in the preface, another group comprised predominantly of Mormons colonized in the Uinta Basin in 1905, after the 1900–1901 Big Horn

Basin colony, but it lacked the church president's official blessings and sponsorship.

11. Welch, *History of the Big Horn Basin*, 64.

12. John Henry Smith was president and Anthony W. Ivins was vice president and general manager. George Teasdale to David McKenzie, April 30, 1904, box 1, fd. 21, George Teasdale Papers. Those arriving in Canada in 1887 later formed the Northwest Coal and Navigation Company. Lee, "The Mormons Come to Canada," 18.

13. J. C. Bentley to John M. Cannon, September 7, 1907, box 1, fd. 22, Teasdale Papers. For extensive documentation of business ventures by general authorities before 1933 in Mexico, Canada, and elsewhere, see Quinn, *Mormon Hierarchy: Wealth and Corporate Power*, Appendix 5, 177–446.

14. Mormon settlements and colonization in Canada were originally met with public outcry, primarily for their practice of polygamy. This later ameliorated, first at the government level, then more broadly as the Mormon settlers brought financial benefits of irrigation and agriculture. The St. Mary's River irrigation canal led to the founding of the towns of Stirling, Magrath, and Raymond. Lee, "The Mormons Come to Canada," 11–17, 22.

15. Late in the development of the Cardston enterprise, John W. Taylor called several Mormon families to boost the mission colonists. About five hundred souls arrived in the months following. Ibid.

16. An apostle within the Latter-day Saints priesthood organization is an honored position. Chosen by the church president, it is a lifetime appointment unless a transgression occurs or the apostle is appointed to the First Presidency. The biblical number of twelve are appointed, and together with the first presidency they constitute the highest ruling body in LDS religious, political, and civil matters. They are usually salaried and can become wealthy through the financial opportunities of their position.

17. It was not until the 1913 Seventeenth Amendment that senators were elected by direct popular vote.

18. The author's great-grandparents John Maxwell and Ellen Russell, as well as his grandparents John Russell Maxwell and Martha Wright, and other extended family were in the 1901 spring colonization. John came to Utah from Scotland in 1854 by way of Glasgow, Liverpool, New Orleans, and an ox team he drove from Westport, Kansas. His fiancée, Ellen Russell, and the remaining Maxwell family followed in 1856 in the Second Handcart Company. They lived first in West Jordan and were called to Summit County in 1861. After nearly forty years of frontier laboring, they left a successful—but not wealthy—farming and sawmill operation along the upper Weber River in Summit County to answer the call to Wyoming. The family of Robert Allen and Ellen Maxwell, John Russell Maxwell's younger sister, together with two Maxwell families and the Gilbert Johnson Marchant family, were the only Summit County Saints in 1900 called to the venture to Wyoming.

19. Sessions's livestock herd was severely depleted by the extraordinarily hard winter of 1888–1889, and this may have influenced his readiness to remove from Cache County. However, his wife, Idella ("Ida"), was blunt when she described their life in Cache County's community of Woodruff: "Here we had all we wanted for six years, then we had to pull up and sell and in 1900 we emigrated to the Big Horn Basin." Sessions collection, MS 15588, LDS Church History Library, Salt Lake City, Utah.

20. John Maxwell, the author's great-grandfather, allegedly attended medical school in Scotland before leaving Glasgow. Although the University of Glasgow's records of medical school attendees reveal several individuals named John Maxwell, the dates of attendance do not match. Proof is lacking that he attended lectures or otherwise studied medicine. Notwithstanding, he worked as a doctor setting broken bones, delivering babies, and extracting teeth, and he was called by the title doctor in his forty years in Summit County, Utah, and in Cowley, Wyoming.

CHAPTER 1. A PRIMER ON LATTER-DAY SAINT POLYGAMY

1. Zina Diantha Huntington Jacobs Smith Young, 1898, cited in Bergera, "Identifying the Earliest Mormon Polygamists," 1.

2. Hardy's 1992 book, *Solemn Covenant*, and Quinn's "LDS Church Authority and New Plural Marriages, 1890–1904," are especially valuable.

3. Hundreds of books have come to print on Mormon polygamist marriages. For byzantine details, see the two-volume set by Newell Bringhurst and Craig Foster, *The Persistence of Polygamy*, 2010 and 2013; the nearly 800-page palmary opus by Todd Compton in 1997; the 2005 work of Gary J. Bergera; the three-volume set by Brian C. Hales and Laura H. Hales, *Joseph Smith's Polygamy*; and George D. Smith's *Nauvoo Polygamy*. There is also Richard Lyman Bushman's 2005 *Joseph Smith: Rough Stone Rolling*. From 1984 are Lawrence Foster's *Religion and Sexuality*, and Linda King Newell and Valeen Tippetts Avery's *Mormon Enigma: Emma Hale Smith*. Other authors whose important works also address LDS polygamy in the post-Nauvoo years include Kenneth L. Cannon II, Richard Van Wagoner, B. Carmon Hardy, and D. Michael Quinn. Laurel Thatcher Ulrich added *A House Full of Females: Plural Marriage and Women's Rights in Early Mormonism, 1835–1870* in 2017.

4. The Edmunds-Tucker Act of 1887 was financially devastating for the LDS church because it mandated the confiscation of church property and assets. Had the 1890 Cullom-Struble Bill passed, it would have resulted in the disfranchisement of *all* church members.

5. Brodie, *No Man Knows My History*, 297. This book has been reprinted and republished in new editions repeatedly.

6. Smith, "Nauvoo Roots of Mormon Polygamy," 138. Quinn, *Mormon Hierarchy: Extensions of Power*, 178.

7. Compton, *In Sacred Loneliness*, 1.
8. Marinda married Orson Hyde in late 1834 in Kirtland. By May 4, 1835, she was pregnant, and Hyde left on missionary assignment to the eastern states. Compton, *Sacred Loneliness*, 231–33. Years later Brigham Young belittled Hyde because of Marinda's liaison with Joseph Smith, and Hyde "on hearing its truth, put away his wife, although they had several children." Brodie, *No Man Knows My History*, 462–63. See also Smith, "Nauvoo Roots," 133.
9. Compton, *Sacred Loneliness*, 238.
10. Ibid., 31–33.
11. Brodie, *No Man Knows My History*, 181. Chauncey G. Webb was the father of Ann Eliza Webb Dee, who became a plural wife of Brigham Young in Salt Lake City. She shortly sought divorce and financial support from Young. In 1875 she wrote a scathing account of her experiences, *Wife No. 19, or The Story of a Life in Bondage.*
12. Compton, *In Sacred Loneliness*, 34–35.
13. Bergera, "The Earliest Mormon Polygamists," 30n75.
14. Bushman, *Joseph Smith: Rough Stone Rolling*, 325.
15. Brodie, *No Man Knows My History*, 460; Van Wagoner, "Sarah Pratt: The Shaping of an Apostate," 70.
16. Compton, *In Sacred Loneliness*, 43.
17. Ibid., 4.
18. Bushman, *Joseph Smith: Rough Stone Rolling*, 403.
19. Smith, *Nauvoo Polygamy*, 552.
20. Brodie, *No Man Knows My History*, 483–84; Compton, *In Sacred Loneliness*, 609.
21. Compton, *In Sacred Loneliness*, 611, 613–14, 616, 619.
22. Bergera, "The Earliest Mormon Polygamists," 1.
23. LeSueur, *The 1838 Mormon War in Missouri*, 117, 125n35, 150, 261. Danites were "a secret armed group organized to intimidate apostates . . . to enforce obedience . . . and to influence state and county elections" as Joseph Smith's secret police force in Missouri and Nauvoo. Bennett, Black, and Cannon, *Nauvoo Legion*, 62, 75. Their meetings' minutes were closed to research for 170 years, until 2016.
24. Turner, *Brigham Young*, 60–62. Boggs's extermination order earned an attempt on his life by Mormon gunman Porter Rockwell.
25. Compton, *In Sacred Loneliness*, 3.
26. Joseph Smith Indictment and Arrest Warrant, MS 3464, LDS Church History Library.
27. Dinger, "Joseph Smith's Indictment for Adultery and Fornication." Dinger explains that Joseph Smith Jr. decided to carry the name Joseph Smith Sr. shortly after the death of his father, who carried this correct name. This complicated the indictment's correctness. See https://rationalfaiths.com/joseph-smiths-indictment-for-adultery-and-fornication/.

28. Whitefield, *Mormon Delusion*, 127–28. Van Wagoner, in *Mormon History*, does not cover Smith's guardianship of the girls' $8,000 estate. Compton treats the estate settlement in more detail but does not specify any gold or its original value. Compton, *In Sacred Loneliness*, 474–75.

29. Brodie, *No Man Knows My History*, 303; Smith, *Nauvoo Polygamy*, 136–37; Bergera, "The Earliest Mormon Polygamists," 2–3.

30. Ulrich, *A House Full of Females*, 132, 423n108.

31. Family Tree of Rebecca Ann Palao Moreno, https://gw.geneanet.org.

32. Rogers, *Unpopular Sovereignty*, 74.

33. Ivins, "Notes on Mormon Polygamy," 311.

34. Hardy, *Solemn Covenant*, 392.

35. Quinn, *The Mormon Hierarchy: Wealth and Corporate Power*, 203.

36. Brodie, *No Man Knows My History*, 188, 294–95.

37. "How They Gobble Up the Land," *Salt Lake Tribune*, May 14, 1871; Maxwell, *Gettysburg*, 135.

38. Compton, *In Sacred Loneliness*, xiv–xv.

39. Yorgason, *Transformation of the Mormon Culture Region*, 37.

40. Compton, personal communication with the author, October 2019.

41. Young, February 4, 1851, *Complete Discourses of Brigham Young*, 1:419.

42. Van Wagoner, *Mormon Polygamy*, 85. This speech was extensively published in the United States and abroad.

43. Cited in Smith, *Nauvoo Polygamy*, 540.

44. Jacob Gates, Jacob Marsden, and John Variah Long, *Report of the London Pastoral Conference of the Church of Jesus Christ of Latter-day Saints*. See also Aird, *Mormon Convert*, 88–90.

45. Smith, *Nauvoo Polygamy*, 540–41. The fall in European membership might have been greater had it not been for the Crimean War; ships needed for it reduced the number of vessels available for emigrating Saints.

46. Maxwell, *Civil War Years*, 57, 171–72, 314, 351.

47. These numbers were personally compiled by the author in 2018 from his extensive search of all the photographic images issues of Camp Floyd's *Valley Tan* and Fort Douglas's *Union Vedette*. See digitalnewspapers.org.

48. From Abraham's union with Hagar "sprang many people," according to Doctrine and Covenants 132:32–34. See also Van Wagoner, *Complete Discourses of Brigham Young* 4:2357.

49. Tanner, *A Mormon Mother*, 1, 56. Under LDS doctrine the Celestial Kingdom is the highest level of reward in heaven. Less valiant Saints earned lesser levels of glory in the Terrestrial or Telestial Kingdoms.

50. For example, note that William Godbe, a polygamist and businessman, was excommunicated for his criticism of Brigham Young's economic policies. Maxwell, *Robert Newton Baskin*, 25, 59, 61, 84, 100–101, 117, 153, 157, 163, 164, 167, 180–81, 189, 193, 207, 210, 211, 222, 223, 228, 249, 252, 254, 256–58, 292–93, 336.

51. Maxwell, *Robert Newton Baskin*, 15, 177, 220n31, 343, 343n6, 344.

52. This was designated as the "Wilderness Revelation." Neilson, *In the Whirl-pool*, 60. See also Baugh, "Wilford Woodruff Chronology," BYU Religious Studies Center, https://rsc.byu.edu/archived/banner-gospel-wilford -woodruff/11-wilford-woodruff-chronology.

53. Cannon and Knapp, *Brigham Young*, 93. For information on the proposed Cullom-Struble Bill, see Lyman, *Political Deliverance*, 124–29; Cannon and Knapp, *Brigham Young*, 85–94; and Bitton, *George Q. Cannon*, 305–7.

54. "Official Declaration," *Deseret News*, October 4, 1890. Woodruff signed the Manifesto on September 24.

55. Journal of Abraham H. Cannon, October 1, 1890, cited in Cannon II, "Beyond the Manifesto," 27.

56. Staker, *Waiting*, 410. The woman's correct full name is Lydia Mary Olive Mamreoff von Finkelstein Mountford. She was the wife of Charles Edward Mountford. Capitals in the original are incorrect.

57. Staker, *Waiting*, 410n4.

58. Anthon H. Lund Diary, December 1, 1897, cited in Quinn, "LDS Church Authority and New Plural Marriages, 1890–1904," 63.

59. Nuttall was far more than a personal secretary; he was also from at least 1880 a Council of Fifty member. Hansen, *Quest for Empire*, 226. President Woodruff included Nuttall in meetings of church apostles. White, *Church, State, and Politics*, 219 (April 3, 1889). *Electronic Edition of the Minutes of the Apostles of The Church of Jesus Christ of Latter-day Saints, 1835–1951* gives evidence of Nuttall's presence and guidance in countless meetings, affairs, and church financial matters. In 1890 he was sent to Washington to assist Congressman John T. Caine over the criticism surrounding the Manifesto. In 1897 Nuttall became "indispensable," helping Woodruff urinate, accompanying him in travel, and handwriting his words. Alexander, *Things in Heaven and Earth*, 258, 308; Quinn, "LDS Church Authority and New Plural Marriages," 64n215.

60. Staker, *Waiting*, 415, 419.

61. Quinn considers the union took place on September 20. "LDS Church Authority and New Plural Marriages," 64.

62. "Personal Mention," *Sacramento Daily Union*, September 11, 1897.

63. Advertisement, "The Clunie," *Sacramento Daily Union*, September 27, 1897.

64. Cowley's statement in "Minutes of the Quorum of the Twelve, May 30, 1911," cited in Quinn, "LDS Church Authority and New Plural Marriages, 1890–1904," 64.

65. *L. John Nuttall, Letterbook, 1895–1903*, 328, Nuttall to Lydia M. F. Mountford, cited in Quinn, "LDS Church Authority and New Plural Marriages, 1890–1904," 64, 64n215.

66. James Jackson Woodruff was Wilford Woodruff's son by wife Mary Ann Jackson. Susa Young Gates was the daughter of Brigham Young and became an editor and well-known lecturer in eastern US cites. She was also the sister of Eudora Lovina Young, who was given by her father to Wilford Woodruff

as his tenth wife in March 1877. Eudora had a son by Wilford who died soon after birth; they were later divorced. Compton, "The Wives of Wilford Woodruff," 6.

67. Staker, *Waiting*, 411.

68. Alexander, *Things in Heaven and Earth*, 328–29.

69. A polygamist himself, Nuttall, for fear of capture, could not approach his own children, whom he had not seen for years, even though he saw them walk past the building where he was sequestered. Not inclined to include personal details in his diary, Nuttall nevertheless kept meticulous records of business dealings, political maneuverings, private correspondence, and leadership decisions. He was a behind-the-scenes observer of the contentious probate settlement of Brigham Young's estate, the Manifesto, and the quest for statehood. Occasionally, he gave voice to anger Mormons felt over non-Mormon influence in Utah. Rogers, *Diaries of L. John Nuttall, 1879–1892.*

70. Compton, "The Wives of Wilford Woodruff," 6; Hardy, *Solemn Covenant*, appendix.

71. Alexander, *Things in Heaven and Earth*, 328–29.

72. Cannon II, "Wives and Other Women," 89; Hardy, *Solemn Covenant*, appendix.

73. Hardy treats the Woodruff-Mountford incident in considerable detail and with extensive documentation. Hardy, *Solemn Covenant*, 227–32.

74. Ibid., 227.

75. "Cordially Welcomed," *American Journal of Education* XXVIII, no. 1 (January 9, 1895).

76. Stanton, et al., eds., *The History of Women's Suffrage*, 6:41.

77. "A Splendid Gift," *Epworth Herald*, Vol. 20, June 12, 1909.

78. Cannon fought vigorously against federal antipolygamy laws, especially against Cullom. He served prison time in 1888 for his plural marriages. Maxwell, *Robert Newton Baskin*, 179–99.

79. *Minutes of the Apostles of the Church of Jesus Christ of Latter-day Saints, 1835–1951*, 2015, Electronic Edition.

80. Ibid.

81. The son of polygamist Joseph Ellis Johnson, Charles Ellis Johnson was born in St. Louis and arrived in Utah in 1860. In Salt Lake City, Johnson worked as a druggist for the ZCMI. In 1889 he partnered with Parley P. Pratt to operate the Johnson-Pratt Drug Company. Johnson made and sold various family patent medicines, including his "Valley Tan Remedies." During the 1890s, he became involved in the American Star Bicycle craze by selling them and becoming vice president of Salt Lake's Social Wheel bicycle club. After dabbling in photography, Johnson joined Hyrum Sainsbury to open a photographic studio. Johnson soon became the Salt Lake Theater's undesignated official photographer. See "Charles Ellis Johnson," wikipedia.org, https://en.wikipedia.org/wiki/Charles_Ellis_Johnson.

82. *Minutes of the Apostles of the Church of Jesus Christ of Latter-day Saints, 1835–1951*, 2015. Electronic Edition.
83. Flake, *Politics of American Religious Identity*, 75–76; Hardy, *Solemn Covenant*, 289–426.
84. Roberts, *Comprehensive History*, 6:401. From age fifty-three to sixty-eight, Joseph F. Smith had sixteen children; two were conceived before and born after the 1890 Manifesto; fourteen children, conceived by him after the Manifesto, were also born.
85. Cannon II, "Wives and Other Women," 101.
86. Quinn, "LDS Church Authority," 9.
87. Hardy, *Solemn Covenant*, appendix II, 389–93. Additional marriages have been added by later research.
88. In 1896, at age eighty-two, Lorenzo Snow, who would become president on the death of Wilford Woodruff, fathered his only post-Manifesto child, Rhea Lucile Snow. She was born to his plural wife Minnie Jensen Snow while she was living in Canada. Cannon II, "Beyond the Manifesto," 31.

CHAPTER 2. IDEALISTS AMONG THE PRAGMATISTS

1. Dale Morgan, from his 1951 review of Samuel Woolley Taylor's *Family Kingdom*, in Saunders, *Dale Morgan on the Mormons*, 259.
2. These four apostles were chosen because of their close associations—interrelationships outlined—and their same geographical loci of work in the Mormon Corridor's northern portions and those outside US jurisdiction. Other church leaders who deserve attention for their persistence in advancing plural marriage include Moses Thatcher, Anthony W. Ivins, George Teasdale, and Alexander Findlay MacDonald Sr.
3. On March 13, 1853, their date of marriage, Woodruff was forty-six and Emma was barely fifteen. Mormon historian Thomas Alexander suggests that Woodruff "probably refrained from sexual relations with Emma until she became older, since she did not deliver her first child until October 4, 1857, seven months after she turned nineteen." Alexander, *Things in Heaven and Earth*, 168.
4. Karl G. Maeser would later teach at the Big Horn Academy in Cowley, Wyoming, after it opened in 1909–1910.
5. Quinn, *Mormon Hierarchy: Wealth and Corporate Power*, 445–46.
6. Jenson, *Latter-Day Saint Biographical Encyclopedia*, 173.
7. Snyder and Snyder, *Post-Manifesto Polygamy*, 9–10.
8. "President Wilford Woodruff, though feeling quite feeble today, went to the Temple and performed the ordinance of marriage between his son Abraham Owen Woodruff and Miss Helen May Winters." Journal History, June 30, 1897, in *Minutes of the Apostles, 1835–1951*.
9. Lindsay, *Bighorn Basin*, 192.
10. Owen would not have been twenty-five until November 27.

11. Cowley to Avery Clark, June 23, 1904, Eliza Avery Clark Woodruff Papers, MS 4021, cited in Erickson, "Star Valley," 154n110.

12. Staker, *Waiting for World's End*, 234. Capitalization in original.

13. Arrington, "Utah and the Depression of the 1890s," 8–10, 12.

14. Woods, *Wyoming's Big Horn Basin to 1901*, 211. See also Fillerup, *Sidon: the Canal that Faith Built*, 8.

15. Elliott makes no mention of Mormons or polygamy in his "Early History of White Pine County, Nevada, 1865–1887."

16. The relationships and roles of five highly important Woodruff men in Wyoming are treated in detail in chapter 5.

17. It is unclear why David Patten Woodruff used Eckersley as an intermediary rather than contacting his father directly. The name Burlington had been chosen to appeal to the railroad of that name.

18. Eckersley's letter might not have reached Woodruff, for he died September 2, 1898.

19. The Melchizedek priesthood office of Seventy has varied widely in LDS history. As envisioned by Joseph Smith in the 1830s, the Seventy were to be composed of several separate quorums of up to seventy individuals; all would be led by seven presidents. The quorums of seventy are directed and supervised hierarchically by the Quorum of Twelve Apostles, who are in turn directed by the First Presidency. At times the Seventy have been classed as general authorities, and at other times they have not.

20. Welch, *History of the Big Horn*, 138–39. McMurrin's father, Joseph William McMurrin Sr., survived three gunshot wounds from a US marshal while acting as a bodyguard to John Taylor. His grandson, Sterling Moss McMurrin, was a renowned professor at the University of Utah, US Commissioner of Education, and discerning student of LDS church history. Madsen, "Sterling M. McMurrin: A Heretic but Not an Apostate," in Sillito and Staker, *Mormon Mavericks*, 285–87.

21. Welch, *History of the Big Horn Basin*, 52. David Patten Woodruff was Wilford Woodruff's son by his fifth wife, Sarah Brown, making Owen and David Patten half brothers. See chapter 5.

22. Welch, *History of the Big Horn Basin*, 48, 52.

23. Entry for January 11, 1899, in *Diaries of Heber J. Grant, 1880–1945*, Abridged, Salt Lake City, 2015. Digital Edition.

24. Ibid., entry for January 6, 1901. Presumably this refers to John Taylor's claimed revelation of September 27, 1886, in which he and others experienced Joseph Smith's resurrected appearance addressing the importance of plural marriage. See chapter 11.

25. *Minutes of the Apostles of The Church of Jesus Christ of Latter-day Saints, 1894–1899* (Salt Lake City: privately published, 2010).

26. Simmons, "Organization of the Big Horn Stake."

27. *Minutes of the Apostles.*

28. Maxwell, *Robert Newton Baskin*, 220n31. Frank J. Cannon, George Q. Cannon's son, completed a four-year term in the US Senate on March 3, 1899. Utah's legislature failed to elect a new candidate, and the seat was vacant from March 4, 1899, to January 23, 1901. George Q. Cannon died after a lengthy illness on April 12, 1901.

29. Ivins Journal, notes, January to May 1903; Eckersley Journal, September 2–6, November 9, 1903; Lund Journal, September 4, 1903; J. H. Smith Journal, October 1, 1903, cited in Alexander, *Mormonism in Transition*, 62–63, 329n9.

30. Jenson, *LDS Biographical Encyclopedia*, 172–74.

31. Willard Done, "In Memoriam," *Improvement Era*, August 1904, 746.

32. Rich, *Elder's Journal of the Southern States Mission*, 40. Cowley performed the post-Manifesto marriage of Rich to Laura Bowring on April 13, 1898, in Preston, Idaho.

33. Cowley's remarkable life is chronicled in a well-written autobiography, which is the primary source for much information, rephrased or quoted, that constitutes this short biography. Cowley, "Family Sketch of the History of Matthias Foss Cowley," n.d., typescript.

34. Cowley, *Wilford Woodruff, Fourth President of the Church of Jesus Christ of Latter-day Saints: History of His Life and Labors, as Recorded in His Daily Journals* (Salt Lake City: Deseret News, 1909).

35. Cowley later gave the figure as $3.00 per week.

36. David Whitmer was one of three witnesses who certified having seen the golden plates from which Joseph Smith allegedly dictated the Book of Mormon. Whitmer later left the LDS church. Doniphan was warmly remembered by Mormons for his refusal to carry out an order to execute Joseph Smith in the 1838 Mormon War in Missouri.

37. Burt and other Salt Lake City police officers were thought to have played a role in the audacious street murder or cover-up of Dr. John King Robinson. Maxwell, *Robert Newton Baskin*, 94–95, 95n49.

38. See Tables 1A and 1B.

39. A revelation given to John Taylor on this date in Salt Lake City, Utah, is listed in Collier, *Unpublished Revelations*, Vol. 1, Pt. 83, 138–40.

40. Briney, *Apostles on Trial*, 109, 111. This revelation appears in Collier, *Unpublished Revelations*, Vol. 1, Pt. 88, 145–46.

41. There was no official president or first presidency following the July 1887 death of John Taylor while in hiding on the polygamy underground. The presidency was reorganized officially on April 7, 1889.

42. In 1916 King sought Utah's Senate seat and was elected on the Democratic ticket.

43. Judge Miner was among those criticized by Utah Bar members as incompetent. "Meeting of the Bar Association," *Deseret News*, January 21, 1902.

44. Cowley, "Family Sketch of the History of Matthias Foss Cowley."

45. Grant's cessation of support did not coincide with the 1911 excommunication.

46. Jenson, *Latter-Day Saint Bibliographic Encyclopedia*, 153.

47. Ibid., 152.

48. Horned, *An Apostle's Record*, 29.

49. Ibid., 158.

50. Janet Marie Wooley Taylor was the niece of polygamy's ardent defender, John Wickersham Wooley; she was given the code name "Mrs. Nettie M. Taylor" while seeking anonymity on the underground when her husband was sought by US marshals and bounty hunters. This marriage was performed during a carriage ride in Salt Lake City's Liberty Park. Taylor, *Taylor-Made Tales*, 195.

51. As noted in the preface, another post-Manifesto polygamist and close friend of Owen Woodruff, William Henry Smart, would be tasked to deal with the LDS church's ecclesiastical and financial problems in this large area within Utah Territory.

52. "Apostle Taylor, His Arrest in Idaho for Alleged 'Inciting Rebellion,'" *Salt Lake Herald Republican*, August 18, 1880.

53. *Edmonton Bulletin*, September 3, 1887, cited in Erickson, "Alberta Polygamists."

54. *Manitoba Daily Free Press*, January 3, 1888, cited in Erickson, "Alberta Polygamists."

55. *McCleod Gazette*, August 14, 1887, cited in Erickson, "Alberta Polygamists."

56. *Lethbridge News*, August 17 and September 21, 1887, cited in Erickson, "Alberta Polygamists."

57. Jenson, *Latter-Day Saint Biographical Encyclopedia*, 155.

58. *Trials for Membership of John W. Taylor and Mathaias [sic] F. Cowley*, 2.

59. Erickson, "Alberta Polygamists?" 158–59, 161, 162, 164n73.

60. Taylor, *Taylor-Made Tales*, vii, 202.

61. Morgan, Review of *Family Kingdom*, in Saunders, *Dale Morgan*, Vol. 1, 258.

62. Taylor, *Family Kingdom*, 119, 139.

63. Saunders, *Dale Morgan*, Vol. 1, 258.

64. Taylor, *Family Kingdom*, viii, 1, 186.

65. Cracroft, "Samuel Woolley Taylor, Maverick Mormon Historian," in Sillito and Staker, *Mormon Mavericks*, 309.

66. Taylor, *Family Kingdom*, x.

67. White, *Church, State, and Politics*, 241.

68. Ibid., 410.

69. Taylor, *Family Kingdom*, 144–45; "Apostle John W. Taylor Makes Startling Charges Against Members of Tabernacle Choir," *Salt Lake Tribune*, October 8, 1898.

70. White, *Church, State, and Politics*, 219.

71. See Table 1A.

72. White, *Church, State, and Politics*, 392.

73. S. W. Taylor reports his mother received $35.00 per month but does not give information relating to other wives. *Taylor-Made Tales*, 188.

74. The junior Crosby married his third wife, Sarah Ann Meeks, post-Manifesto in June 1894, six years before their move to Cowley, Wyoming.
75. White, *Church, State, and Politics*, 239–40.
76. The Mormon Pioneer Overland Travel database cites Atkinson as the captain.
77. Jenson, "Marriner Wood Merrill," *Biographical Encyclopedia*, 158–59.
78. White, *Church, State, and Politics*, 438.
79. Peterson, "Changing Times," 16n34, 21, 346.
80. Ibid., 443.
81. See Table 3.
82. Quinn, *Mormon Hierarchy: Extensions of Power*, 211–12, 508n96.
83. Ibid., 166, 491n15.

CHAPTER 3. THE BIG HORN BASIN AS FRONTIER

1. Robert Kaplan, *Earning the Rockies*.
2. "Aside from possible wandering Spaniards, Larocque was the first white man to explore northern Wyoming." S. J. Kowrach in Larocque's *Journal of François Larocque*.
3. Edward J. Kowrach, in Larocque's *Journal of François Larocque*, 7, 8.
4. Bryant, "Bad Pass Trail," 90–92. The first Euro-Americans known to pass through the Big Horn Canyon were Edward Gillette and N. S. Sharpe; they did not utilize boats but waited until severe cold weather solidified the river. Gillette, born in 1854 in New Haven, Connecticut, was a graduate of Sheffield Scientific School of Yale University and was appointed in 1878 to the United States Surveys West of the One-hundredth Meridian's staff. He subsequently became the major surveyor for western railroads. He and Sharpe, of Sheridan, Montana, started down the canyon on March 7, 1891, completing their journey in about thirty days. The first whites to travel through Big Horn Canyon in boats were T. E. Calvert and M. W. Ensign of Burlington, Wyoming. In the summer of 1893, a four-man group from Sheridan, Wyoming, composed of W. G. Griffen, Judge James P. and Thomas Robinson, and J. W. Newell traversed the canyon. They noted the offensive odor at the Stinking Water River's headwaters and deduced it arose from contact with sulphur deposits near present-day Cody, Wyoming. The National Parks Committee recommended in 1923 that the Big Horn, Devil's, and Black Canyons be set aside as a national park, as they compared favorably with Yellowstone and Glacier. Gillette, *Locating the Iron Trail*, 78–102.
5. LeRoy R. Hafen's descriptions in *The Mountain Men and The Fur Trade of the Far West* required a multivolume set to identify and recognize the large number of early mountain explorers. Historian Charles Lindsay and other investigators cite the French Canadian Vérendrye brothers crossing the basin in 1742–1743. *Big Horn Basin*, 17–21, 17n1.
6. Manuel Lisa left St. Louis in the spring of 1807 hauling keelboats up the Missouri. By chance he intercepted Colter going downstream, near the Platte's

mouth. Lisa, together with George Drouillard, John Potts, and Peter Weiser, also Lewis and Clark veterans, convinced Colter to join their adventuring party. Bryant, "Bad Pass Trail," 92.

7. Hardee, *Pierre's Hole!*, 58; Mattes, *Colter's Hell and Jackson Hole*, 19. One active hot springs is now underwater in the reservoir created on the Shoshone River in 1910 by the Buffalo Bill Dam. Jim Hardee, personal communication with the author, September 2019; Jeremy Johnston, personal communication with the author, November 2019.

8. The Jefferson River, about eighty miles in length, is about fifty miles west of Bozeman and 125 miles north and west of present-day West Yellowstone, Montana.

9. Mattes, *Colter's Hell*, 17; Tubbs and Jenkinson, *Lewis and Clark Companion*, 75.

10. Grenville Dodge, "Biographical Sketch of James Bridger," cited in Lowe, *The Bridger Trail*, 24.

11. Lowe, *The Bridger Trail*, 64–65, 291.

12. Ibid., 20–21.

13. W. F. Raynolds, *Report on the Exploration of the Yellowstone*, cited in Lowe, *The Bridger Trail*, 67–68.

14. Stegner, *Wolf Willow*, 287–88.

15. Today's Pryor Mountains are not lumber rich, but in 1900–1901 colonists harvested logs there to build their earliest dwellings.

16. Gillette, *Locating the Iron Trail*, 149.

17. Woods, *Wyoming's Big Horn Basin*, 225. Historian Gregory Nickerson clarifies that railroad names are a confusing issue in recounting Wyoming's railroad progress. The CB&Q operated under several names in Wyoming. It financed construction in the state through entities like the Grand Island and Northern Wyoming Railroad Company and the Big Horn Railroad Company. After construction ended, the CB&Q bought these paper companies and incorporated them into its network. Wyoming residents rarely used the construction companies' names. Instead, they referred to the new lines as the Burlington and Missouri Railroad, the B&M, or simply "The Burlington," a nickname that signified the CB&Q's financial control over all the lines. Nickerson, "The Burlington Route: Wyoming's Second Transcontinental Railroad," November 8, 2014, www.wyohistory.org, https://www.wyohistory .org/encyclopedia/burlington-route-wyomings-second-transcontinental -railroad.

18. Gillette, *Locating the Iron Trail*, 39; Kelley, *Images of America: Gillette*, 22.

19. Athearn, *Union Pacific Country*, 211. According to Vileisis, in the United States a standard-gauge track is 4 feet 8 1/2 inches. Any size smaller is narrow-gauge. Narrow-gauge rails can be as narrow as 1 foot 11 5/8 inches, with the largest at 3 feet 6 inches. Vileisis, "Working on Desert Rails."

20. Vileisis, "Working on Desert Rails," 1; Athearn, *Union Pacific Country*, 361–62.

21. Partridge, *With Book and Plow*, 15. Although many colonists arrived by animal-powered wagons, they quickly came to depend on the railroad for their supplies.
22. Arrington, *Great Basin Kingdom*, 259.
23. J. Francis to John W. Taylor and A. O. Woodruff, February 15, 1904, typescript, box 4, fd. 13, A. O. Woodruff papers.
24. Edward Gillette, the distinguished Burlington surveyor, reported, "In the spring of 1899 we located the Burlington line from Toluca, Montana, to Cody, Wyoming. The distinguishing feature of this line was the development necessary in the shape of a boot to go through Pryor Gap on the grade desired." "Locating the Iron Trail," 146.
25. S. W. Eccles, General Traffic Manager, and D. E. Burley, in Salt Lake City, to Mr. E. L. Lomax, General Passenger and Ticket Administrator, UPRR, in Omaha, Nebraska, February 20, 1901, typescript, box 5, fd. 2, A. O. Woodruff papers.
26. Burley to Woodruff, March 8, 1901, typescript, box 5, fd. 2, A. O. Woodruff Papers.
27. Ibid.
28. Meyers, "The Cody Route to Yellowstone," 13.
29. "Line to Cody City," *Wyoming Industrial Journal*, No. 12, May 1, 1900.
30. Woods, *Big Horn Basin*, 204.
31. "The Burlington in Wyoming," *Cody Enterprise*, January 2, 1902.
32. Woods, *Wyoming's Big Horn Basin*, 225. Nickerson, "The Burlington Route." See also "Railroad Notes," *Salt Lake Tribune*, June 15, 1900.
33. David W. Harvey, "Chicago, Burlington & Quincy Railroad—Toluca-Cody Line," The Pryor Mountains Railroad, 1974. Excerpted with permission from Harvey, "A General Historical Survey of the Pryor Mountains," Western Interstate Commission for Higher Education, Boulder, CO, 1974, http://www.pryormountains.org/cultural-history/homestead-era/railroad/.
34. This date is roughly corroborated by George C. Gustin's letter of February 23, 1904, to the Utah Sugar Company's general manager, Thomas R. Cutler, box 5, fd. 1, A. O. Woodruff Papers.
35. Kirby is about twelve miles north of Thermopolis, Wyoming.
36. BNSF Railway, "Our Railroad," https://www.bnsf.com/about-bnsf/our-railroad/index.html.
37. Gregory Nickerson, "The Burlington Route: Wyoming's Second Transcontinental Railroad," www.wyohistory.org, https://www.wyohistory.org/encyclopedia/burlington-route-wyomings-second-transcontinental-railroad.
38. Woods, *Wyoming's Big Horn Basin*, 10.
39. Roberts, "Watering a Dry Land: Wyoming and Federal Irrigation," 2.
40. Frison, *Calendar of Change*, 129–30.
41. Meeteetse is the area's only town still in existence of four tiny towns shown on an 1890 map of Wyoming. Davis, *Goodbye, Judge Lynch*, 24.

42. Turner, *Frontier in American History*, 2. See also Woods, *Wyoming's Big Horn Basin*, 9, 9n1. Wyoming became the Union's forty-fourth state; Cheyenne, in the southeast corner and outside the Big Horn basin, was its largest city and capital. Utah Territory, with an ample population of more than 211,000, was still burdened by the albatross of secret polygamy and undisguised theocratic rule. Utah Territory required another six years of struggle before statehood was granted.

43. May, *Three Frontiers*, 6–7.

44. Turner, *Frontier in American History*, 3.

45. Loveland, *Sagebrush and Roses*, 21, 69. Otto's population in 2000 was listed as only fifty people.

46. Lustin to Thomas R. Cutler, February 23, 1904, box 5, fd. 1, A. O. Woodruff Papers. Excessive irrigation was soon noted to have negative consequences.

47. In 1901 the river's name was changed by the state of Wyoming from Stinking Water to Shoshone, likely due to pressure from Bill Cody and George Beck.

48. Smith, "The W. C. Partridge Family and the Settling of Cowley, Wyoming: Worth the Cost?"

49. The width, depth, and drop were not made up as it was built but stipulated by the canal permit. Partridge, *With Book and Plow*, 17, 289n7.

50. Ibid., 9, 13.

51. Davis, *Goodbye, Judge Lynch*, 9, 13, 38, 100, 141. Davis cites a study by Zangrando, *The NAACO Crusade Against Lynching, 1909–1950*, 5–8.

52. Davis, *Goodbye, Judge Lynch*, 8, 188–96. The cattle war of 1892 in Johnson County, beyond the scope of this work, is thoroughly treated by Wyoming attorney John W. Davis in *Wyoming Range War*, 2010.

CHAPTER 4. DISPOSSESSION AND ELIMINATION

1. Royal Charter, Massachusetts Bay Colony, 1628.

2. "When the Tribes Sold the Hot Springs," December 3, 2018, www.wyohistory .org, https://www.wyohistory.org/encyclopedia/when-tribes-sold-hot-springs.

3. Ibid. Thermopolis, Wyoming, boasts a beautiful naturally heated spring-water resort that produces 16 million gallons of hot water daily.

4. Ibid. Later financial installments "were not forthcoming." A recent publication tells of an 1895 dispute near today's Jackson, Wyoming, with whites and a party of Bannocks who had traveled from Fort Hall in Idaho to hunt elk, as was their right of treaty with the US government. The tensions were resolved in a much-maligned 1896 US Supreme Court decision, known as the *Race Horse* case. More than a century later, in a 2019 case known as *Herrera*, the Supreme Court fully repudiated its *Race Horse* principles. See John Clayton, "Who gets to hunt Wyoming's elk? Tribal Hunting Rights, U.S. Law and the Bannock 'War' of 1895," September 29, 2020, www.wyohistory.org, https://www.wyohistory.org/encyclopedia/who-gets-hunt-wyomings-elk -tribal-hunting-rights-us-law-and-bannock-war-1895.

5. Welch, *History of the Big Horn Basin*, 74–76, 174; US Census Bureau, 1910 Federal Census.
6. Bagley, *The Whites Want Every Thing*, 486.
7. James Duane Doty, a man dedicated to the protection of Indian rights, was Indian superintendent until Irish's appointment in 1864. To Brigham Young's discomfort, Doty worked with P. Edward Connor to execute treaties with the Utah tribes. Doty's very puzzling onset of violent pain of June 6 prevented his attendance at the Spanish Fork Treaty. Doty died June 13, but his wife made no public statement of suspicion regarding the possible cause of his unexpected death. Maxwell, *Civil War Years in Utah*, 327–30.
8. Bagley, *The Whites Want Every Thing*, 502, 502n36.
9. Ibid.
10. William H. Smart's dedicated efforts are treated in detail in the preface of this work.
11. O'Neil, "An Anguished Odyssey," 317.
12. Cutch, *History of Utah's American Indians*, 203–6.
13. The Utes left Whiterocks, Utah, traveled not far from Evanston, Wyoming, then northeast to Douglas, then to Gillette, Wyoming, then briefly into the southeastern tip of Montana, then to Belle Fourche, Rapid City, and Thunder Butte, South Dakota. They did not enter the Wind River Mountains, the Big Horn Basin, or the Bighorn Mountains. O'Neil, "An Anguished Odyssey," 319.
14. Beard, *Wyoming: From Territorial Day to the Present*, Vol. 1, 561–62. Uneasiness regarding the White River Utes' presence is understandable, since in 1879 they massacred Colorado Indian agent Nathan Meeker and ten of his staff. Meeker had abusively demanded the Utes adopt an in-residence provisional farming lifestyle and had punished the tribal leader's lack of obedience beyond their tolerance. "I shall propose to cut every Indian down to bare starvation point if he will not work," Meeker wrote. Dunn, *Massacres of the Mountains*, 690. On the same day of Meeker's killing, Ute Chief Colorow attacked the nearby force of Major Thomas T. Thornburgh, killing him and thirteen officers, all above the rank of captain.
15. Laudenschlager, "Utes in South Dakota," 237.
16. George Case to Summary Court, Camp Thunder Butte, S. Dak., Sworn Testimony, January 31, 1908, File 9757, RG 75, NA.
17. O'Neil, "An Anguished Odyssey," 323, 327.
18. Winchester, *Land*, 131.
19. The Doctrine of Discovery, 1493, The Gilder Lehrman Institute of American History, https://www.gilderlehrman.org/history-resources/spotlight-primary-source/doctrine-discovery-1493.
20. Winchester, *Land*, 133.
21. That George Washington and other elites had already taken ownership of lands west of the Appalachian line also stoked the actions for independence in 1776.

22. The Doctrine of Discovery, 1493.

23. Winchester, *Land*, 123; "United States, ex rel. Standing Bear, v. George Crook, a Brigadier-General of the Army of the United States," 25 F. Cas. 695, 5 Dill. 453 (D. Neb. 1879).

24. Dahl, *Empire of the People*, 1–2. Italics added.

25. Wolfe, "Settler Colonialism," 388. Much of the published work similar to Wolfe's and Dahl's seems to be complex polemics for academic specialists. The interested reader might consider Gerald Horne, *The Apocalypse of Settler Colonialism: The Roots of Slavery, White Supremacy, and Capitalism in 17th Century North America* (New York: Monthly Review Press, 2017); and Walter L. Hixson, *American Settler Colonialism: A History* (New York: Palgrave MacMillan, 2013).

26. Harris, "How Did Colonialism Dispossess?" 168–70.

27. From 1847 Brigham Young sought converts primarily from poor, landless people in predominantly white Scandinavian nations and British Isles, denoting underlying racism.

28. Wolfe, "Settler Colonialism and the Elimination of the Native," 390.

29. Dahl, *Empire of the People*, 13.

30. Deloria, book review of *Tecumseh and the Prophet: The Shawnee Brothers Who Defied a Nation*, by Peter Cozzens, in *The New Yorker*, November 2, 2020, 80.

31. Maxwell, *Civil War Years in Utah*, 185–94, 403n53.

32. Dahl, *Empire*, 101–2. Brigham Young recruited colonists, but once they arrived and contributed to his empire, their leaving was fraught with danger. Historian Polly Aird's ancestors, Peter and Agnes McAuslin, became so frightened from threatened violence that they secured a US Army escort to take them safely to California. Polly Aird, "Ladder to the Moon," in Geisner, *Writing Mormon History*, 1–36.

33. Bagley, *The Whites Want Every Thing*, 138.

34. In the keepsake edition of *The Whites Want Every Thing*, Bagley honors Floyd A. O'Neil's seminal work, "An Anguished Odyssey: The Flight of the Utes, 1906–1908. A New Edition of Floyd A. O'Neil's Landmark 1968 Article."

CHAPTER 5. PENURY, DEPRESSION, AND OVERPOPULATION

1. Cowley, ed., *Wilford Woodruff*, 573; Diary of Wilford Woodruff, August 9 and November 1, 1894, cited in Arrington, *Great Basin Kingdom*, 402, 514n109.

2. Arrington, *Great Basin Kingdom*, 372–74.

3. Woodruff Journal, 8:421, cited in Neilson, *In the Whirlpool*, 64. Historian Susan Stone emphasizes Woodruff's long history of seeing the earth's violent end brought on by God as punishment of those who refused the LDS message. Stone, "Waiting for World's End," 11–16.

4. Arrington, *Great Basin Kingdom*, 400–403. Measured by GDP per capita. "Seven Ways to Compute the Relative Value of a U.S. Dollar Amount," http://www.measuringworth.com/uscompare/.

5. Bell, "Windows of Heaven," 50.
6. Ibid., 61–63; Quinn, *The Mormon Hierarchy: Extensions of Power*, 202.
7. Joseph Eckersley of Wayne County received $250 per year as stake tithing clerk. Alexander, *Mormonism in Transition*, 100.
8. Bell, "Windows of Heaven," 53.
9. Harold R. Laycock, "Academies," https://eom.byu.edu/index.php/Academies. Originally named the Woodruff Academy for Owen Woodruff, the school began by alternating its location from Lovell to Cowley to Byron. After a beautiful brick building was constructed in Cowley, the academy was moved there, and the name was changed to Big Horn Academy. Partridge, *With Book and Plow*, 75.
10. Alexander, *Mormonism in Transition*, 100.
11. Bell, "Windows of Heaven," 53.
12. Maxwell, *Robert Newton Baskin*, 237–38.
13. Richard Holzapfel, *Every Stone a Sermon*, 15.
14. "To Complete the Temple," *Deseret News*, April 23, 1892.
15. The Salt Lake City and County Building was completed in December 1894.
16. Stone, "Waiting for World's End," 15. Capitalization in original.
17. At its unveiling, "an immense congregation assembled . . . estimated at not less than 6,000 persons." "Meeting of the First Presidency and others," in Journal History, July 1, 1897, CR 100 137, reel 85, v. 337, image 4. Jokesters would observe that Young's empty left hand was held out as though reaching out to Zions Bank on the corner opposite the monument.
18. Arrington, *Great Basin Kingdom*, 401. Measured by GDP per capita. "Seven Ways to Compute the Relative Value of a U.S. Dollar Amount," http://www.measuringworth.com/uscompare/.
19. Journal History, June 8, 1899, CR 100, 137 reel 93, v. 361, image 131.
20. "The Church of Jesus Christ of Latter-day Saints membership history," wikipedia.org.
21. Clawson married Lydia Spence on March 29, 1883.
22. Payne, "Rudger Clawson's Report," 171.
23. Quinn, *The Mormon Hierarchy: Extension of Power*, 201.
24. Alexander, *Mormonism in Transition*, 100; also cited in Larson, "A 'Meeting of the Brethren,'" 90n35.
25. Clawson and Larson, *Prisoner for Polygamy*, 18.
26. Hardy, *Solemn Covenant*, 401.
27. Arrington, "Utah and the Depression of the 1890s," 3, 5. Measured by GDP per capita. "Seven Ways to Compute the Relative Value of a U.S. Dollar Amount," http://www.measuringworth.com/uscompare/.
28. Maxwell, *Robert Newton Baskin*, 261–70. Emphasis added.
29. Arrington, "Utah and the Depression of the 1890s," 8–10.
30. Cache Stake "High Priests Minute Book B," 104, cited in Sherlock, "Mormon Migration and Settlement," 54.

31. Sherlock, "Mormon Migration and Settlement," 54.

32. Arrington, *Great Basin Kingdom*, 364.

33. F. A. Hammond, "On the Way to San Juan," *Deseret News Weekly*, April 24, 1885.

34. Sherlock, "Mormon Migration and Settlement," 54.

35. The valley was originally part of the Oregon Trail. The Grand Ronde River is a tributary to the Snake. It arises in the Blue Mountains and is used for irrigation.

36. Journal History, July 1, 1897, CR 100 137, reel 85, v. 337, image 4.

37. Quinn, *The Mormon Hierarchy: Extensions of Power*, 124, 125, 126, 218, 509n122, 510n123.

38. Journal History, January 19, 1899, CR 100 137, reel 90–91, v. 356, images 222–24. Provisions of Edmunds-Tucker also dissolved what was left in the Perpetual Emigrating Fund and prevented Utah from forming any organization bringing people into Utah "for any purpose whatsoever." Arrington, *Great Basin Kingdom*, 382.

39. As noted, Latter-day Saints had colonized areas of Colorado earlier, as when John W. Taylor formed a mission there in 1899.

40. "Want 'Mormon' Beet Raisers . . . Inducements Offered . . . Many Families are Going," *Deseret News*, January 20, 1900.

41. Abraham H. Cannon Journal, May 28, 1889, vol. 40, p. 20, A. H. Cannon papers.

42. Quinn lists the company president as A. H. Cannon, with trustees Wilford Woodruff, George Q. Cannon, Seymour B. Young, Heber J. Grant, and Abraham Owen Woodruff. Quinn, *The Mormon Hierarchy: Wealth and Corporate Power*, 232. Note that all six men were polygamists.

43. Fox was Matthias Cowley's stepfather from the marriage to his widowed mother, Sarah Elizabeth Foss Cowley.

44. Abraham H. Cannon Journal, October 4, 1889, vol. 11, p. 124, A. H. Cannon papers.

45. In a meeting at the Gardo House, each First Presidency member also decided to invest in a section of land. Abraham H. Cannon Journal, July 1, 1889, p. 46, A. H. Cannon papers.

46. Journal History, August 10, 1905, CR 100 137, reel 112, v. 421, image 278. During this era, Mormon Apostle John W. Taylor was among those interested in private for-profit investments in Canada that were independent of church monies.

47. Journal History, July 1, 1897, CR 100 137, reel 85, v. 337, image 5. Emphasis added.

CHAPTER 6. FIVE WOODRUFF MEN

1. Chief Joseph. Sadly, this Wallowa band, Nez Perce leader, and his people were doggedly pursued across the Rocky Mountains and forced to surrender to their white captors.

2. Abbott, *Woodruff Genealogy: Descendants of Mathew Woodruff of Farmington, Connecticut*, 418–19.
3. Homsher, "Wyoming Zephyrs," 91.
4. Riter, "Biographical Sketch of John Dwight Woodruff," 214.
5. Their daughter, Clara A. Woodruff, was married in Salt Lake City; she died there and is also buried in Mount Olivet Cemetery. Their son, Harry L. Woodruff, lived until 1968; he died in Los Angeles, California.
6. A draft registration card dated June 30, 1863, for Buffalo, Ogle County, Illinois, and signed by Captain John V. Eustace, Provost Marshal, lists Dwight's age at twenty-six, his occupation as a carpenter, and that he was married. Ancestry.com Military Records, accessed 2019. Buffalo, Ogle County, was only about fifty miles from Bonus, Illinois, where he appears in the 1860 federal census.
7. Davis, *Goodbye, Judge Lynch*, 7. Woods, *Wyoming's Big Horn Basin*, 80.
8. Riter, "Biographical Sketch of John Dwight Woodruff," 216–17. See also Walker, *Stories of Early Days in Wyoming*, 48.
9. Riter, "Biographical Sketch of John Dwight Woodruff," 219.
10. Woodruff Cabin Site, wikipedia.org; https://en.wikipedia.org/wiki /Woodruff_Cabin_Site; J. D. Woodruff Cabin Site, "Read All About It," Wyoming State Preservation Office, http://wyoshpo.state.wy.us/index .php/programs/national-register/wyoming-listings/view-full-list/593-j-d -woodruff-cabin-site.
11. Woods, *Wyoming's Big Horn Basin to 1901*, 66.
12. Walker, *Stories of Early Days in Wyoming*, 45–55.
13. Ibid., 54.
14. Ibid., 45–55. Named for Jim Lysite is the small unincorporated community of Lysite in Fremont County; it is not far from the Bridger Trail and about twenty-four miles directly east of the Wind River Reservation.
15. Riter, "Biographical Sketch of John Dwight Woodruff," 224–25.
16. "Biographical Notes," Benjamin Franklin Riter Papers, MSS B 46, Utah State Historical Society. The Woodruff-Riter-Stewart mansion was later remodeled and remains as a posh bed and breakfast. Another impressive structure owned by E. D. Woodruff was located in Darlington Place, about 900 East and Third Avenue.
17. Shepard and Marquardt, *Lost Apostles*, 3, 143, 189; LeSuer, *The 1838 Mormon War in Missouri*, 117, 125n35, 150, 261. Gideon Carter and Patrick O'Bannion also died, and seven Mormons were wounded. Metcalfe, "Firm and Steadfast in the Faith," 1899.
18. Wilson, Lycurgus A., *Life of David W. Patten: The First Apostolic Martyr*, cited in "David W. Patten," wikipedia.org, https://en.wikipedia.org/wiki /David_W._Patten.
19. While David Patten Woodruff fathered eleven children, he was not a polygamist.

20. Packard was born in Springville, Utah, in 1851. He moved to Cache County, then to Uintah County, as did David P. Woodruff. Packard and his wife Christine had nine children. He died in 1918 in Glenwood, Alberta, Canada. Loveland, *Sagebrush and Roses*, 71.

21. Henry Griffin's wife, Sylvia Perry, was the sister of Cynthia Perry, who married Willian H. Packard. This likely explains why the two families moved together.

22. Loveland, *Sagebrush and Roses*, 71.

23. Welch, *History of the Big Horn Basin*, 49.

24. Woods, *Wyoming's Big Horn Basin to 1901*, 209–10.

25. Lindsay, *The Bighorn Basin*, 164–65; Welch, *History of the Big Horn Basin*, 50; Davis, *Goodbye, Judge Lynch*, 36, 190.

26. These jurors were Charles Duncan, born in Utah about 1877; Charles Emil Nielson, from Juab County, Utah, who was temporarily working near Cody; and Charles Walker.

27. Davis, *Goodbye, Judge Lynch*, 168, 190–92.

28. Abraham Owen Woodruff was born November 23, 1872, in Salt Lake City. David Patten Woodruff was born in 1854 in Salt Lake City and died on January 20, 1937, in Long Beach, California; his mother was Sarah Elinor Brown. David's two wives were sequential; he married Arabella Jane Hatch on February 19, 1877, in Logan, Utah. She died January 13, 1923, and he married Sarah Rolfe on July 26, 1924.

CHAPTER 7. WHETHER CALLED OR VOLUNTEERED, PLANS AND PROGRESS FOLLOW

1. This was President Lorenzo Snow's opinion regarding the 1900 Big Horn colonization. Abraham O. Woodruff Journal, 171–72.

2. "Good Report from the Big Horn," *Deseret Evening News*, March 27, 1897. Italics added.

3. Journal History, June 18, 1899, CR 100 137, v. 362, reel 93, image 132.

4. Ibid.

5. Simmons, "The Organization of the Big Horn Stake," presentation at the Mormon History Association Conference, May 25, 2006. Note that Owen Woodruff also said that on February 25, 1899, he and Cowley were "trying to bring about the accomplishment of the mission assigned us." See chapter 3.

6. Fillerup, *Sidon*, 3. It is curious that David P. Woodruff wrote to Governor Richards, yet Richards anticipated a response from Owen Woodruff. Owen may have made earlier contact through the engineer Mr. Ham, or perhaps David was aware of Owen's visit and was competing with his younger brother.

7. "The Big Horn Basin, Idaho [*sic*]," *Deseret Evening News*, November 11, 1899.

8. Fillerup, *Sidon*, 18.

9. Life sketch of William Benoma Graham, 1852–1926, available with a subscription at https://www.familysearch.org.

10. Author personal communication with Roland Simmons, 2015.

11. Italics added. Snow's use of the word "sacred" may have implied a more-than-ordinary meaning. He had been cautious in approving marriages in Mexico, for which he held final authority, and he might also have seen Wyoming as a place to continue the sacred ordinances on US soil with approval via a few apostles. The laws of punishment would then fall on the individuals married or those performing the rites. Cowley said he was instructed not to tell other apostles about the authority given him verbally to perform plural marriages. Hardy, *Solemn Covenant*, 187–88.

12. Abraham Owen Woodruff Journal, 171–72.

13. Journal History, January 23, 1900, CR 100 137, v. 369, reel 96, image 126–27.

14. Lindsay, *The Bighorn Basin*, 195, 197.

15. Bowen, "Migration," 212–13.

16. Bagley, *Blood of the Prophets*, 349.

17. Abraham Owen Woodruff Journal, Johnson to Woodruff, box 5, fd. 9. Note that David King Udall was already a polygamist when Matthias Cowley performed a third marriage—post-Manifesto—in 1903 to Mary Morgan. D. K. Udall's grandson, Stewart Lee Udall, from first wife Eliza Luella Stewart, had a distinguished career as an Arizona congressman and as US secretary of Interior from 1961 to 1969.

18. Ibid.

19. Bowen, "Migration to and from a Northern Wyoming Mormon Community," 215.

20. Ibid., 216.

21. Fillerup, *Sidon*, 12.

22. Loveland, *Sagebrush and Roses*, 144–45.

23. Welch, *History of the Big Horn Basin*, 53–54. Trains served both Red Lodge and Bridger in 1900, although Mormon records indicate that Bridger was the nearest to their needs.

24. Welch, *History of the Big Horn Basin*, 54, 58.

25. John Croft of Burlington did not attend due to illness.

26. Partridge, *With Book and Plow*, 4–5.

27. "Big Horn Basin Colonization," *Deseret Evening News*, February 5, 1900. Appointed by President Ulysses Grant, George W. Emery was the eleventh Utah Territorial governor, serving from 1875 to 1880. While a Republican from Tennessee, Emery had formerly been a supervisor of Internal Revenue for the Confederate states.

28. Erickson, "Star Valley," 135–36.

29. Fillerup, *Sidon*, 4. Wyoming received another million acres of federal land in 1908.

30. Charles Kingston's little-known role as a special railroad agent for the Latter-day Saints is treated in chapter 10.

31. Because Kingston could not travel to Wyoming at the time, John Croft was elected to fill his position. Welch, *History of Big Horn Basin*, 64.

32. Lindsay, *The Bighorn Basin*, 121, 122, 194, 194n120.
33. Welch, *History of the Big Horn Basin*, 65.

CHAPTER 8. TREKS, TRIALS, AND FINANCES

1. Arthur C. Clarke, *2010: Odyssey Two*, unnumbered.
2. Eliza Lythgoe describes Ham's Fork as a small settlement near the present site of Kemmerer, Wyoming, in "Colonization of the Big Horn Basin by the Mormons," 14. Other sources indicate the meeting place was Kemmerer Bridge, to which Woodruff had traveled by Oregon Shortline and Union Pacific rail. His wagon and horse team had been sent ahead with instructions to meet there. Fillerup, *Sidon Canal*, 23.
3. Welch, *History of the Big Horn Basin*, 65–66. See map by Mark N. Partridge, "Life history of Mark N. Partridge," by himself. LDS_CHL, M270.1 P2755p 1990.
4. "Settlement in the Big Horn Country," *Deseret Evening News*, June 16, 1900. Charles A. Welch appears to be the author of this detailed description.
5. The data in Welch's record regarding wagons, people, and horses are incomplete for Company 7, neither is there a full accounting of officers in Company 6 and 7. Welch, *History of the Big Horn Basin*, 66–69.
6. "Settlement in the Big Horn Country," *Deseret Evening News*, June 16, 1900.
7. Welch, *History of the Big Horn Basin*, 67–68.
8. Salisbury and wife Anna May Clinger were from Utah County.
9. Orson Frost and wife Rebecca Taggart were from Morgan County, Utah.
10. Partridge, *With Book and Plow*, 11–12, 12–14. William Henderson Dickson and wife Edna Seviah Despain were from Morgan County, Utah.
11. Smith, "The W. C. Partridge Family and the Settling of Cowley, Wyoming: Worth the Cost?"
12. Partridge, *With Book and Plow*, 15.
13. Lindsay, "The Big Horn Basin," 197.
14. This is almost certainly an underestimate.
15. Partridge, *With Book and Plow*, 17. George Hartson and wife Idabell Horne were from Salt Lake County.
16. "Settlement in the Big Horn Country," *Deseret News*, June 16, 1900.
17. Woods, *Wyoming's Big Horn Basin*, 217n23.
18. Bowen, "Migration," 209–10. Henry Clay Lovell trailed two herds of cattle into Wyoming in 1879. In 1883 Lovell, partnered with Anthony L. Mason of Kansas City, established a ranch near Nowood Creek, and in the following year a second ranch on Shell Creek. At one time the partnership controlled 25,000 head.
19. Partridge, *With Book and Plow*, 46–47.
20. Wallace Wright Maxwell was born October 14, 1901, in Cowley. He died there on May 17 in 1907.
21. A copy of the manuscript is owned by the author.

22. Welch lists 104 scrapers purchased from Hiram Haskins, a hardware merchant in Bridger, Montana, plus an unknown but small number brought by the colonists. "Settlement in the Big Horn Country," *Deseret Evening News*, June 16, 1900. Partridge explains that very few more advanced scrapers with wheels or with a strengthened center "tongue" were available. Partridge, *With Book and Plow*, 4, 18.

23. Smith, "The W. C. Partridge Family and the Settling of Cowley, Wyoming: Worth the Cost?" See also Partridge, *With Book and Plow*, 17.

24. Jesse W. Crosby Jr. to Owen Woodruff, April 10, 1901, box 5, fd. 4, A. O. Woodruff Papers.

25. Historian Woods adds that William H. Packard gave bond for the contract but for an unknown reason would not sign it. Woods, *Wyoming's Big Horn Basin*, 216, 216n21.

26. Lindsay notes that the ten-hour workday was soon reduced to eight. Lindsay, "The Big Horn Basin," 200–210.

27. Ibid., 201, 201n140.

28. Partridge, *With Book and Plow*, 17–18. Welch contends that $7.20 was "all the cash that any man under the canal had to pay for each 40 acres of water right." Welch, *History of the Big Horn Basin*, 91.

29. Crosby to Woodruff, handwritten on letterhead of Big Horn Basin Colonization Company, April 4, 1901, box 5, fd. 4, A. O. Woodruff Papers, underscore in original. Smallpox vaccination was occurring among Wyoming's citizens at this time, as noted by a letter from W. Dean Hays of Meeteetse bank. Hays expressed regrets to David Patten Woodruff for missing church conference since his smallpox vaccination had made his arm too painful to attend. Ibid., box 5, fd. 8.

30. Woods, *Big Horn Basin*, 216, 217n23.

31. Loveland, *Sagebrush and Roses*, 146.

32. Welch, *History of the Big Horn Basin*, 87.

33. Partridge, *With Book and Plow*, 17–18, 25–27. Measured by GDP per capita. "Seven Ways to Compute the Relative Value of a U.S. Dollar Amount," https://www.measuringworth.com/calculators/uscompare/.

34. Welch, *History of the Big Horn Basin*, 107.

35. Ibid., 89.

36. Ibid., 147.

37. Ibid., 107.

38. Partridge, *With Book and Plow*, 53, 93; Welch, *History of the Big Horn Basin*, 107.

39. See photo in Partridge, *With Book and Plow*, 62.

40. Harvey, David W., "Chicago, Burlington & Quincy Railroad—Toluca-Cody Line," The Pryor Mountains Railroad, 1974. Neils, wife Ester Jane, and four daughters had come from Parowan, Utah, after the birth of daughter Alice in August 1900. Welch, *History of Big Horn Basin*, 87.

41. Loveland, *Sagebrush and Roses*, 148–49.
42. Harvey, "Chicago, Burlington & Quincy Railroad."
43. "'Still Look to the Future of Faith,' Religion and Life in Rich County," Parson, *History of Rich County*, 236–37.

CHAPTER 9. PROMISES AND ACCOMPLISHMENTS
1. Partridge, *With Book and Plow*, 20.
2. Chatterton, *The State of Wyoming*, 27.
3. Welch, *History of the Big Horn Basin*, 91.
4. Ariel R. Doty Journals, MS 23715, fd. 3.
5. Lythgoe, "Colonization of the Big Horn Basin by the Mormons," 44.
6. Partridge, *With Book and Plow*, 20.
7. Welch, *History of the Big Horn Basin*, 140.
8. Fillerup, *Sidon Canal*, 103–4.
9. Conference Minutes, p. 163, from the Big Horn Stake Archives, in Cowley, Wyoming, cited in Lindsay, *The Bighorn Basin*, 196; Fillerup, *Sidon Canal*, 109. Welch, *History of the Big Horn Basin*, 108. Lund was one of only a few monogamists among topmost LDS church leaders of this era. Italics added.
10. Journal of Charles Ora Card, cited in Lehr, "Polygamy, Patrimony, and Prophecy," 118. Lehr does not suggest that Card went to Canada for the secrecy of polygamous unions, but in large part as a haven to avoid a life on the run from arrest by US marshals. "Polygamy, Patrimony, and Prophecy," 116, 120.
11. Embry, "Exiles for the Principle: Polygamy in Canada," 109.
12. *University of Wyoming Agricultural Experimental Station*, Bulletin No. 205, May 1935, "Economic Studies of Irrigated Farms in Big Horn County," 18.
13. Phil Roberts, "Watering a Dry Land: Wyoming and Federal Legislation," Wyohistory.org, October 28, 2019, https://www.wyohistory.org/encyclopedia/watering-dry-land-wyoming-and-federal-irrigation.
14. J. A. Widtsoe to Owen Woodruff, January 13, 1904, typescript, box 4, fd. 13, A. O. Woodruff Papers.
15. A 1917 deposit of sodium and potassium nitrate was found in Washakie County, on the Big Horn Mountain's flanks, but it was insufficient to be of commercial value. Some potash nitrate in the Leucite Hills on North Table Butte in Sweetwater County was reported in a 1932 Department of the Interior report. Mansfield and Boardman, "Nitrate Deposits of the United States," 99. A 1983 report of "Alum Minerals in Wyoming," by Ray E. Harris and Jonathan K. King, indicates that alum has been found in the Yellowstone Park area but no verified occurrences in the basin. Gary B. Glass, "The Geological Survey of Wyoming," 1986, https://www.wsgs.wyo.gov/products/wsgs-1986-ofr-24.pdf
16. Bowen, "Migration," 217.
17. Partridge, *With Book and Plow*, 120.

18. Quinn, *Wealth and Power*, does not list the Great Western Sugar Company in his compilation of more than 1,880 companies with general authority involvement before 1933.
19. Welch, *History of Big Horn Basin*, 103.
20. Ibid.
21. Bowen, "Migration," 217–18.
22. Ibid., 220–21.
23. Stockmore came into existence in 1905 after two swindlers paid for their drinks in Park City with a gold nugget. They claimed to have found a gold strike on the upper Duchesne River near present-day Hanna. Immediately, there arose a small settlement of tents and temporary wooden buildings, but the scheme was quickly revealed as being on the Ute Uintah Reservation and without gold ore. The promotors fled before they could be arrested. By 1910 little remained of the town. Barton, *History of Duchesne County*, 87.
24. This tiny city was named for Tabby-To-Kwanah, a Ute Indian chief who lived in the Uinta Basin in 1867.
25. With great difficulty, the remains of both John and Ellen were taken across the 9,400 feet of Wolf Creek pass to be buried at home in Peoa City Cemetery, Summit County, Utah.
26. When John Russell Maxwell died in Cowley at age seventy-eight, he had lived alone for nineteen years, for his wife Martha Wright Maxwell died in 1915.
27. See chapter 12.
28. Barnes, "Mormon Colonizers in Wyoming's Bighorn Basin," wyohistory .org, August 3, 2015, https://www.wyohistory.org/encyclopedia/mormon -colonizers-wyomings-bighorn-basin.
29. Bowen, "Migration," 220–21.
30. Beard, *Wyoming*, vol. 2, 427–28.
31. Quinn, *The Mormon Hierarchy, Wealth and Corporate Power*, 224.
32. Dr. Horsley was very interested in roses and was attracted to Lovell, where he considered the environment ideal for their successful growth. Over time his efforts led to citizens creating many rose gardens and Lovell being named "The City of Roses." The claim was made that Dr. Horsley was removed from the hospital staff for pedophilia. He remained in outpatient practice from his home until his death in 1971. Colliflower, *Misfits of Medicine*, n.p.
33. Elizabeth Shaw Smith, "The W. C. Partridge Family and the Settling of Cowley, Wyoming: Worth the Cost?" Presented at Casper, Wyoming, Mormon History Association Annual Meeting, May 25, 2006.
34. "To Register on Shoshone Land," *Cowley Progress*, vol. 1 no. 1, 2.
35. "Salutatory," *The Cowley Weekly Progress*, June 15 and 22, 1906.
36. "Ward Reunion Biggest Event Cowley's History," *Cowley Progress*, June 24, 1920. Despite its claim of never turning a profit, the *Progress* and *Cowley Progress* somehow remained in publication until 1948.
37. Yorgason, *Transformation of the Mormon Culture Region*, 2–4.

38. Stegner, *Wolf Willow: A History, a Story, and a Memory of the Last Plains Frontier*, 306.

CHAPTER 10. AN INNOCENT IN THE BIG HORN BASIN?

1. Bonner, *Buffalo Bill Cody*, 450.
2. Bonner, *Wyoming Empire*, 118. "Settlement in the Big Horn Country," *Deseret News*, June 16, 1900. See also Journal History, CR 100 37, reel 98, v. 379.
3. Woods, *A Late Frontier*, 213–14.
4. Bonner, *Wyoming Empire*, xix–xxi, 273n4.
5. Cody had associated previously with Beck in 1892 on the Sheridan Inn. Wealthy sportsmen were delivered by the Burlington & Missouri Railroad to stay at the inn while hunting guides took them into the Big Horn Mountains.
6. Bonner, *Wyoming Empire*, 9.
7. George Albert Smith, the son of John Henry Smith and his first wife Sarah Farr Smith, became the LDS church president in 1945.
8. Jenson, *Latter-day Saint Biographical Encyclopedia*, vol. 1, 331–32.
9. Quinn, "Big Horn Basin Colonization Company," *The Mormon Hierarchy: Wealth and Corporate Power*, 193.
10. Woods, *A Late Frontier*, 211, 213.
11. If Charles Kingston had allegedly married Mary Ann Wass, she would have been forty-seven years old at the time of their marriage, making children from such a union unlikely.
12. Foster and Watson, *American Polygamy*, 95, 253–57.
13. Mondell to Woodruff, October 14, 1903, typescript, box 4, fd. 19, A. O. Woodruff Papers.
14. Malmquist, *The First 100 Years*, 206–7.
15. Woodruff to Kearns, January 1, 1904, typescript, box 4, fd. 18, A. O. Woodruff Papers.
16. The Whistle Creek and Wilwood tract were on the same ground as had been the Cincinnati Canal. Wilwood was named by Owen Woodruff to honor his father, Wilford Woodruff.
17. Also known as the Oregon Basin proposition, this was an effort of Omaha businessman Solon L. Wiley to build a canal from the Greybull River; it was later called the Bench Canal. By 1902 Wiley expanded the idea, wishing to control all irrigation on the remaining portions on the Shoshone's south side. In March 1902 Cody accepted the deal. Bonner, *Wyoming Empire*, 145.
18. Woodruff to Kearns, January 1, 1904, typescript, box 4, fd. 18, A. O. Woodruff Papers.
19. Ibid., 5. The unnamed company was likely the Utah Sugar Company, whose principals at the time were Joseph F. Smith, Heber J. Grant, John Rex Winder, John Henry Smith, and George Albert Smith. Quinn, *The Mormon Hierarchy: Wealth and Corporate Power*, 424. All five were polygamists. In 1916 the Great Western Sugar Company built a factory at Lovell. Woods,

Big Horn Basin, 216. The company originated in Colorado and involved New York businessman Henry O. Havenmeyer, who became a dominant force in the sugar industry. It is not listed by Quinn as connected to LDS owners or the LDS church.

20. Woodruff to Kearns, January 1, 1904, typescript, box 4, fd. 18, A. O. Woodruff Papers.

21. Edward A. Whitney, Horace C. Alger, and C. H. Grinnell formed the Sheridan Land Company that built the inn in 1893 directly across the street from the Burlington and Missouri Depot. Cody became part owner in 1894. Blair, *Images of America, Sheridan*, 39.

22. Woods, *Big Horn Basin*, 200–201. Bonner, "Elwood Mead," 40, 42. Mead had a remarkable but not seamless career, including heading the US Bureau of Reclamation from 1924 to 1936; the lake on the Colorado River created by the Hoover Dam was named for him.

23. Bonner, *Buffalo Bill Cody*, 438–39.

24. Bonner, *Buffalo Bill Cody*, 423, 450.

25. Walker, *Railroading Religion*, 104, 109, 193, 239.

26. In 1888 Joseph F. Smith accused Young of unethically using church funds to maintain a lavish lifestyle.

27. Athearn, *Union Pacific Country*, 232–89.

CHAPTER 11. POLYGAMY AMONG THE COLONISTS AND ITS RESIDUE

1. Niccolo Machiavelli Quotes. BraineyQuote.com, BraineyMedia2021.

2. Erickson, "Star Valley, Wyoming: Polygamous Haven," 135, 136.

3. For example, certain parts of LDS Church History Library MS 4734 have been and may remain closed to outside researchers. Portions of Abraham Owen Woodruff Journals, from 1894–1902, and perhaps including his diary for February 1899 shared with Cowley in MS 30345, have not been available to the author.

4. Quinn, "LDS Church Authority and New Plural Marriages, 1890–1904," 52–53.

5. Welch, *History of the Big Horn Basin*, 147.

6. Partridge, *With Book and Plow*, 173.

7. Jenson, *Biographical Encyclopedia*, vol. 1, 543.

8. Hardy, *Solemn Covenant*, appendix.

9. Welch, *History of the Big Horn Basin*, 159.

10. Hendrick, "The Mormon Revival of Polygamy," 459.

11. In *Church Chronology*, Nephi Jensen notes: "Saturday, October 8, 1892, in the Third District Court, Salt Lake City, Gilbert J. Marchant was sentenced to three months imprisonment for u. c. [unlawful co-habitation]." An added handwritten note dated December 23, 1892, reads: "Gilbert J. Marchant was discharged from the Penitentiary."

12. Bagley, *Blood of the Prophets*, 151, 154.

13. Ancestry.com federal census records for 1900, 1910, and 1920. William Willis's grandfather, who shared the same name, was a three-wife polygamist and father of ten children.

14. Loveland, *Sagebrush and Roses*, 341.

15. Reilly, "Warren Marshal Johnson," 5, 19. William W. Slaughter, "Faith through Extreme Adversity," *Ensign*, April 1997.

16. Polygamist Edwin Dilworth Woolley Jr. was the brother of fundamentalist polygamist John Wickersham Woolley.

17. Loveland, *Sagebrush and Roses*, 152.

18. Reilly, "Warren Marshal Johnson," 21–22.

19. US Census Bureau, 1900 Federal Census, Wyoming, Big Horn County, Lovell.

20. Hardy, *Solemn Covenant*. Quinn and Whitefield give the marriage date as September 14, 1903. Whitefield, *The Mormon Delusion*, 223. Anthon H. Lund Diary, September 14, 1903, and December 1, 1910; statement of Matthias F. Cowley in Minutes of the Quorum of the Twelve, May 10, 1911; Byron Sessions Family Group Sheets.

21. Welch, *History of the Big Horn Basin*, 144–145.

22. Helen Sessions was born December 30, 1905. Although she appears in the 1920 federal census as the child of William G. Peterson and Janet Easton (Sessions), she was Peterson's stepchild. Helen's marriage to Orvel Jesse Wilcock resulted in one child. Helen died in Lehi, Utah, on July 2, 1997. However, she is interred in the Lovell, Wyoming, cemetery, where her headstone inscription reads Helen Sessions Wilcock. William G. Peterson and Janet Easton had three children. Janet died in Sacramento, California, on December 20, 1966.

23. Parson, *History of Rich County*, 236–37.

24. Foster and Watson, *American Polygamy*, 66. Musser's role with Smart is described in the preface.

25. Bennion, *Polygamy in Primetime*, 34–35.

26. Janet Bennion, "Apostolic United Brethren," *World Religions and Spirituality*, May 27, 2019.

27. Ervil Morrell LeBaron was accused of more than thirty-five murders between 1972 and 1981. He was arrested in 1979 in Mexico and imprisoned. He died in prison in 1981. Wikipedia, s.v. "Apostolic United Brethren," last modified July 27, 2021.

28. Survey respondents also wrote that the AUB is acknowledged by many in Lovell, where if you have meat to be butchered or plumbing to be done, you will likely be interacting with AUB polygamists.

29. Calls were not entirely random, since some colonists were selected for their skills or occupations.

30. Welch, *History of the Big Horn Basin*, 90, 140.

31. Willard Done, "In Memoriam," *Improvement Era*, August 1904, 746.

32. Rich, *Elder's Journal of the Southern States' Mission*, 140. Owen Woodruff's kindness did not purge him of prevalent Democratic Party racism during this period. On March 6, 1902, he penned in his diary: "Boarded the Great Northern for Great Falls [Montana]. Had trouble with an insolent 'Nigger' Conductor, told him what I thought of him and wished for a while that the 'Slave Days' might return." MS 30345, box 1, A. O. Woodruff Papers.

33. Jorgensen and Hardy, "The Taylor-Cowley Affair," 14.

34. Snyder and Snyder, *Post-Manifesto Polygamy*, 162. Hyrum Don Carlos Clark's first marriage was November 11, 1880, to Ann Eliza Porter; she lived until June 12, 1927. The 1900 federal census for Star Valley, Lincoln County, Wyoming lists Annie E. Clark, wife of Hyrum Clark, age thirty-seven, born October 1862, married nineteen years, with nine children born, nine living. The 1930 federal census for Utah gives Mary A. Clark's birth year as 1878, with her first marriage at age twenty-five or in 1903. From 1903 to 1927 Clark had two wives.

35. Hendrick, "The Mormon Revival of Polygamy," 451.

36. Ibid.

37. Cannon II, "Beyond the Manifesto," *Sunstone*, 31.

38. Roberts, B. H., *Comprehensive History*, 6:399–400, cited in Quinn, "LDS Church Authority and New Plural Marriages," 12.

39. Erickson, "Star Valley, Wyoming: Polygamous Haven," 133.

40. Flake, "Emotional and Priestly Logic," 2–3. Flake adds that these charges have been brought against monogamy as well.

41. Quinn, *The Mormon Hierarchy: Wealth and Corporate Power*, front and back of book cover.

42. Jon Swaine, Douglas MacMillan, and Michelle Boorstein, "Mormon Church has misled members on $100 billion tax-exempt investment fund, whistleblower alleges," *Washington Post*, December 17, 2019.

43. John G. Turner, "Mormons and money: An unorthodox and messy history of church finances," *The Conversation*, December 20, 2019. Turner also authored *Brigham Young: Pioneer Prophet*, a 2014 biography.

44. Tad Walch, "Church responds to allegations made by former employee in IRS complaint," *Deseret News*, December 17, 2019.

45. Ian Lovett and Rachael Levy, "The Mormon Church Amassed $100 Billion. It Was the Best-Kept Secret in the Investment World," *Wall Street Journal*, February 8, 2020. See also Nate Carlisle, "LDS Church discloses the $37.8 billion stock portfolio of its biggest investment fund," *Salt Lake Tribune*, March 8, 2020. By historical precedent, the presiding bishop oversees the faith's vast financial, real estate, and investment operations, an office in 2020 held by Presiding Bishop Gérald Caussé. The fund increased from $40 billion in 2012 to $100 billion in 2019. Peggy Fletcher Stack, "LDS Church kept the lid on its $100B fund," *Salt Lake Tribune*, February 9, 2020.

CHAPTER 12. A PLATFORM FOR POLYGAMY'S SURVIVAL

1. "I make this prophecy in the name of Jesus Christ," said Owen Woodruff at a 1901 conference in Colonia Juarez, Mexico. This was recorded by polygamist Joseph Charles Bentley in his journal. According to Quinn, the LDS Presidency's first counselor Joseph F. Smith was on the stand next to Owen and made no effort to correct him, while Seymour B. Young, president of the Seventy, stood in the conference and endorsed the statement. Historian B. Carmon Hardy points out the "nearly identical remarks the previous year by Apostle Marriner W. Merrill." *Solemn Covenant*, 190, 205n133, 205n134.

2. Romney, *The Mormon Colonies in Mexico*, 38.

3. White, *Church, State, and Politics*, 136.

4. Quinn, "John W. Woolley as a Faithful Mormon from September 1886 to December 1913," 1–2. According to Foster and Watson, the date was July 18, 1887, when John Taylor told Joseph F. Smith of his 1886 revelation and gave Smith the same special appointment. Emphasis added.

5. Quinn, "John W. Woolley as a Faithful Mormon," 3.

6. Foster and Watson, *American Polygamy*, 40. Charles Henry Wilcken is a little-known recipient of allegedly shaking the hand of a resurrected prophet. Born in Germany in 1830, Wilcken served in the military and immigrated to America in 1857, joining the Utah Expedition under Colonel Albert Sidney Johnston. Captured by the Mormons, Wilcken was brought to Salt Lake City by Porter Rockwell. Wilcken became "knight errant for the First Presidency . . . and for Wilford Woodruff." Wilcken helped with the underground life of various LDS leaders, including carrying John Taylor's mail. Wilcken formed strong ties with Abraham H. Cannon, George Q. Cannon, Joseph F. Smith, and Wilford Woodruff. By 1890 Wilcken's relationship with Woodruff was "based more on collegiality and companionship than of . . . a bodyguard." When polygamist L. John Nuttall was hiding in Provo, Wilcken visited him with messages from George Q. Cannon and Joseph F. Smith to not give up for arrest. Wilcken had business dealings with railroad companies and in 1911 was named a church patriarch. He served as a guide on Temple Square and died in 1915. Seifert, "Charles Henry Wilcken, An Undervalued Saint," 308–21.

7. Ibid., 46–47.

8. Also called by some as "Council of Seven Friends."

9. Bennion, "Apostolic United Brethren," *World Religions and Spirituality*, May 27, 2019, https://wrldrels.org/2019/05/27/apostolic-united-brethren/.

10. Quinn, *Biography of J. Reuben Clark*, 183–84.

11. Quinn, "LDS Church Authority and New Plural Marriage," 57, 62.

12. "Discourse delivered at St. George, Utah, Thursday, May 8, 1899 by Pres. Lorenzo Snow," *Deseret Evening News*, June 3, 1899.

13. These plural marriages were William Cole Ockey to Ovena Jorgensen, September 14, 1898; Miles Archibald Romney to Lilly Burrell, October 23, 1898; Joseph Morrell to Mary Ann Davis, October 23, 1898, by Matthias F. Cowley;

Heber Manassah Cluff to Susan Carolyn Sims, October 30, 1898; Pierre Droubay to Martha Jane Dunn, January 1899, in Mexico City; Matthias F. Cowley to Harriet Bennion, January 1899; Winslow Farr Jr. to Sarah Mitchell, January 10, 1899. Hardy, *Solemn Covenant*, 394–426.

14. Foster and Watson, *American Polygamy*, 32. Roberts's mother, Ann Reed Everington, had been divorced twice and widowed once. She married Benjamin Roberts in 1848; William John Nichols in 1863; and Seth Dustin in 1869.
15. Jorgensen and Hardy, "The Taylor-Cowley Affair," 20. From 1904 to 1907, senate hearings on the seating of Reed Smoot kept President Joseph F. Smith's focus on denying secret continuing polygamy and habitation with plural wives.
16. *Deseret Evening News*, January 8, 1900.
17. "Polygamy and Unlawful Cohabitation," *Deseret Evening News*, January 8, 1900.
18. Italics added. Cited in Park City's biweekly newspaper, the *Park Record*, September 1, 1900. The *Park Record's* non-Mormon publishers, William O. Raddon and former *Salt Lake Tribune* editor Samuel L. Raddon, commented, "It is not to be much wondered at that the Mormons are made the subject of severe criticism ... when they allow their leaders to utter such words ... and counsel his hearers to disobey the law—according to the manifesto—of his church and of God on the polygamy question."
19. Allred to Woodruff, January 27, 1901, box 4, fd. 6, A. O. Woodruff Papers.
20. Briney, *Apostles on Trial*, 182.
21. Cannon and O'Higgins, *Under the Prophet*, 176–79, 237.
22. David Hoagland Cannon died of heart failure in October 1892 while in Germany serving a mission. David had never married. Quinn, "LDS Church Authority and New Plural Marriages," 84n303.
23. Quinn, "Plural Marriages After the 1890 Manifesto," address given at Bluffdale, Utah, August 11, 1991.
24. Utah Select Marriages, 1887–1937, available by paid membership to Ancestry .com.
25. Benjamin Cluff Presidential Papers, 1898 Series.
26. US Census Bureau, 1900 Federal Census, Utah, Emery County, Castle Dale.
27. Hardy, *Solemn Covenant*, appendix.
28. See Jorgensen and Hardy, "The Taylor-Cowley Affair," 18–20.
29. Bradley, "Polygamy," in *Historical Atlas of Mormonism*, 116.
30. Erickson, "Star Valley, Wyoming: Polygamous Haven," 131.
31. Snyder and Snyder, *Post-Manifesto Polygamy*, 21, 171n55.
32. Hendrick, "The Mormon Revival of Polygamy," 452.
33. Van Wagoner, *Mormon Polygamy*, 167–68.
34. "Fine of $300 is Imposed on Joseph F. Smith for Unlawful Cohabitation," *Salt Lake Telegram*, November 23, 1906; "Joseph F. Smith Pleaded Guilty Before Judge Ritchie," *Salt Lake Tribune*, November 24, 1906.

35. Paulos, "Under the Gun at the Smoot Hearings," 224–25.
36. Hardy, *Solemn Covenant*, appendix.
37. Erickson, "Star Valley, Wyoming: Polygamous Haven," 157.
38. Lambert, "Autobiography and Recollections, 1882–1953."
39. Carlos Ashby Badger Diaries, October 8, 1904, MS 2056, LDS Church History Department. Rosannah was well positioned to hear such talk and share it with her husband, as she was born out of wedlock to Frank Jenne Cannon but was raised in the George Q. Cannon household.
40. Hardy, *Solemn Covenant*, 182, 295, 305n65.
41. LDS_CHL, MS 3420_f001, Matthias Cowley Marriages, 1898–1903.
42. Ivins Journal, January to May 1903; Eckersley Journal, September 2–6, November 9, 1903; Lund journal, September 4, 1903; J. H. Smith Journal, October 1, 1903; all cited in Alexander, *Mormonism in Transition*, 62–63, 329n9.
43. Melvin Joseph Ballard was a monogamist, but his father, Henry Ballard, had three wives. Henry went on a two-year mission to England, a move suggested by Apostle Franklin D. Richards, as a stratagem for avoiding arrest from US marshals who had long been in his pursuit. Hardy, *Doing the Works of Abraham*, 335.
44. Romney, *The Mormon Colonies in Mexico*, 308. Wholesale and retail manufacturing of union suits, unique LDS garments, and all kinds of goods of silk, wool, and cotton were produced by the Logan firm. Eliza Avery Clark was attending the Agricultural School in Logan in 1900 and continued attending after her secret marriage to Owen Woodruff.
45. Merrill had eight wives, the last married in April 1901. Parkinson had two wives, last married in 1903. Nibley had three wives and seventeen children. Nibley's substantial wealth came from lumber businesses in Oregon, the Sumpter Valley and Payette Valley railroads, and as the Lewiston Sugar Company's president. Quinn, *Wealth and Corporate Power*, 305.
46. "A Sugar Factory for Lewiston Idaho," *Sugar Beet Gazette*, June 20, 1903.
47. Reed Smoot to C. E. Loose, January 6, 1904, Reed Smoot Collection, cited in Flake, *Politics of Religious Identity*, 51, 188n50.
48. According to historian H. Michael Marquardt, the Law of Retribution, or Oath of Vengeance, was first administered in Nauvoo and was included in the Mormon temple endowment ceremonies until February 1927. The target of vengeance changed over time. Joseph Smith, speaking to Stephen Markham of his premonition of being killed, extracted a promise that "my loyal friends will avenge my blood, that you and your posterity after you will not rest until *the last member of this mob is killed.*" Marquardt cites Increase Van Deusen's writing in 1847: "We will avenge the blood of Joseph Smith *on this Nation.*" Marquardt, personal communication, October 2011. By the Civil War era, the vengeance was interpreted as directed against the nation's entire non-Mormon population. Baskin, *Reminiscences of Early Utah*, 98–99.

49. Beside President Smith, those included were Francis W. Lyman, John Henry Smith, and Hyrum Mack Smith. George Teasdale fled to Mexico, where he remained until August 1906 after the hearings had ended; Heber J. Grant had already fled to Europe, where he remained until November 1906.

50. Lund to Woodruff, February 14, 1904, box 4, fd. 10, A. O. Woodruff Papers.

51. "Bethel" for Salt Lake City; "Chicago" for Byron, Wyoming; "Chief" for Joseph Fielding Smith; "Clarence" for Owen Woodruff; "Hettie" and "Nellie" for Helen May Winters Woodruff; "Illinois" for the Big Horn Basin; and "Maggie" for Eliza Avery Clark Woodruff are examples cited in Snyder and Snyder, *Post-Manifesto Polygamy*.

52. George F. Gibbs, as secretary to the First Presidency, advised Apostle Heber J. Grant in 1903 to marry a plural wife and take her on a mission to England, where she would not be recognized or known. Quinn, "Plural Marriages After the 1890 Manifesto."

53. Grant to Woodruff, June 21, 1904, typescript, box 4, fd. 8, A. O. Woodruff Papers.

54. Michael Quinn to the author, personal communication, January 2016.

55. Abraham Owen Woodruff, Journal, 147.

56. "Schools Close Indefinitely," *Deseret Evening News*, January 29, 1900.

57. Cowley to Aunt Emma, June 28, 1904, box 4, fd. 7, A. O. Woodruff Papers.

58. Snyder and Snyder, *Post-Manifesto Polygamy*, 82; Erickson, "Star Valley, Wyoming," 155.

59. Snyder and Snyder, *Post-Manifesto Polygamy*, 27, 39. Heber Erastus Farr, born in Ogden in 1875, baptized by John W. Taylor in 1883, was called on a mission to Colonia Dublan from 1897 to 1899. His plural marriage to Hilda Bluth was performed there on March 25, 1904, by Anthony W. Ivins. Hardy, *Solemn Covenant*, appendix.

60. *The Diaries of Heber J. Grant*.

61. Snyder and Snyder, *Post-Manifesto Polygamy*, 40.

62. *The Diaries of Heber J. Grant*.

63. *The Diaries of Heber J. Grant*.

64. Joseph F. Smith to J. C. Burrows, April 15, 1904, Reed Smoot Collection, cited in Flake, *Politics of American Identity*, 102, 199n68.

65. Alexander, *Mormonism in Transition*, 24.

66. Smoot to the First Presidency, December 9, 1905, Reed Smoot Collection, cited in Flake, *Politics of American Identity*, 107, 200n92.

67. Quinn, "Plural Marriages After the 1890 Manifesto."

68. Smoot to Owen Woodruff, January 21, 1904, typescript, box 4, fd. 11, A. O. Woodruff Papers.

69. Flake, *Politics of American Identity*, 101.

70. Cowley, "Family History."

71. Flake speculates that this vague explanation may have been to facilitate the men's later return to full privileges, *Politics of American Identity*, 205n26.

72. Flake, *Politics of American Identity*, 205n13.

73. Quinn, "Plural Marriages After the 1890 Manifesto."

74. Briney, *Apostles on Trial*, 89, 92, 112, 133, 142, 173, 178, 197.

75. Quinn, "Plural Marriages After the 1890 Manifesto."

76. Ibid.

77. Briney, *Apostles on Trial*, emphasis added.

78. This revelation is included in Collier's *Unpublished Revelations*, 2011 Edition, vol. 1, part 114, 374–75.

79. The word count for this revelation is 275. Author not given, *The Trials for the Membership of John W. Taylor and Matthias F. Cowley*, Post Office Box 473, West Jordan, Utah, 84084, 1, 4.

80. *The Trials for the Membership of John W. Taylor and Matthias F. Cowley*, 6.

81. Briney, *Apostles on Trial*, 109–10, 111.

82. Quinn, "John W. Woolley as a Highly Trusted Mormon from September 1886 to December 1913," 7, 7n4, 11, 11n8.

83. Quinn, "John W. Woolley as a Highly Trusted Mormon," 8. The word count for this handwritten photographed version is 289. Briney, *Apostles on Trial*, 109–10.

84. Briney, *Apostles on Trial*, 123.

85. Briney, *Apostles on Trial*, 143; *The Trials for the Membership of John W. Taylor and Matthias F. Cowley*, 11–12. The name of Taylor's sixth wife, Ellen Georgina Sandberg, was not given in the record.

86. Quinn, *Extensions of Power*, 786.

87. Five years earlier, when Heber J. Grant was in Europe and learned that Taylor and Cowley were to lose their apostleship, Grant was outraged and wrote to the church president to not allow this, because he felt he was equally involved in post-Manifesto polygamy. Grant wrote, "If you drop them, you should drop me, because the only thing that has kept me from being in their situation is that the circumstances just did not workout." Quinn, "Plural Marriages After the 1890 Manifesto."

88. Of Cowley's forty-six marriages performed, only three were after Smith's 1904 Manifesto. Cowley's final documented marriage was in 1909 of John W. Taylor to his sixth wife, Ellen G. Sandberg. See Table 1A.

89. Briney, *Apostles on Trial*, 195.

90. Hardy, *Solemn Covenant*, 266, 281n142. Hardy does not identify the two leaders who held for Cowley's punishment.

91. One source claims that Cowley's salary was $150 per month; another source cites $35 per month for one of Taylor's wives.

92. Cowley, "Family History Sketch," 17.

93. Taylor, *Taylor-Made Tales*, 3.

94. Hardy, *Solemn Covenant*, 267, 282n150; Samuel W. Taylor, "Interviews with Nettie Taylor," 14–15, January 1936.

95. Taylor, *Family Kingdom*, 298. Penrose was Owen Woodruff's replacement in the Twelve.

96. Taylor, *"Record of Reinstatement,"* 1; Taylor, *Taylor-Made Tales*, 200.

97. Taylor, *Taylor-Made Tales*, 202.

98. Hardy, *Solemn Covenant*, 282; "Reconciliation, Letters Passing between the First Presidency and Elder Matthias Cowley," *Deseret Evening News*, April 3, 1936, cited in Hardy, *Solemn Covenant*, 282n148.

99. "LDS Will Hear Mission Worker," *Salt Lake Tribune*, October 23, 1938; "Services Set for Churches in Salt Lake City," *Salt Lake Tribune*, October 23, 1938.

100. Quinn, "LDS Church Authority and New Plural Marriages," 57–58, 63–65. Quinn argues that Woodruff married Mountford in September of 1897 on a steamship on the Pacific Ocean, between San Francisco and Portland.

101. Quinn, "John W. Woolley, as a Highly Trusted Mormon," 2.

102. Foster and Watson, *American Polygamy*, 55–56. It is uncertain whether Woolley invoked the revelation of 1886.

103. "Excommunication of John W. Woolley," *Salt Lake Tribune*, April 1, 1914.

104. Wood, Benjamin, "Utah Senate votes unanimously to decriminalize polygamy," *Salt Lake Tribune*, February 18, 2020. The article makes no mention whether the law required a husband to financially support wives and children.

Bibliography

COLLECTIONS

Cannon, Abraham H. Abraham Hoagland Cannon Journals, 1879–1895, MSS 0003. Special Collections, J. Willard Marriott Library, University of Utah, Salt Lake City, Utah.

Clayton, David Cowley. "Matthias Cowley." Typescript, 12 pages. Matthias F. Cowley Family, Accn 1223, Special Collections, J. Willard Marriott Library, University of Utah, Salt Lake City, Utah.

Cluff, Benjamin, Jr. Register of the Brigham Young University President's Records, 1893–1903, UA 1093, L. Tom Perry Special Collections, Harold B. Lee Library, Brigham Young University, Provo, Utah.

Cowley, Matthias Foss. "Family Sketch of the History of Matthias Foss Cowley," n.d. Typescript, 17 pages. Matthias F. Cowley Family, Accn 1223, Special Collections, J. Willard Marriott Library, University of Utah, Salt Lake City, Utah.

Doty, Ariel R. Ariel R. Doty Journals, MSS 23715. LDS Church History Library, Salt Lake City, Utah.

Journal History of The Church of Jesus Christ of Latter-day Saints, 1830–2008, CR 100 137 and CR 100 93. LDS Church History Library, Salt Lake City, Utah.

Lambert, Eliza Avery Clark Woodruff. "Autobiography and Recollections, 1882–1953," Box 6, Folder 21, L. Tom Perry, Special Collections, Harold B. Lee Library, Brigham Young University, Provo, Utah.

Riter, Benjamin Franklin. Benjamin Franklin Riter Papers, 1882–1966, MSS B 46. Utah State Historical Society, Salt Lake City, Utah.

Sessions, Edwin S. Edwin S. Sessions Collection, ca. 1900–1940, MSS 15588. LDS Church History Library, Salt Lake City, Utah.

Woodruff, Abraham Owen. Abraham Owen Woodruff Papers, MSS 777. L. Tom Perry Special Collections, Harold B. Lee Library, Brigham Young University, Provo, Utah.

Woodruff, Etha Mayo. Etha Mayo Woodruff Memorial Collection of Family Papers, 1863–1925, MSS HM 70372-70384. Manuscripts Department, The Huntington Library, Art Collections, and Botanical Gardens, San Marino, California.

GOVERNMENT DOCUMENTS

Committee on Privileges and Elections, of the United States Senate, in the Matter of The Protests Against the Right of Hon. Reed Smoot, a Senator from the State of Utah, to Hold His Seat. 2 vols. Washington, DC: Government Printing Office, 1906.

Hearings Before the Committee on Invalid Pensions, House of Representative, House of Representative, Seventy Sixth Congress on HR 1006 HR, 3996, HR 4924, HR 4991, HR 4999, HR 7899, HR 8030, and HR 9149. Bills to Liberalize the Now Existing Benefits with Reference to Liberalize the Now Existing Benefits with Reference to Veterans and Dependents of Veterans of the Indian Wars, January 22 and 23, 1940. Washington, DC: United States Government Printing, 1940.

Mansfield, G. R., and Leona Boardman. "Nitrate Deposits of the United States." *Bulletin 838 US Department of the Interior.* Washington, DC: Government Printing Office, 1932.

BOOKS AND PUBLISHED WORKS

Abbott, Susan Emma Woodruff. *Woodruff Genealogy: Descendants of Mathew Woodruff of Farmington, Connecticut.* New Haven, CT: Harty Press, 1963.

Alexander, Thomas G. *Mormonism in Transition, A History of the Latter-day Saints, 1890–1930.* Urbana: University of Illinois Press, 1996.

———. *Things in Heaven and Earth: The Life and Times of Wilford Woodruff, a Mormon Prophet.* Salt Lake City: Signature Books, 1991.

———. "'To Maintain Harmony': Adjusting to External and Internal Stress, 1890–1930." *Dialogue: A Journal of Mormon Thought* 15 (Winter 1982): 44–58.

Arrington, Leonard J. *Great Basin Kingdom: An Economic History of the Latter-day Saints, 1830–1900.* Salt Lake City: University of Utah Press and Tanner Trust Fund, 1993.

———. "Utah and the Depression of the 1890s." *Utah Historical Quarterly* 29 (January 1961): 3–20.

Athearn, Robert G. *Union Pacific Country.* Chicago: Rand McNally & Company, 1971.

Bagley, Will. *Blood of the Prophets: Brigham Young and the Massacre at Mountain Meadows.* Norman: University of Oklahoma Press, 2002.

Bagley, Will, ed. *The Whites Want Every Thing: Indian–Mormon Relations, 1847–1877.* Norman: Arthur H. Clark Company, 2019.

Barnes, Darcee. "Mormon Colonizers in Wyoming's Bighorn Basin," wyohistory .org. August 3, 2015. https://www.wyohistory.org/encyclopedia/mormon -colonizers-wyomings-bighorn-basin

Barton, John D. *A History of Duchesne County*. Salt Lake City: Utah State Historical Society and Duchesne County Commission, 1998.

Baskin, Robert N. *Reminiscences of Early Utah*. 1914; Salt Lake City: Signature Books, 2006.

Beard, Francis Birkhead. *Wyoming: From Territorial Day to the Present*. 3 vols. New York: American Historical Society, 1933.

Bell, E. Jay. "The Windows of Heaven Revisited: The 1899 Tithing Reformation." *Journal of Mormon History* 29 (Spring 1994): 45–83.

Bennett, Richard E., Susan Easton Black, and Donald Q. Cannon. *The Nauvoo Legion in Illinois: A History of the Mormon Militia, 1841–1846*. Norman: Arthur H. Clark, 2010.

Bennion, Janet. "Apostolic United Brethren." World Religions and Spirituality. https://wrldrels.org/2019/05/27/apostolic-united-brethren/.

———. *Polygamy in Primetime, Media, Gender, and Politics in Mormon Fundamentalism*. Waltham, MA: Brandeis University Press, 2012.

Bergera, Gary James. "Identifying the Earliest Mormon Polygamists, 1841–44." *Dialogue: A Journal of Mormon Thought* 38 (Fall 2005): 1–74.

Bitton, Davis. *George Q. Cannon: A Biography*. Salt Lake City: Deseret Book, 1999.

Blair, Pat, Dana Prater, and the Sheridan County Museum. *Images of America: Sheridan*. Charleston, SC: Arcadia Publishing Company, 2008.

Bonner, Robert E. "Buffalo Bill Cody and Wyoming Water Politics." *Western Historical Quarterly* 33 (Winter 2002): 432–51.

———. "Elwood Mead, Buffalo Bill Cody, and the Carey Act in Wyoming." *Montana: The Magazine of Western History* 55 (Spring 2005): 36–51.

———. *William F. Cody's Wyoming Empire: The Buffalo Bill Nobody Knows*. Norman: University of Oklahoma Press, 2007.

Bowen, Marshall. "Migration to and from a Northern Wyoming Mormon Community, 1900 to 1925." *Pioneer America* 9, no. 2 (1977): 208–27.

Bradley, Martha. "Polygamy." In *Historical Atlas of Mormonism*. New York: Simon & Shuster, 1994.

Briney, Drew. *Apostles on Trial*. Hindsight Publications, 2012.

Brodie, Fawn M. *No Man Knows My History: The Life of Joseph Smith, The Mormon Prophet*. 2d ed. New York: Random House, 1971.

Brown, S. Kent, Donald Q. Cannon, Richard H. Jackson, eds. *Historical Atlas of Mormonism*. New York: Simon & Shuster, 1994.

Brooks, Bryant G., ed. *The State of Wyoming*. N.p., 1905.

Bryant, Mike. "Bad Pass Trail: Gateway between the Wind and Yellowstone Rivers." *Rocky Mountain Fur Trade Journal* 11 (2017): 86–111.

Bushman, Richard Lyman. *Joseph Smith: Rough Stone Rolling*. New York: Alfred A. Knopf, 2005.

Campbell, Eugene H. *Establishing Zion: The Mormon Church in the American West, 1847–1869*. Salt Lake City: Signature Books, 1988.

Cannon, Frank J., and George L. Knapp. *Brigham Young and His Mormon Empire.* New York: Fleming H. Revell Co., 1913.

Cannon, Frank J., and Harvey J. O'Higgins. *Under the Prophet in Utah.* Boston, MA: C. M. Clark Publishing Company, 1911.

Cannon, Kenneth L., II. "After the Manifesto Mormon Polygamy, 1890–1906." *Sunstone* 8 (January–April 1983): 27–35.

———. "After the Manifesto: Mormon Polygamy, 1890–1906." in *The New Mormon History: Revisionist Essays on the Past.* Edited by D. Michael Quinn. Salt Lake City: Signature Books, 1992.

———. "Beyond the Manifesto: Polygamous Cohabitation among LDS General Authorities after 1890." *Utah Historical Quarterly* 46 (Winter 1978): 24–36.

———. "Wives and Other Women: Love, Sex, and Marriage in the Lives of John Q. Cannon, Frank J. Cannon, and Abraham H. Cannon." *Dialogue: A Journal of Mormon Thought* 43 (Winter 2010): 71–130.

Chatterton, Fennimore. *The State of Wyoming: An Official Publication Containing Reliable Information Concerning the Resources of the State.* Wyoming Secretary of State, 1904.

Childers, Christopher. *The Failure of Popular Sovereignty: Slavery, Manifest Destiny, and the Radicalization of Southern Politics.* Lawrence: University of Kansas Press, 2012.

Clarke, Arthur C. *2010: Odyssey Two.* New York: Del Ray Books, 1982.

Clawson, Rudger. *Prisoner for Polygamy: The Memoirs and Letters of Rudger Clawson at the Utah Territorial Penitentiary, 1884–1887.* Edited by Stan Larson. Urbana: University of Illinois Press, 1993.

Collier, Fred C. "New Light on the Lorin Woolley Story and Early Fundamentalist Beginnings." http://josephsmithspolygamy.org/new-light-on-the-lorin-woolley-story-and-early-fundamentalist-beginnings/.

Collier, Fred C., comp. *Unpublished Revelations of the Prophets and Presidents of the Church of Jesus Christ of Latter-Day Saints.* Salt Lake City: Collier's Publishing Co., Vol. 1, 1979, Vol. 2, 1993.

Colliflower, William W. *Misfits of Medicine.* Victoria, BC, Canada: Friesen Press, 2019. Electronic edition.

Compton, Todd. *In Sacred Loneliness. The Plural Wives of Joseph Smith.* Salt Lake City: Signature Books, 1997.

Cuch, Forrest S., ed. *A History of Utah's American Indians.* Salt Lake City: Utah Division of Indian Affairs and Utah Division of State History, 2003.

Dahl, Adam. *Empire of the People: Settler Colonization and the Foundations of Modern Democratic Thought.* Lawrence: University of Kansas Press, 2018.

Davis, John W. *Goodbye, Judge Lynch: The End of a Lawless Era in Wyoming's Big Horn Basin.* Norman: University of Oklahoma Press, 2005.

———. *Wyoming Range War.* Norman: University of Oklahoma Press, 2010.

Deloria, Philip. Book Review of *Tecumseh and the Prophet: The Shawnee Brothers Who Defied a Nation,* by Peter Cozzens New York: Knopf, 2020. In *The New Yorker,* November 2, 2020, 76–80.

Dunn, JR., J. P. *Massacres of the Mountains: A History of the Indian Wares of the Far West*. Mechanicsburg, PA: Stackpole Books, 2002.

Elliott, Russell Richard. "The Early History of White Pine County, Nevada, 1865–1887." *Pacific Northwest Quarterly* 30 (April 1939): 145–68.

Embry, Jessie L. "Exiles for the Principle: LDS Polygamy in Canada." *Dialogue: A Journal of Mormon Thought* 18 (July 1985): 108–116.

Erickson, Dan. "Alberta Polygamists? The Canadian Climate and Response to the Introduction of Mormonism's Peculiar Institution.'" *Pacific Northwest Quarterly* 86 (Fall 1995): 155–64.

———. "Star Valley, Wyoming: Polygamous Haven," *Journal of Mormon History* 26 (Spring 2000): 123–64.

Fillerup, Melvin M. *A Pioneer History: Sidon, the Canal that Faith Built*. Cody, WY: Ptarmigan Company, 1988.

Flake, Kathleen. "The Emotional and Priestly Logic of Plural Marriage." Arrington Annual Lecture, Leonard J. Arrington Mormon History Lectures, Utah State University, 2009.

———. *The Politics of American Religious Identity: The Seating of Senator Reed Smoot, Mormon Apostle*. Chapel Hill: University of North Carolina Press, 2004.

Foster, Craig L., and Marianne T. Watson. *American Polygamy: A History of Fundamentalist Mormon Faith*. Charleston, SC: History Press, 2019.

Frison, Paul. *Calendar of Change*. Worland, WY: Serl Kay, Inc. Printing, 1975.

Geisner, Joseph W., ed. *Writing Mormon History*. Salt Lake City: Signature Books, 2020.

Gibson, Richard I. "Mining City History: Butte's First Railroad was Clandestine." *Montana Standard,* August 26, 2019.

Gillette, Edward. *Locating the Iron Trail*. Boston: Christopher Publishing House, 1925.

Gordon, Sarah Barringer. *The Mormon Question: Polygamy and Constitutional Conflict in Nineteenth Century America*. Chapel Hill: University of North Carolina Press, 2002.

Graham, D. Kurt. "The Mormon Migration to Wyoming's Big Horn Basin." Master's thesis, Brigham Young University, 1994.

Grant, Heber J. *The Diaries of Heber J. Grant, 1880–1945 Abridged*. Salt Lake City: 2015. Digital edition.

Hales, Brian C., and Laura H. Hales. *Joseph Smith's Polygamy*. 3 vols. Salt Lake City: Greg Kofford Books, 2013.

Hardee, Jim. *Pierre's Hole! The Fur Trade History of Teton Valley, Idaho*. Pinedale, WY: Museum of the Mountain Man and Sublette County Historical Society, 2010.

Hardt, Michael. *Empire*. Cambridge, MA: Harvard University Press, 2001.

Hardy, B. Carmon. *Doing the Works of Abraham: Mormon Polygamy, Its Origins, Practice, and Demise*. Norman, OK: Arthur H. Clark Co., 2007.

———. "Mormon Polygamy in Mexico and Canada: A Legal and Historiographical Review." In *The Mormon Presence in Canada*. Edited by Brigham Young Card. Logan: Utah State University Press, 1990.

————. *Solemn Covenant: The Mormon Polygamous Passage*. Urbana: University of Illinois Press, 1992.

Hardy, B. Carmon, and Dan Erickson. "'Regeneration—Now and Evermore!': Mormon Polygamy and the Physical Rehabilitation of Humankind." *Journal of the History of Sexuality* 10 (January 2001): 40–61.

Harris, Cole. "How Did Colonialism Dispossess? Comments from an Edge of Empire." *Annals of the Association of American Geographers* 94 (March 2004): 165–82.

Hendrick, Burton J. "The Mormon Revival of Polygamy." *McClure's Magazine* 36 (February 1911): 458–64.

Homer, Michael W. *Joseph's Temples: The Dynamic Relationship Between Freemasonry and Mormonism*. Salt Lake City: University of Utah Press, 2014.

Homsher, Lois M. "Wyoming Zephyrs." *Ann. of Wyoming* (January 1953): 91.

Horne, Dennis B., ed. *An Apostle's Record: The Journal of Abraham H. Cannon*. Clearfield, UT: Gnolaum Books, 2004.

Ivins, Stanley S. "Notes on Mormon Polygamy." *Utah Historical Quarterly* 35 (Fall 1967): 309–21.

Jenson, Andrew. *Latter-Day Saint Biographical Encyclopedia*. Vol. 1. Salt Lake City: Andrew Jenson Company and Deseret News, 1901.

Jorgensen, Victor W., and B. Carmon Hardy. "The Taylor-Cowley Affair and the Watershed of Mormon History." *Utah Historical Quarterly* 48 (Winter 1980): 4–36.

Kelley, Mary. *Images of America: Gillette*. Charleston, SC: Arcadia Publishing Company, 2010.

Kenner, S. A., *Utah As It Is: With a Comprehensive Statement of Utah As It Was*. Salt Lake City: Deseret News, 1904.

LaRocque, Francois-Antione. *The Journal of Francois LaRocque*. Fairfield, WA: Ye Galleon Press, 1981.

Larson, Stan. "A 'Meeting of the Brethren.'" *Dialogue: A Journal of Mormon Thought* 31, no. 2 (1998): 77–95.

Laudenschlager, David D. "The Utes in South Dakota, 1906-1908." *South Dakota History* 9, no. 3 (1979): 234-47.

Lee, B. Lawrence. "The Mormons Come to Canada, 1887–1902." *Pacific Northwest Quarterly* 59 (January 1968): 11–22.

Lehr, John Campbell. "Polygamy, Patrimony, and Prophecy: The Mormon Colonization of Cardston." *Dialogue: A Journal of Mormon Thought* 21 (Winter 1988): 114–21.

LeSuer, Stephen C. *The 1838 Mormon War in Missouri*. Columbia: University of Missouri Press, 1987.

Lindsay, Charles. *The Big Horn Basin*. Lincoln: University of Nebraska Press, 1930.

Loveland, Carla Neves. *Sagebrush and Roses: A History of Otto and Burlington, Wyoming*. Lindon, UT: Alexander's Digital Printing, 2003.

Lowe, James A. *The Bridger Trail: A Viable Alternative Route to the Gold Fields of Montana Territory in 1864*. Spokane, WA: Arthur H. Clark Co., 1999.

Lyman, Edward Leo. *Political Deliverance: The Mormon Quest for Utah Statehood*. Urbana: University of Illinois Press, 1986.

Lythgoe, Eliza R. "Colonization of the Big Horn Basin by the Mormons." *Annals of Wyoming* 14 (January 1942): 39–50.

MacKinnon, William P. *At Sword's Point, Part I: A Documentary History of the Utah War to 1858*. Norman: University of Oklahoma Press, 2008.

Malmquist, O[rvin]. N[ebeker]. *The First 100 Years: A History of the Salt Lake Tribune, 1871–1971*. Salt Lake City: Utah State Historical Society, 1971.

Marquardt, H. Michael. *Joseph Smith Revelations: Text and Commentary*. Salt Lake City: Signature Books, 1999.

———. "The Strange Marriages of Sarah Ann Whitney to Joseph Smith, the Mormon Prophet, Joseph C. Kingsbury, and Heber C. Kimball." 1973; Rev. ed., 1982. https://user.xmission.com/~research/family/strange.htm

Mattes, Merrill J. *Colter's Hell and Jackson Hole*. Yellowstone Library and Museum Association, Grand Teton Natural History Association, and National Park Service, 1962.

Maxwell, John Gary. *The Civil War Years in Utah: The Kingdom of God and the Territory That Did Not Fight*. Norman: University of Oklahoma Press, 2016.

———. *Gettysburg to Great Salt Lake: George R. Maxwell, Civil War Hero and Federal Marshal, among the Mormons*. Norman, OK: Arthur H. Clark Company and University of Oklahoma Press, 2010.

———. *Robert Newton Baskin and the Making of Modern Utah*. Norman: Arthur H. Clark Company and University of Oklahoma Press, 2013.

May, Dean L. *Three Frontiers: Family, Land, and Society in the American West, 1850–1900*. New York: Cambridge University Press, 1994.

Metcalfe, Erin B. "'Firm and Steadfast in the Faith': Patterson O'Bannion and the Battle of Crooked River." *Mormon Historical Studies* 14 (Fall 2013): 189–201.

Meyers, Rex C. "The Cody Route to Yellowstone." *Annals of Wyoming* 81 (Autumn 2009): 11–29.

Minutes of the Apostles of The Church of Jesus Christ of Latter-day Saints, 1835–1951. Salt Lake City: privately published, 2015. Digital edition.

Neilson, Reid L., ed. *In the Whirlpool: The Pre-Manifesto Letters of President Wilford Woodruff to William Atkin Family, 1885–1890*. Norman: University of Oklahoma Press, 2011.

Nichols, Robert L. *With Courage Not Words: Ancestors and Descendants of Sidney James Tebbs*. Privately published, 2000.

O'Neil, Floyd A. "An Anguished Odyssey: The Flight of the Utes, 1906–1908," *Utah Historical Quarterly* 36 (Winter 1968): 315–27.

———. "The Reluctant Suzerainty: The Uintah and Ouray Reservation." *Utah Historical Quarterly* 39 (Spring 1971): 134–37.

O'Neil, Floyd A., and John D. Sylvester, eds. *Ute People: An Historical Study*. Salt Lake City: Uintah School District and the Western History Center, University of Utah, 1970.

Ostling, Richard N., and Joan K. Ostling. *The Power and Promise of Mormon America*. San Francisco: Harper Collins, 1999.

Parson, Robert E. *History of Rich County*. Salt Lake City: Utah State Historical Society and Rich County Commission, 1996.

Partridge, Mark N. *With Book and Plow: History of a Mormon Settlement*. Rev. ed. Bountiful, UT: Family History Publishers, 2003.

Paulos, Michael Harold. "Under the Gun at the Smoot Hearings: Joseph F. Smith's Testimony." *Journal of Mormon History* 34 (Fall 2008): 181–225.

Payne, Body, ed. "Rudger Clawson's Report on LDS Church Finances at the Turn of the Twentieth Century." *Dialogue: A Journal of Mormon Thought* 31 (Winter 1998): 165–79.

Peterson, Charles S. "The Americanization of Utah's Agriculture." *Utah Historical Quarterly* 42 (Spring 1974): 108–25.

———. "Changing Times: A View from Cache Valley, 1890–1915." *USU Faculty Honor Lectures*, Paper 9. 1979.

Peterson, John Alton. *Utah's Black Hawk War*. Salt Lake City: University of Utah Press, 1998.

Quinn, D. Michael. *Elder Statesman: A Biography of J. Reuben Clark*. Salt Lake City: Signature Books, 2001.

———. "John W. Woolley as a Highly Trusted Mormon from September 1886 to December 1913." Rev. September 1, 2019, in possession of the author.

———. "LDS Church Authority and New Plural Marriages, 1890–1904." *Dialogue: A Journal of Mormon Thought* 18 (Spring 1985): 9–105.

———. *LDS Church Authority and New Plural Marriages, 1890–1904*. Salt Lake City: Pioneer Press, 2001.

———. "Lorin C. Woolley as a Faithful Mormon from September 1886 to December 1913." Rev. September 1, 2019, in possession of the author.

———. *The Mormon Hierarchy: Extensions of Power*. Salt Lake City: Signature Books, 1997.

———. *The Mormon Hierarchy: Wealth and Corporate Power*. Salt Lake City: Signature Books, 2017.

———. "Plural Marriages After the 1890 Manifesto." Address given at Bluffdale, Utah, August 11, 1991, in possession of the author.

Rich, Benjamin Erastus. *Elder's Journal of the Southern States Mission*. Vol. 1. Atlanta, GA: Ben E. Rich, June 1904.

Rielly, P. T. "Warren Marshall Johnson, Forgotten Saint." *Utah Historical Quarterly* 39 (Winter 1971): 3–22.

Riter, Lesley Day Woodruff. "Biographical Sketch of the Life of John Dwight Woodruff." *Annals of Wyoming* 3, no 4 (April 1926): 212–27.

Roberts, Brigham H. *A Comprehensive History of the Church of Jesus Christ of Latter-day Saints.* 6 vols. Salt Lake City: Deseret News Press, 1930.

Roberts, Phil. "Watering a Dry Land: Wyoming and Federal Legislation," October 28, 2019. WyoHistory.org.

Rogers, Brent M. *Unpopular Sovereignty: Mormons and the Federal Management of Early Utah Territory.* Lincoln: University of Nebraska Press, 2017.

Rogers, Jedediah S. *In the President's Office: The Diaries of L. John Nuttall, 1879–1892.* Salt Lake City: Signature Books, 2007.

Romney, Thomas Cottam. *The Mormon Colonies in Mexico.* Salt Lake City: University of Utah Press, 1938.

Saunders, Richard L., ed. *Dale Morgan on the Mormons, Collected Works, Part I, 1939–1951.* Norman: Arthur H. Clark Company, 2012.

Seifrit, William C. "Charles Henry Wilcken, an Undervalued Saint." *Utah Historical Quarterly* 55 (Fall 1987): 308–21.

Sheppard, William, and H. Michael Marquardt. *Lost Apostles: Forgotten Members of Mormonism's Original Quorum of Twelve.* Salt Lake City: Signature Books, 2014.

Sherlock, Richard. "Mormon Migration and Settlement After 1875." *Journal of Mormon History* 2 (1975): 53–68.

Sillito, John, and Susan Staker, eds. *Mormon Mavericks: Essays on Dissenters.* Salt Lake City: Signature Books, 2002.

Simmons, Roland. "The Organization of the Big Horn Stake." Presented at the 41st Annual Meeting of the Mormon History Association, Casper, Wyoming, May 2006.

Smart, William B. *Mormonism's Last Colonizer: The Life and Times of William H. Smart.* Logan: Utah State University Press, 2008.

Smith, Elizabeth Shaw. "The W. C. Partridge Family and the Settling of Cowley, Wyoming: Worth the Cost?" Presented at the 41st Annual Meeting of the Mormon History Association, Casper, Wyoming, May 2006.

Smith, George D. *Nauvoo Polygamy: "But We Called It Celestial Marriage."* Salt Lake City: Signature Books, 2008.

———. "Nauvoo Roots of Mormon Polygamy, 1841–46: A Preliminary Demographic Report." *Dialogue: A Journal of Mormon Thought* 27 (Spring 1994): 1–72.

Smith, Joseph F., Jr., and Richard C. Evans. *Blood Atonement and the Origins of Plural Marriage.* Salt Lake City: Deseret News Press, 1905.

Snyder, Lu Ann Taylor, and Phillip A. Snyder, eds. *Post-Manifesto Polygamy: The 1899–1904 Correspondence of Helen, Owen, and Avery Woodruff.* Logan: Utah State University Press, 2009.

Staker, Susan. "Waiting for World's End: Wilford Woodruff & David Koresh." *Sunstone Magazine* 16 (December 1993): 11–16.

Staker, Susan, ed. *Waiting for World's End: The Diaries of Wilford Woodruff.* Salt Lake City: Signature Press, 1993.

Stegner, Wallace. *Wolf Willow: A History, A Story, and A Memory of the Last Plains Frontier*. New York: Penguin Books, 2000.

Stenhouse, Mrs. T. B. H. *Expose of Polygamy in Utah. A Lady's Life Among the Mormons. A Record of Personal Experience as One of the Wives of a Mormon Elder During a Period of More Than Twenty Years*. New York: American News Company, 1872.

Tanner, Annie Clark. *Mormon Mother, An Autobiography*. Salt Lake City: Signature Books, 1983.

Taylor, Raymond Woolley. "Record of the Reinstatement of the Last Apostle John Whittaker Taylor, 1858–1916." Provo, Utah: n.p., 1965. Copy in LDS Church History Library, Salt Lake City, Utah.

Taylor, Samuel W. *Taylor-Made Tales*. Murray, UT: Aspen Books, 1994.

Taylor, Samuel Woolley. *Family Kingdom*. New York: McGraw-Hill Book Company, 1951.

Traxel, David. *The Birth of the American Century*. New York: Knopf, 1998.

The Trials for the Membership of John W. Taylor and Mathaias [sic] Cowley. West Jordan, UT: Mormon Underground Press, 1976.

Tubbs, Stephanie Ambrose, with Clay Straus Jenkinson. *The Lewis and Clark Companion: An Encyclopedic Guide to the Voyage of Discovery*. New York: Henry Hold and Company, 2003.

Turner, Frederick Jackson. *The Frontier in American History*. New York: Henry Holt and Company, 1921.

Turner, John G. *Brigham Young, Pioneer Prophet*. Cambridge, MA: Belknap Press of Harvard University Press, 2012.

Ulrich, Laurel Thatcher. *A House Full of Females: Plural Marriage and Women's Rights in Early Mormonism, 1835–1870*. New York: Knopf, 2017.

Van Wagoner, Richard S. *Complete Discourses of Brigham Young*, 5 vols. Salt Lake City: The Smith-Pettit Foundation, 2009.

———. *Mormon Polygamy: A History*. 2d ed. Salt Lake City: Signature Books, 1989.

———, "Sarah M. Pratt: The Shaping of an Apostate." *Dialogue: A Journal of Mormon Thought* 19 (Summer 1986): 69–99.

Vileisis, Ann E. "Working on Desert Rails: A Social and Environmental History." MA thesis, Utah State University, 1992.

Walker, David. *Railroading Religion: Mormons, Tourists, and the Spirit of the West*. Chapel Hill: University of North Carolina Press, 2019.

Walker, Tacetta B. *Stories of Early Days in Wyoming: Big Horn Basin*. Casper, WY: Prairie Publishing Company, 1936.

Welch, Arthur H. *Frederick Arza Welch: Laborer in the Lord's Vineyard, 1889–1954*. N.p., 1987.

Welch, Charles A. *History of the Big Horn Basin*. Salt Lake City: Deseret News Press, 1940; reprinted, 1998.

White, Jean Bickmore, ed. *Church, State, and Politics: The Diaries of John Henry Smith.* Salt Lake City: Signature Books, 1990.

Whitefield, Jim. *The Mormon Delusion: The Truth Behind Polygamy and Secret Polyandry.* Vol. 1. Raleigh, NC: Lulu Press, 2009.

Wilson, Lycurgus A. *Life of David W. Patten: The First Apostolic Martyr.* Salt Lake City: The Deseret News Company, 1904.

Winchester, Simon. *Land: How the Hunger for Ownership Shaped the Modern World.* New York: Harper, an Imprint of Harper Collins Publishers, 2021.

Wolfe, Patrick. "Settler Colonization and the Elimination of the Native." *Journal of Genocide Research* 8 (December 2006): 387–409.

Woods, Lawrence M. *Wyoming's Big Horn Basin to 1901: A Late Frontier.* Spokane, WA: Arthur H. Clark Company, 1997.

Wyoming Editorial Board of Immigration. *The Territory of Wyoming.* Laramie Sentinel Print: Prairie Publishing Company, 1874.

Yorgason, Ethan R. *Transformation of the Mormon Culture Region.* Urbana: University of Illinois Press, 2003.

Zangrando, Robert L. *The NAACO Crusade Against Lynching, 1909–1950.* Philadelphia: Temple University Press, 1980.

Index